WILHELM WUNDT
AND THE MAKING OF A
SCIENTIFIC PSYCHOLOGY

PATH IN PSYCHOLOGY
Published in Cooperation with Publications for the
Advancement of Theory and History in Psychology (PATH)

Series Editors:
David Bakan, *York University*
John Broughton, *Teachers College, Columbia University*
Miriam Lewis, *Manhattanville College*
Robert Rieber, *John Jay College, CUNY, and Columbia University*

WILHELM WUNDT AND THE MAKING OF A SCIENTIFIC PSYCHOLOGY
Edited by R. W. Rieber

WILHELM WUNDT
AND THE MAKING OF A
SCIENTIFIC PSYCHOLOGY

EDITED BY

R.W. RIEBER
John Jay College, CUNY and
Columbia University College of Physicians and Surgeons
New York, New York

In collaboration with

ARTHUR L. BLUMENTHAL
University of Massachusetts — Boston
Boston, Massachusetts

KURT DANZIGER
York University
Toronto, Ontario, Canada

SOLOMON DIAMOND
California State University
Los Angeles, California

PLENUM PRESS · NEW YORK AND LONDON

Library of Congress Cataloging in Publication Data

Main entry under title:

Wilhelm Wundt and the making of a scientific psychology.

  Publications for the advancement of theory and history in psychology (PATH)
  Includes index.
  1. Wundt, Wilhelm Max, 1832—1920. 2. Psychology, Experimental—History.
3. Psychology—History. I. Rieber, Robert W. II. Series.
BF105.W54   150'.92'4 [B]   80-15877
ISBN 0-306-40483-4

©1980 Plenum Press, New York
A Division of Plenum Publishing Corporation
227 West 17th Street, New York, N.Y. 10011

Printed in the United States of America

PREFACE

The creation of this book stems largely from the current centennial celebration of the founding in Leipzig of Wundt's psychological laboratory. Wundt is acknowledged by many as one of the principal founders of experimental psychology. His laboratory, his journal, and his students were all influential in the transmission of the new psychology from Germany to all parts of the world. Nevertheless, until recently, psychologists and historians of science hardly recognized the scope and breadth of Wundt's influence, not to mention his contributions.[1] It was first through E. B. Titchener, and then through Titchener's student, E. G. Boring, that psychology got to know the somewhat biased and distorted picture of this great German psychologist. The picture painted by Titchener and Boring was unquestionably the way they saw him, and the way they wished to use him as a part of the scientific psychological Zeitgeist of their time.

This volume of essays on Wundt from the perspective of our times would therefore provide a fresh and, hopefully, more accurate point of view for current as well as future scholarship, not only on German psychology, but on occidental psychology and the history of ideas. The diverging points of view of each of the contributors in this book provide a unique and important scholarly dimension that could not have been possible if written by a single author. At the present time there is no biography or book of scholarly essays available in English on Wilhelm Wundt; therefore, it is especially appropriate that we issue this book during the centennial year of the founding of Wundt's psychological

---

[1]D. A. Lieberman's paper in *The American Psychologist,* April 1979, is a good example of an attempt to develop a contemporary variation of introspectionism based in Wundt and Titchener.

laboratory. The cooperative approach in putting this book together for publication is particularly appropriate for this series, Publications for the Advancement of Theory and History in Psychology (PATH), for it is quite compatible with many of the basic objectives that PATH has set for its goals.

The book is comprised of four parts: (1) Wundt's personal history before Leipzig, (2) Wundt's influence after Leipzig, (3) Wundt and English translations, and (4) a critical appreciation of Wundt as reflected in the literature of the past.

Part I, written by Solomon Diamond, is a comprehensive and detailed contribution, consisting of one chapter, covering Wundt's early career between the years 1856–1873. The chapter presents an original contribution in the form of new information about Wundt's personality and how it related to his theory and research.

Part II contains four chapters, the first two by Kurt Danziger, the next by Arthur Blumenthal, and the last by Robert W. Rieber.

Danziger's paper on the two traditions of psychology shows that Wundt, contrary to the interpretations of Titchener and Boring, rejected the psychological tradition of mental and individual atomism, but, rather, prompted a psychology of "apperception." In his next chapter on the theory of behavior and volition, Danziger discusses Wundt's psychology of "voluntarism," which extended the concept of volition to cover both conative and affective processes. With this theory, Wundt additionally distinguished between a developmental process of psychological differentiation and a process defined as "automatization." Danziger indicates that Wundt's theories prompted opposition from those who adhered to the sensationalist doctrine of mental life.

Blumenthal's chapter dealing with Wundt and the theory of American psychology focuses on the distinction and clash between the American and German experimental traditions and applications. As Wundt's objects of investigations derived from German philosophical traditions concerning levels of consciousness, emotion and will, and priority of mind over matter, the American testing notions were exemplary of the Anglo-French Enlightenment tradition concerning mechanistic laws, utilitarianism, and priority of matter over mind. Although these academic communities maintained close relations under the stress of conflicting cultural viewpoints, nonetheless, this is a source of much misunderstanding and misinterpretation still unresolved today.

The fourth chapter, by Rieber, on the Americanization of Wundt defines the Americanization process and its influence on the groundwork of psychology. A vivid example of the influence of this process is expressed in G. Stanley Hall's glowing tribute to and criticism of Wundt. The functionalist–structuralist debate is also reviewed. Wundt and his "disciples" are placed within this framework. Additionally, major factors fueling this debate are considered. A consideration of Wundt's criticism of Darwin's theories, particularly Darwin's theory of emotional expression, is commented upon. Wundt's criticism of Darwin, crediting Darwin for his observational powers and nothing more, coupled with the influence of biological and physiological accounts of both mind and body, lend further understanding to the criticism of Wundtian psychology. The wavering influence of Wundt on James Mark Baldwin is discussed.

Part III is composed of two chapters. Chapter 6 comprises excerpts from Wundt's *Principles of Physiological Psychology*. Solomon Diamond has provided both a translation and a commentary on this work. The translation of Wundt's *Outlines of Psychology* is the focus of Chapter 7.

Part IV consists of Chapters 8, 9, and 10. James's review of Wundt's *Grundzuge*, Feldman's paper on "Wundt's Psychology," and Haeberlin's paper on "The Theoretical Foundations of Wundt's Folk-Psychology" constitute the critical appreciation of Wundt as reflected in the literature of the past.

The following list of Wundt's works translated into English will be of interest to those who wish to read further:

Einführung in die Psychologie [*An introduction to psychology*] (R. Pinter, trans.). London, 1912.

Elemente der Völkerpsychologie [*Elements of folk psychology*] (E. L. Schaub, trans.). London, 1916.

Ethik [*Ethics: An Investigation of the facts and laws of the moral life*] (E. B. Titchener, M. F. Washburn, and J. H. Gulliver, trans.). London, 1897.

Grundriss der Psychologie [*Outlines of Psychology*] (C. H. Judd, trans.). Leipzig, 1897.

Grundzüge der physiologischen Psychologie [*Principles of physiological psychology*] (E. B. Titchener, trans.). London, 1904.

Vorlesungen über die Menschen- und Tierseele [*Lectures on human and animal psychology*] (J. E. Creighton and E. B. Titchener, trans.). London, 1894.

Über den wahraften Kreig. Rede 1914 [*Concerning true war*] (G. E. Hadow, trans.). Oxford: Oxford Pamphlets, 1915.

It is our hope that this volume will set the stage for a better understanding of Wundt's contribution to psychology.

R. W. Rieber

January, 1980

CONTENTS

I

PERSONAL HISTORY BEFORE LEIPZIG

Solomon Diamond

WUNDT BEFORE LEIPZIG*

It is possible to sum up the first 40 years of Wundt's life, in the style of an introductory textbook of psychology, by saying that he was the son of a country parson, that he studied medicine at Heidelberg and subsequently served for several years as assistant to Helmholtz at that university, and that he was by profession a physiologist until, in his 40th or 41st year, he set about writing what Boring (1950) called "the most important book in the history of modern psychology" (p. 322). All this would be accurate, but also completely uninformative. The Wilhelm Wundt who is regularly depicted in much fuller yet still fragmentary accounts is a myth based on the misconceptions of some of his students, both embellished and softened by the complementary processes of "sharpening" and "leveling" that are familiar to all psychologists as phenomena of recall and rumor and that are unavoidable in that form of information transfer that we call history. In the case of Wundt, the resulting distortions have passed acceptable limits. Until we put his career in proper perspective, our view of the process by which psychology became an experimental science will be seriously defective.

This chapter has a limited scope. It deals with the first half of Wundt's life, including the period that Titchener (1921b) aptly called "seventeen years of depression" (p. 171n)—years during which he worked as a physiologist with only modest success, before the appearance of the *Physiological Psychology* suddenly made him the most prominent figure in

*This paper is an expanded version of an invited address to Division 26 of the American Psychological Association, Toronto, Canada, August 29, 1978. In its present form, it has profited from critical readings by Karl Danziger and William R. Woodward—and would doubtless have profited more if the author were more flexible in his views.

an emerging science. This chapter is motivated by a conviction that it is not possible to understand the part that Wundt played in the development of psychology as an independent science without a serious study of his early career. If Wundt was half so great a force in the history of modern psychology as he is commonly thought to have been, a full-length portrait of him is long overdue. This chapter is a beginning.

Why this task remains to be done sixty years after his death is itself something of an enigma. Before he died in 1920 at the age of 88, Wundt had been honored worldwide for more than four decades as the world's leading psychologist. At that time, it would have seemed safe to assume that his life and work would before long engage more than one enthusiastic biographer. In fact, the closest approach to a full account is that by Petersen (1925), which is explicitly directed primarily to elucidating Wundt's position as a philosopher rather than as a psychologist. One searches the literature in vain for any comprehensive treatment that is written with historical perspective. The imposing presence that overawed his students seems still to inhibit the work of even his most recent chroniclers. Furthermore, some recent articles (Eschler, 1962; Kossakowski, 1966) make such arbitrary selections of facts and quotations as to introduce new distortions.

This situation is in striking contrast to the intensive treatment that has been given to the life of William James (e.g., H. James, 1920; MacLeod, 1969; Perry, 1935), who in much the same period passed through the same progression from physiologist to psychologist to philosopher, and whose name was often linked with that of Wundt during their lifetimes. For example, in 1896, at a time when enthusiasm for the "new psychology" was running high on both sides of the Atlantic, a leading German newspaper reporting on the Third International Congress of Psychology at Munich commented that "the psychological pope of the Old World, Wundt, and the psychological pope of the New World, James, were both distinguished by their absence" (Perry, 1935, Vol. 2, p. 145). There was more than a little truth in this hint of schism in the new faith, but the relative importance of the two leaders in the eyes of their knowledgeable contemporaries was probably correctly reflected in the fact that Villa's *Contemporary Psychology* (1903) cited Wundt on 95 pages and James on 37.

The scope of this chapter is indicated by its title. Wundt went to Leipzig in 1876, at the age of 44. He was to die at 88. Our intent is to establish a foundation that will permit a meaningful discussion of his work during the second half of his life, but that task is left to future papers, not necessarily by this writer. Readers who are unhappy with some of the interpretations offered will, it is hoped, be stimulated to seek others consistent with the facts, and not simply to asseverate the myth.

A Question of Lifestyle

It is often said of Wundt that he led the quiet, withdrawn life of a scholar and a scientist, in which intellectual pursuits were always dominant. If this were true, it would be oddly out of keeping with his own insistence that his psychology is fundamentally "voluntaristic" rather than intellectual in its orientation and emphasis. He said of himself that his strongest motivations were political and that this was especially true at the high points of his life (1920, p. iv). This statement led Titchener (1920) to comment that "whatever else Wundt learned in the course of his long life he had not learned fully to know himself" (p. 75). It is nevertheless unwise to dismiss Wundt's self-characterization lightly, although we need not limit our conception of political motivation to his definition of it as "concern for the welfare of state and society." We should keep in mind also Spranger's concept of the "political style of life" (usually translated as *political type*) as applicable not only to those involved in "politics" in the narrow sense but also to those who seek to dominate some special field, even if this is done with the intention of benefiting others. Specifically, said Spranger (1925/1928), the term applies to "whoever strives to dominate through knowledge" and by assuming the role of authority (p. 233). That sentence could have been written with Wundt in mind! Both varieties of political interest coexisted in Wundt's complex personality.

Wundt's autobiography is invaluable for our purpose, and on every rereading of it one discovers fresh, illuminating sidelights. However, it is not always accurate in detail, and it shows from time to time the sort of defensiveness that must be expected in even the best-intentioned work of that genre. Specific reference to it will not be made in reporting facts about which there can be no question. Similarly, we shall not clutter the text with references to the many standard biographic sources that have been useful. They are listed separately at the end of the chapter, with an indication of the articles used in each. Throughout, we shall use the unqualified name Wundt only to refer to Wilhelm Wundt, always designating others who bear the same surname by their relationship to him.

Early Childhood and Family

Wundt was born August 16, 1832, at Neckarau, a suburb of Mannheim, which was already an important commercial center, situated as it
was at the upper limit of the then navigable Rhine. Neckarau is scarcely
two kilometers from the heart of Mannheim and from its great ducal
palace, the largest in Germany, with a facade that stretches 600 meters
along gardens sloping to the Rhine. Within Wundt's infancy, construction had begun on the harbor facilities that made Mannheim the second
greatest inland port of all Europe. In short, Wundt was not born in the
rural environment we associate with the term *country pastor*. However, he
was only about four years old when his parents moved to Heidelsheim,
which he described as "a small town or rather a large village." It was
situated about one league (a brisk hour's walk) from the sizable provincial
town of Bruchsal, where he later experienced the most traumatic year of
his life, his first year of formal schooling away from home. The transfer
from Neckarau to Heidelsheim is just the first of a number of facts that
show that Wundt's father, despite some fine qualities, was a rather
ineffectual person, a circumstance that was not without effect on his son.
It was in Heidelsheim that Wundt spent most of his childhood, virtually
without peer companionship, though fortunate in attracting the kindly
interest of sympathetic adults who also helped to shape his character and
interests. (Heidelsheim is not in the vicinity of Heidelberg, where Wundt
either studied, taught, or summered for long periods of his life. The
similarity in names means only that the common blueberry was plentiful
in both regions.)

In Heidelsheim, on the afternoon of the final day of his first year's
schooling, he watched from his doorstep as a crowd of peasants erected a
"freedom tree" in the public square. Then he saw the burgomaster's
house set ablaze by the demonstrators and later—while the local bailiff
paced up and down inside the Wundt cottage—he saw them dispersed by
a squadron of dragoons. To this childhood experience Wundt immediately added pictures of scenes witnessed in the greater revolution, to
which this incident was a minor prelude. Early in 1849, the Republic of
Baden was established, and in June of that year, Wundt, not yet 17, from a
high vantage point near Heidelberg, watched the distant flashes of cannon that signaled the suppression of that republic by a Prussian army.
After the reaction of the 1850s came the liberalism of the 1860s, during

which Wundt was active in the Workers' Educational League and served for a time as a member of the Baden diet.

These, except for two early memories that relate to his father, are the events with which Wilhelm Wundt chose to open his autobiography because they were "more vivid in [his] memory than many others." It would be unwise, therefore, as we have said, to dismiss all these experiences as not pertinent to an understanding of his career. If Spranger's definition of the political lifestyle is valid, the priority that Wundt gave to these events (some of which are described in greater detail later) should alert us to the likelihood that coming to terms with power, whether in exercising it or in resisting it, was to be a critical issue in much of his future conduct. Perhaps this was even the root of his later insistence that "will" is the most primitive, most fundamental psychic process.

Wundt (1920, p. 58) tells us that his father, Maximillian (1787–1846), had not become a minister by his free choice but because his older brother had been "untrue" to the study of theology, thus leaving to Maximillian the onus of carrying on the family's long-standing pastoral tradition. Those who worked in that tradition were often simultaneously active in academic life. However, Heidelberg's theological faculty was primarily Catholic in its orientation, and severe limits were placed on advancement for Protestant theologians. From standard biographical sources (including an article by Wundt's daughter [E. Wundt, 1928]), we learn that his paternal grandfather had been a professor, apparently of Baden's history and geography, at the University of Heidelberg, while acting also as pastor of a church at Wieblingen, a small town in the vicinity. The great-grandfather and two great-uncles had also been on the university faculty, one as a greatly honored professor of rhetoric who received attractive offers from other institutions. A son of the latter was for a time on the medical faculty (Stübler, 1926). All these persons were deceased before Wundt's birth, but they left numerous issues, including a cousin named Justus (Bringmann, oral communication, September 2, 1979), who was the "university architect Wundt" who directed the construction of a maternity ward in 1828 and of the university hospital in 1843 (Stübler, 1926).

Wundt mentioned no paternal relative other than the grandfather he never knew and the unnamed uncle who had been "untrue" to theology; his daughter ignored the latter. It would seem, therefore, that the "country pastor" had virtually lost contact with the better-placed members of his family, perhaps because Wundt's father clearly was not an achiever—a fact reflected, as we have already noted, in his transfer from Neckarau to more rural Heidelsheim.

Wundt described him as a jovial and generous person, but generous to a fault: he too readily yielded to parishioners who pleaded hardship in meeting their obligations for support of the church, and hence of the pastor's family, and he displayed embarrassment when his wife tried to stretch their inadequate income by energetic bargaining with tradespeople—a normal practice of the times. In the end, relatives (doubtless on the maternal side) brought about an understanding that Wundt's mother would take charge of the family finances, something that could hardly have taken place unless they had been called on to give some financial assistance. Wundt described his father also as a loving parent who called him by endearing names and from whom he might expect consoling caresses whenever his mother, who took the more active part in his early education, administered some painful reproof.

Wundt opened his autobiography with two "earliest memories," both of which concern his father. The first was of a traumatic tumble down a flight of cellar stairs, and its recall was always accompanied by a vague feeling that this had happened while he was attempting to follow his father into the cellar. In the other, Wundt was roused from a classroom reverie by a blow on the ear and looked up to see his father glowering over him. The office of school inspector was an appurtenance to the position of pastor, and on this day, his father had stepped out of his usual role of passive observer to become a not-altogether-loving parent. How shall we interpret these memories? Wundt only said that they show how the persistence of even very early memories depends on contextual reinforcement. If we look for some more dynamic process as being responsible for their selection from the fullness of a child's experience, we are struck by the ambivalence that turns a loving father, in each instance, into a source of pain. Clinically, we know that a boy's identification with such a father can lead to distrust of himself.

Wundt's relatives on the maternal side played a much greater part in his life than the Wundts. His mother's grandfather had owned property and managed church lands in the Palatinate, but after his death and the unsettling Napoleonic wars her father, Zacharias Arnold (1767–1840), sold his property and moved to Heidelberg, on the more safely German side of the Rhine. During Wundt's boyhood, Grandfather Arnold divided his time between his piano and a roomful of plants in a home that was run by his youngest, unmarried daughter. While he lived, Wundt and his parents visited there for a few weeks each summer, providing the young boy with a masculine model very different from his own father. Wundt described him as "a man of the greatest precision," who frowned upon the slightest deviation from the established household order and always treated his grown sons and daughters as children. He took an active interest in Wundt's education, and during those summer visits, grandfather and grandson had daily walks together—except when his uncle's daughters, older than himself, also visited, on which occasions Wundt would be turned over to the care of a servant girl, which cannot have been an ego-building experience. One summer, they went each day to observe the construction of Heidelberg's first railway station, and together they witnessed the departure of the first train to leave that station for Mannheim, with an Englishman in the engineer's cab giving instruction to a German understudy. These vacations were not all amusement. Discipline in the Arnold household was strict, and Wundt recalled especially his terror at being confined in a dark closet as punishment for some infraction—a punishment that "even [!] aroused [his] mother's deepest sympathy" (1920, p. 37).

Wundt's mother, Maria Friederike née Arnold (1797–1868), had acquired a knowledge of French from her childhood governess—an unusual accomplishment in the wife of a country pastor in Baden. She had apparently also acquired some of her father's traits of character. She had two sisters, the unmarried one who ran their father's home and another in whose home Wundt was to live during part of his intermediate schooling. She also had two brothers, both of whom studied medicine at Heidelberg and who started their professional careers teaching there. Johann Wilhelm (1801–1873), after becoming assistant professor of physiology at Zurich, returned to private practice in Heidelberg, where he continued research in physiology, often writing in collaboration with his brother. Wundt spoke of him as having the "nominal title" of professor, without mentioning that he had an active, though short, university career. Philipp Friedrich (1803–1890) became assistant professor at Heidelberg, then went on to full professorships of anatomy and physiology (which were commonly joined in one chair in that period) at Zurich, Freiburg, and Tübingen before returning to end his career with twenty years of service as director of the Anatomical Institute at Heidelberg. He received very special honors at the time of his retirement in 1873 (Hinz, 1961). Each of these persons had some part to play in Wundt's life. Uncle

Friedrich's part was especially important and apparently decisive at a critical period. He was also instrumental in bringing Helmholtz to Heidelberg in 1858, a circumstance that cannot have been without influence on Wundt's success in winning the post of assistant to Helmholtz at that time. After the death of Wundt's father, when Wundt was 14, it was the Arnold family that passed on the plans for his education, in addition to providing the role models that obviously helped to determine its direction.

Wundt grew up in effect as an "only child." One sibling died before his birth, another he did not remember, and Wundt was only two years old when the only other survivor, Ludwig (1824–1902), eight years older than himself, was sent to live with their aunt in Heidelberg to attend the gymnasium there. The fact that her husband was an official in the tax service (Fürbringer, 1903) may have played a part in directing Ludwig's university studies and career toward the field of law.

Boyhood and Early Youth

Wundt attended the village school at Heidelsheim for the first two grades. The curriculum of that school would not have prepared him to continue toward a professional career, especially since it lacked the all-important ingredient, Latin. However, when Wundt was eight years old, his father acquired an assistant pastor, and Wundt thereby acquired a tutor, although one who proved to be more sympathetic than efficient. Soon young Friedrich Müller became "closer to [him] than mother or father." During that period, Wundt's only chum was a somewhat older mentally retarded youngster with very defective speech, who waited for him each day outside the Wundt cottage door. An occasional game with other village boys was more a tribulation than a pleasurable experience, and this was true even of the annual Easter egg hunt and the egg-tapping contest that followed it, which he "was not spared." He usually left empty-handed, having lost all his eggs to other boys, who were often less scrupulous about observing the rules.

Wundt sought by preference the less threatening companionship of adults. He was an almost daily visitor at the home of the two spinster daughters and the crippled son of the former pastor. The brother, a bookbinder, had a great fund of tales about fictitious adventures that he told with dramatic embellishments in which his sisters participated, even to the point of dressing in costume for their parts. Might this have stimulated Wundt's later active interest in the theater, which led him at one time to write theatrical reviews? He also visited often at the home of a Jewish family with whom his mother had occasional dealings, where the grandmother kept various wares for sale and the husband ordinarily tramped the roads as a peddler, bent under his sack. Sometimes he invited Wundt to the synagogue, or to the Feast of Tabernacles, the harvest festival that is traditionally celebrated in the home under a bower of greenery. Late in life, Wundt "still felt the uplifting impression" he had received when he witnessed the dignified manner in which this peddler then recited the ritual prayers. We must set this memory (on p. 32) alongside another "shadowy recollection" (on p. 199) to appreciate the full impact of this experience on the impressionable boy. His earliest literary project, before he had learned the cursive script, was to write a history that would show what is common to all religions. Thus, the roots of his interest in ethnic psychology apparently ran back to this early warm relationship with members of an alien culture.

Meanwhile, his father's library helped to mature Wundt's early passion for reading, which progressed in time from romantic novels to historical novels to history, and which gave rise to literary aspirations that were destined to go unfulfilled. The precocity of Wundt's literary tastes showed in the fact that when he was about ten, he made his first acquaintance with Shakespeare in translation, which initiated a lifelong enthusiasm.

But possibly the most important consequence of Wundt's lack of peer companionship in his childhood, and one that left its imprint to some extent on all his future life, was his inordinate surreptitious indulgence in daydreams while staring into his open book, pen in hand, without reading a line. Sometimes he "waited longingly" for his tutor to leave to tend to his other duties so that he might then "abandon [himself] to all sorts of imaginary experiences," often taking up on one day where he had left off the day before. (Boring, 1950, took some latitude with this passage, describing Wundt as "longing always for the vicar's return from his parish duties." But though Wundt loved his tutor, he loved his fantasies more. Schlotte, 1956, took even greater liberty, writing that "The boy used a great part of this time to pursue his own thoughts. This habit of directing his attention to his own inner life certainly prepared the ground for the later return of his psychological interests." There is a great difference between introspective analysis and fantasy.) This daydreaming "gradually became a passion" that brought in its wake "an ever increasing inattention to everything going on about [him]," one result of which was that even in his university days, he was a very inattentive auditor, and many lectures that greatly impressed his fellow students "passed over [him] without leaving a trace." Wundt speculated on the influence that such exercise in fantasy, and the general habit of working alone, might have had on his future work habits. Although the thought could not have occurred to him, it seems not unreasonable to regard this facility in daydreams as an incipient stage of what Titchener (1921a) gently described as Wundt's "imperative need to systematize the unripe" (p. 590) or, bluntly stated, his disposition to advance unsubstantiated hypotheses of a scope and grandeur that makes them at times hardly more substantial than daydreams, and tending to serve the same purpose of self-aggrandizement. We suggest, further, that the habitual inattentiveness to which Wundt confessed was not unrelated to his lifelong disposition to disregard hypotheses put forward by others. Within the scope of this chapter, we shall see several instances of how he imposed much harsher criteria on the hypotheses of others than on his own.

Four years after Herr Müller assumed the direction of his education, Wundt entered the Bruchsal gymnasium (high school). A year before that, however, the young vicar obtained his own church at a village not very distant from Heidelsheim. The resulting separation produced in the pupil such "unutterable" desolation that Wundt's parents accepted the tutor's suggestion that the boy be allowed to live with him at Münzesheim for the year remaining before he would be sent off to school. When the time finally came, his parents arranged for Wundt to live with a Protestant family in Bruchsal, which, because it had once been a bishop's residence, was still a predominantly Catholic town. This precaution, and Wundt's gradual weaning from his family, were of no avail. It soon appeared that he was both inadequately prepared for the work expected of him and unable to adjust emotionally to the new situation. He was a timid, frightened youngster who would have found it difficult under the most favorable circumstances to enter into the sort of peer relationships that might have given him emotional support to endure the mistreatments routinely meted out to unsuccessful pupils, which were made all the more damaging by his own feelings that he deserved no better. At one time, he ran home, only to be returned to the school by his determined mother. The year was a total loss academically, and his future—any future beyond, perhaps, one in the postal service, which a "kind" teacher recommended to him as the proper level for his aspiration—was placed in doubt.

Wundt's family—which is to say, the Arnolds—saw to it that he was given another chance. At 13, he joined Ludwig in their aunt's home, to attend the Heidelberg gymnasium and do his studying in the same room with his industrious brother, with no daydreaming nonsense allowed.

Wundt was then of an age when it is not uncommon for adolescent boys to experience a happy change of self-concept when placed in a favorable environment. He formed friendships, entered into the extracurricular activities expected of his age group, and felt himself "as if reborn." Being a year older than most of his classmates, as a result of the Bruchsal fiasco, may have helped him to overcome his feelings of physical inferiority. However, this still does not explain why he acquired close friendships with classmates whose academic performance was as outstanding as his was, and continued to be, mediocre. What was it about Wundt that made this possible?

At this point, we do well to recall Wundt's emphasis on his political interests and his vivid recollections of the Baden revolution. It was in the fall of 1845 that Wundt entered the Heidelberg gymnasium. Early in 1846, Polish peasants in Galicia, who always had the sympathy of Baden's liberals, were in revolt against Austria. (Wundt tells us that the more radical element in Heidelsheim called themselves "Poles" as a residue of their earlier sympathies with Polish peasants in revolt against Russian landlords.) The Galician revolt was suppressed with atrocities that shocked all Europe. By 1847, demands were being voiced throughout Baden to turn the army into a national militia pledged to support the constitution, and to institute various economic reforms. In March 1848, these demands were backed by the Diet, and soon after, the government proclaimed amnesty and promised reforms. In that same month, armed revolution broke out in Vienna. Wundt kept a diary of the revolutionary developments, recording "with immense agitation" such events as the Vienna uprising and the martyrdom of Robert Blum, leader of the Left wing in the Frankfort provisional parliament. Later, there was insurrection in Baden, and a republic was established, but in June 1849, Prussian troops commanded by the future emperor Wilhelm I crushed its army, which was commanded by a Polish general. Wundt, surely standing side by side with his comrades, watched the distant flashes of cannon from a mountaintop near Heidelberg.

"There are today few persons still living," Wundt wrote on almost the first page of his autobiography, "who remember the time when Baden was an independent republic for half a year. Still fewer is the number of those who experienced the preceding decade, at least in part, with clear awareness. I am among those few." There are few circumstances so effective in overcoming introverted isolation as a popular revolutionary movement, which draws people together by common bonds of interest, gives them common heroes, and provides an external focus of attention and never-failing topics of daily discussion. A lively interest in the political events of that period, to which Wundt himself attested, would have fostered the bonding of friendships with classmates who shared that interest. This must have been an important factor in the change that Wundt experienced during this period, which was indeed one of the "high points" of his life, a period in which he felt "as if reborn." (Bringmann, 1975, quite correctly emphasized the importance of the personality changes that Wundt experienced between 1845 and 1874, but he did not, in this writer's judgment, correctly characterize them or adequately explain them.)

Choice of a Career

At 19, after six years of normal but unspectacular progress through the gymnasium, Wundt faced the need to select a professional objective. Many generations of Wundts had studied at the University of Heidelberg, and quite a few of that number, including his own grandfather, had served on its faculty. Many, again like his father and his grandfather, had been Protestant churchmen, yet not always by free personal choice. Nor was that choice one to Wundt's liking. He would have preferred a literary career, but he saw that as ruled out by the uncertainties attached to it, especially in view of the fact that his mother, living on the meager pension of a pastor's widow, could give him no financial assistance. (Only at this point in his autobiography do we learn from Wundt that his father had died five years earlier, during his first year at the gymnasium.) The need for assistance meant that whatever choice he made must be acceptable to a family council in which the Arnolds would be dominant. He was disinclined to teaching as a profession because the very school environment was abhorrent to him. Indeed, his overriding motivation was to get away from Heidelberg, from home and city, to become at last an independent person. The reference here to escape from his "parental home" reminds us that Wundt's mother would almost certainly have come to Heidelberg immediately after her husband's death, and that since that time, Wundt had probably been living with her rather than with his aunt, just as he would be doing later as a student and still later as a young faculty member at the university. At this time, he found the arrangement irksome. We must also assume that his desire to get away from Heidelberg was motivated in part by the dread of the inevitable comparisons at a university where many members of his family had held posts of distinction. It is a common syndrome in our own time on much less cause, and it must have played a part in Wundt's motivation, even if unverbalized.

Wundt did escape from Heidelberg, if only for a year, by taking advantage of two more-or-less accidental circumstances. His scholastic record was so mediocre that despite the special consideration he could expect as the descendant of a long line of pastors, he did not qualify for state aid to attend the university. If this failure disappointed his widowed mother, it seemed a stroke of good luck to him. The loss of a possible state stipend was a misfortune in which he secretly rejoiced, since receiving it would have given him no choice but to attend the University of Heidelberg. However, he still needed a plausible pretext for attending a "foreign" university, in view of the added expense that it would entail. He found this excuse in the fact that one of his uncles, Friedrich Arnold, was then professor of anatomy and physiology at Tübingen, and Wundt reasoned that if he chose medicine as a career, it would seem quite natural that he should pursue his studies there, even though Heidelberg's status in the natural sciences was higher. He therefore announced that to be his intention, and the family council gave its consent on condition that he complete the course within four years, the minimum time required. We may be sure that Wundt's mother asked her younger brother, Friedrich, to keep an eye on his nephew and to see that he did not neglect his studies.

Let us review what we have learned of Wundt's early years. His mother, largely as a result of her upbringing in the Arnold household, was much stricter with him than was his father, and she was probably also more determined to see that he made a mark in the world. He received affection from his father but little guidance. (Wundt's statement that even if his father had been alive, he would not have interfered with his free choice, can be interpreted in more ways than one.) The lame bookbinder and the Jewish peddler were both father surrogates to some degree, but it was the young assistant vicar who filled this role most nearly, yet ineffectually. The relationships that Wundt established with these men must have been an expression of his own need, not theirs. We would expect, therefore, that as long as his role in life remained uncertain he would seek other father surrogates and suffer disappointments when they failed to live up to his hopes. We shall see that this disappointment clearly happened in his relations with Du Bois-Reymond, probably in his relations with Friedrich Arnold, and possibly in his relations with Helmholtz, although, of course, the manner in which he sought their approbation was quite different from the open hunger of a small boy for simple affection.

Like any child, Wundt also had a need for the satisfaction of mastery. This need was frustrated in his rare contacts with other village boys. It was fulfilled to some degree in his relationship with his mentally retarded playmate, who was so gratifyingly dependent on him, but it was fulfilled to a greater degree in fantasy. We are all entitled to privacy in our fantasies, and we cannot be surprised that Wundt told us nothing about the content of his. However, he did tell us that they were usually accompanied by rhythmic movements of his pen, up and down, and this statement suggests that in them he took active rather than passive roles. The daydreaming boy was father to the man who one day would write to his fiancée, "I am too ambitious to be vainglorious" (Schlotte, 1956, p. 337).

Student Years

If Wundt's mother hoped, when he went off to Tübingen, that he would return a changed person, she was not to be disappointed. Let us look first at that aspect of his experience there that might be called college life. During his final year at the gymnasium, Wundt and several close friends agreed to join a certain student corps (fraternity) when they became university students. He did in fact join the affiliated group at Tübingen, but he found its members less congenial than he had hoped, and he was therefore relieved when it disbanded early in the semester because it had attracted too few members. He then became attached to another corps on a trial basis, but he soon withdrew from that as well "to surrender [himself] to a solitary life" and to a single-minded pursuit of his studies in anatomy. This is the first evidence we have of serious application to any interest not literary. Meanwhile, there were dances, the best being the weekly faculty dance. This was open to fortunate students by faculty invitation, in which respect Uncle Friedrich must have been helpful. There was music and theater—the best in distant Stuttgart, which might be reached on a rare adventure. There were forbidden duels, more exciting than in Heidelberg because in these narrow streets, the danger that the authorities might appear quite suddenly was heightened. In these, Wundt participated only as a spectator. All these things evidently played a larger part in Wundt's life during the first semester than during the second, when he was caught up in the spirit of his work.

We turn now to the scholastic life. Wundt mentioned attending lecture courses in botany, chemistry, and physics, in all of which the professors were hampered by inadequate, antiquated equipment. The first semester of a course in aesthetics turned out to be the only philosophy course of his entire student career. The professor, he wrote, held his attention only when he dealt with Karl Gutzkow's *Die Ritter vom Geiste*, the influential novel, published in 1850, that depicted "the detrimental characteristics of a police state and its demoralizing influence" and included among its characters "recognizable portraits" of persons who had been active in the Berlin revolution of 1848 (Kurz and Wedel, 1927, p. 698). The fact that Wundt did not continue with that course for the summer semester is less an evidence of disinterest than of his growing passion for cerebral anatomy, which he studied under the guidance of his uncle, Friedrich Arnold. During the entire summer semester, he worked "from early till late," acquiring a knowledge of this special field out of all proportion to his superficial learning of other subjects. This was perhaps the decisive turning point of his career, not because of the relevance of cerebral anatomy to his future interest in physiological psychology, but because for the first time in his life, he experienced the joy of mastery based on his own solid accomplishment. Suddenly, he had become the industrious, seemingly indefatigable Wundt who would be so astonishingly productive in future years. Uncle Arnold deserves most of the credit for bringing this change about. Perhaps in emulation of him, Wundt resolved during that semester that he would make physiology his life's work.

It was the period in which Germany displaced France as the world leader in physiology and changed its nature by the introduction of quantitative methods. Although Arnold was not equipped by his training to participate fully in that advance, he correctly assessed its importance when he explained in his lectures why the kymograph was destined to open new paths of physiological research. (Or perhaps it was really Vierordt speaking through Arnold, who, Wundt observed, "hardly knew how to handle the kymograph." That instrument had been introduced by Karl Ludwig in 1848 as an outcome of his efforts to produce tracings of the pulse, and it was quickly put to further use by Helmholtz in his development of the myograph and in measuring the speed of the nervous impulse. However, it was given its name by Vierordt, then an assistant professor of physiology at Tübingen.)

During the next three years, Wundt completed his medical course at Heidelberg, not Tübingen. A reader who relies solely on the autobiography would conclude that the change came about because Wundt's expenses had been running above his anticipated budget and because facilities in the natural sciences were inferior to those at Heidelberg. There is no mention of the compelling reason for the change: his uncle had accepted a chair at Heidelberg, where for the next twenty years he was director of its Anatomical Institute (Hinz, 1961). The pretext that Wundt had used to attend Tübingen thus no longer existed. However, he no longer needed it, because he had proved his competence to himself and had found a direction for his ambition. At any rate, it was at Heidelberg, if anywhere, that his uncle could now be of help, as he doubtless was from time to time. Among Arnold's students at Heidelberg we find the names—to select only a few well known to psychologists—of Sigmund Exner, David Ferrier, and Krafft-Ebing (Fürbringer, 1903).

The first of Wundt's three years as a student at Heidelberg was still chiefly devoted to making up deficiencies in basic sciences because he had given no thought to a scientific career during his gymnasial studies. He took private instruction in mathematics, while pursuing lecture courses in physics and chemistry and a laboratory course in chemistry. His return to Heidelberg coincided with the arrival there of Robert Bunsen, of whom it has been said, in words much like those that have often been applied to Wundt, that his greatness as a teacher "is attested by the scores of pupils who flocked from every part of the globe to study under him, and by the number of those pupils who afterwards made their mark in the chemical world" (Encyclopaedia Britannica, 11th ed.). Wundt was very nearly seduced into deserting physiology for chemistry, but he went no farther along that path than to perform a physiological experiment touching on a problem of body chemistry. For several days, he limited his dietary salt intake as much as possible; as a result, he experienced metabolic disorders and an intensified hunger for salt that lasted for some time afterward. He had the immense satisfaction to achieve thereby his first publication (Wundt, 1853) and later to see his work cited in Ludwig's *Textbook of Human Physiology* (1858–1861).

The last two years of his medical study were devoted to the required courses in the various areas of medical practice. Because of his need to compress these courses into a shorter time than customary, he generally took the corresponding lecture and clinical courses simultaneously rather than in the usual successive pattern. Again, he seized an opportunity for experiment by entering a prize contest for experimental study of the effect of sectioning the vagus nerve on the respiratory organs.

At this time, Wundt tells us, he had just begun hearing lectures on pathology and had no training whatever in pathological anatomy. The problem assigned was to study the effect on respiration of sectioning the vagus nerve, and it assumed some practice in vivisection as well as a knowledge of pathological anatomy. Relying for guidance on a textbook, he performed the experimental work in his mother's kitchen, enlisting her as his surgical assistant. It was the custom, Wundt wrote (1920, p. 82ff.) to work on prize problems of the medical faculty

> in the clinic or the Institute of the professor who set the problem. Therefore the winner was as a rule known in advance, and my paper, submitted anonymously according to the rules, aroused some measure of surprise to the faculty. It had been prepared in my own study, so that no one outside my home knew anything about it.

Wundt's results nevertheless matched those reached by his leading competitor "with the assistance of his professor," raising a question as to who should be declared the winner. The prize was divided between them. Wundt's paper was also accepted for publication by Johannes Müller (Wundt, 1855), and Müller's letter became a prized possession.

The preceding paragraph is based solely on Wundt's account. The episode takes on greater interest if we add a detail that he omitted: the professor who set the problem that year—and stood ready to give guidance to students working in his laboratory, with a selfless dedication that made him one of the university's best-loved teachers—was none other than Friedrich Arnold (Fürbringer, 1903). It is of course possible that Wundt's "surgical assistant" did not keep the secret from her brother, but that is unimportant. The fact that the paper was accepted for publication attests to its quality. What is important is the proudly individualistic manner in which Wundt carried out his difficult project while rejecting the opportunity to receive guidance. The necessary motivation must have come largely from a desire to gain his uncle's applause. We shall see similar behavior on Wundt's part with respect to two other mentors, DuBois-Reymond and Helmholtz. In each instance, the relations between Wundt and these older men became strained.

In the summer of 1855, ten years after he had left Bruchsal in disgrace, Wundt passed the state examinations for admission to the practice of medicine. Separate examinations were given in internal medicine, surgery, and obstetrics, and when the names of the successful candidates were published, Wundt's name stood at the top of each list! He modestly explained this result by the fact that because the examinations were devised and graded by practicing physicians rather than by university professors, success depended less on a knowledge of the latest findings than on "a certain superficial skill in expression combined with some knowledge of the history of medicine" (1920, p. 93). He was not alone in regarding the examination practice at this time as superficial (Stübler, 1926). Be that as it may, success brought Wundt face to face once again with the need to make a decision regarding his future course of action.

Postgraduate Training

So far as the "family council" was concerned, once Wundt had passed his examinations they could see no problem: he had qualified for a respected profession, and therefore, he should practice it and make a decent contribution to the support of his mother. However, although the examination results attested to the fact that he had mastered a great many bookish facts, Wundt felt unprepared for the responsibilities of medical practice. He would have taken a post as a military physician if it were available, on the theory that in times of peace, he could do little harm to healthy young soldiers, but on inquiry, he discovered that openings did not exist. He recoiled from the offer of a position at a health spa, feeling that the social services expected of him would be more onerous than his medical duties in treating the anemic daughters of government functionaries. He was rescued from his difficulty when an acquaintance, who had been working as assistant in a municipal hospital directed by one of the university professors, asked Wundt if he would spell him for six months while he prepared for his own examinations. So Wundt stepped into something like a medical internship early in this century: on call 24 hours a day, in full charge of the women's ward of a public hospital save for the daily visits of the hospital director. The patients included some peasant women, more servants from the town, and a sizable contingent of prostitutes, who were isolated in a separate section but nevertheless saw to it that the ward was never quiet. It was, as Wundt observed, a trying situation for a young doctor, but one from which he could gain a great deal of practical experience. Two special aspects of this hospital experience received repeated mention in Wundt's later writings. Let us call them the *iodine affair* and the *localization problem*.

The Iodine Affair

Wundt's fullest account of this incident appears in his slender book on *Hypnotism and Suggestion* (1892a), which was reprinted in the *Philosophische Studien* the following year and later in his *Kleine Studien* (Vol. 2) and was also translated into French, Italian, Russian, Bulgarian, and Spanish! In it, Wundt attacked the then-popular notion that post-hypnotic suggestions could provide even more valuable experimental data than the conventional psychological laboratory. In the course of his argument that the suggestibility of the subject invalidates the results obtained under such circumstances, he told at length of an occasion on which he was awakened from a deep sleep by a hospital attendant and summoned to help a patient in great pain. He went about administering a narcotic but instead took the bottle of tincture of iodine, which had much the same appearance but was clearly labeled, and poured a spoonful into the patient's mouth, all the while aware in his somnolent state that it was iodine and yet thinking of it as a narcotic. Fortunately, the patient was more awake than the doctor and instantly spat it out, yet even this action did not fully awaken him, and it was only after returning to his room that he grasped what had happened. Although no harm was done to the patient, the incident revived Wundt's apprehension about entering the practice of medicine. For weeks, as he stated in the autobiography, he was troubled "by doubts whether someone who could commit such an error was competent to practice the medical profession" (1920; p. 99ff.). Wundt's account of this incident leaves little question that his hesitation about entering practice was not based solely on reservations about the training he had received; it was also based, at least in part, on a still-persisting sense of personal inferiority.

The Localization Problem

There were at the hospital, during the period of Wundt's service, some patients who suffered sensory paralysis as a result of leg injuries and the like. In checking on the course of recovery, Wundt made fairly systematic observations on the impairment of localization of touch sensations, and he came to the conclusion that the results could not be harmonized with Weber's theory (E. H. Weber, 1846) that localization is based on a mosaic organization of the sensory innervation of the skin. Indeed, he concluded that the results could not be harmonized with *any* purely physiological hypothesis and that they required a psychological explanation. Thus, said Wundt, it was by experiment that he was led for the first time into thinking about a psychological problem. Why he thought a purely physiological explanation must be inadequate and how he attempted to construct a psychological explanation are matters to be discussed when we deal with his *Contributions to the Theory of Sensory Perception* (1862a).

Wundt's experience in the hospital ward did nothing to reduce either his aversion to the private practice of medicine or his desire to become a research physiologist. On the other hand, the Arnolds were evidently unwilling to subsidize his education further. However, by pooling his own meager resources, including his nest egg of prize money and a small sum that his mother could provide, he had enough to support himself through one semester of residence at some "foreign" university. He gave some thought to going to Zurich, where Karl Ludwig, the inventor of the kymograph, had been professor of anatomy and physiology since 1849, but if he had done so, he would have been disappointed to discover that Ludwig had left Zurich in 1855 to become professor at the Josephinum, a school for military surgeons in Vienna! (This trifling detail is one of several that show that Wundt did his planning, like his work, as an isolate. If he had spoken to his uncle about his plans, he would at least have learned that Ludwig had left Zurich for Vienna. Perhaps he would even have received some financial help. But Wundt, as we shall see again and again, coupled a fierce pride with his sense of inferiority.) Wundt decided in favor of Berlin, where he could maximize the yield of his one short semester by studying under both Johannes Müller, whose letter of encouragement he treasured, and Emil Du Bois-Reymond.

Both men were famous. Müller's *Handbook of Human Physiology* (1840) was, and still is, regarded as the work that marked the transition to physiology as a science, while Du Bois-Reymond's *Researches on Animal Electricity* (1848) had made him the foremost worker in the field of electrophysiology. Only two years later, Müller would be dead at 56, and Du Bois would succeed to his chair. Wundt, perhaps unwisely, undertook to work simultaneously in the laboratories of both men. As it turned out, this meant that he worked along with four others in Müller's laboratory in the mornings, and by himself in the upstairs corridor set aside for Du Bois-Reymond's students in the afternoon.

Müller questioned him about his interests and then proposed that he work on extirpating nerve centers in invertebrates—a project that we may think of as a sort of miniaturization of his student prize work on the effects of interfering with respiratory innervation in mammals. In this case, Wundt wrote, he obtained no results sufficiently noteworthy to warrant publication.

Du Bois set him to measuring the elasticity of muscles, and specifically to checking on the validity of a finding by E. Weber (1846) that the extension of a resting muscle did not vary directly with the load placed upon it, but that successive equal increments of load produce smaller and smaller extensions. Wundt spent the semester wrestling with problems of method and only finished the project several months after his return to Heidelberg. In a paper (Wundt, 1857) submitted in November 1856, he concluded, on the basis of experiments conducted with nerves, tendons, and arteries as well as muscles, (1) that if time is allowed for the tissue to reach its maximum extension, this is proportional to the load, and (2) that within certain (unspecified) limits, this is true for the immediate extension as well. However, the illustrative data provided suggest that Weber's statement was correct for muscle, and later literature has sustained it. One is left wondering why Wundt blurred the issue by stating general conclusions about all "moist, organic tissues" when the matter of concern was the role of elasticity in muscular contraction.

Before the end of the year, Wundt was habilitated as docent at the university. Though he still had not escaped Heidelberg, he had at least escaped the need to practice medicine, and he could go forward with the plan he had stated in a letter written from Berlin to his mother (who apparently still hoped that her son would be a practicing doctor) that "he would teach so that he could remain a physiologist" (Schlotte, 1956, p. 334).

Some Fresh Frustrations

With characteristic lack of caution, Wundt undertook to teach a general survey of experimental physiology in his first semester as a docent, that is, starting in April 1857. It attracted four students. The course was soon interrupted by severe illness that showed itself in a sudden violent hemorrhage. Wundt perceived that his doctors had no hope for his recovery, and this confrontation with death produced in him (as he told it), a "perfect tranquillity" that brought about "a complete reversal of [his] outlook on life" (1920, p. 116ff.). Objectively, we recognize the tranquillity as an effect of the nature of his illness, although this explanation does not elucidate what further effects it may have had on his thinking. Indeed, his new outlook, tinged with religiosity, became explicit only in later retrospect, and by degrees, as a sense that there was an intimate relatedness between his subjective and objective experiences, between the external world and his awareness of it (whence his autobiography derived its title, *Erlebtes und Erkanntes*), and that the true meaning of immortality lay in the uniqueness of personal existence. This new outlook also included, as it ripened, a conviction that scientific knowledge and philosophic knowledge are inseparable. Whether or not these attitudes were ultimately traceable to this traumatic experience, as Wundt implied, they were characteristic of much of Wundt's later work, and the reader must therefore be prepared to accept the fact that Wundt's empiricism, except in his earliest period, had mystical as well as experimental aspects.

Meanwhile, we must not think that this "perfect tranquillity" immediately took hold of his life. Schlotte (1956) found among Wundt's papers the following poem, which can hardly have been written at any other time:

> The world has much of evil in it,
> Much that I don't like a bit,
> Yet of misfortunes only one,
> Nothing but this single one,
> That strikes alike at young and old,
> Against which no defense can hold:
> To lose the best before 'twas won,
> To die before life has begun!

(My rendering is "free" only in the sixth line, where a literal translation would be "against which no power gives protection.") It is hard not to read these lines as a proof that Wundt at 25 was not as philosophically acceptant of death as at 88. Another short poem that Schlotte placed in the same period is no less pessimistic, stating that earth's smallest hamlet has room enough for pain but that the universe has not space enough to hold one untrammeled pleasure. It had to be ambition, not tranquillity, that lifted Wundt from this depression and gave him the resilience soon to produce his first book and to launch a program that would culminate in the second.

By Wundt's account, a full year passed in illness and convalescence before he was able to resume his work. This account cannot be accurate, since the preface to his book (Wundt, 1858b) is dated October 1857, not more than 14 months at the outside after his return from Berlin, 11 months after submitting his previous publication, and probably not more than 6 months after the first traumatic episode of his illness. The book's title may be translated as "The Present State of Knowledge Concerning Muscular Action." The subtitle promised a treatment based on the author's own experiments. It was a bold step for a young scientist who was, after all, still a novice in a field in which many distinguished workers were engaged. A reviewer (*Literarisches Centralblatt*, 1858) chided the author for presenting a series of disconnected experiments on the mechanical characteristics of muscular tissue along with some unrelated discussions under a title that promised much more. Nevertheless, the reviewer conceded that the author showed skill and promise, and that if the yield from his experiments was not proportional to the energy expended on them, it might be because it takes luck as well as talent and industry to arrive at noteworthy results.

Needless to say, this assessment of the book's worth fell far below the expectations of its luckless author. More than 60 years later, 13 pages of Wundt's autobiography expounded the book's merits and excused its failure. He took pride in the fact that his measures of elasticity (on the gastrocnemius of frog) were performed on living animals without disturbing the principal nerves and blood vessels. Although he saw this as an innovation important enough in itself to have attracted attention, a passage in the book shows that he was aware that Schwann had earlier measured the strength of this muscle in living and intact animals, in a procedure that measured the load that the already contracted muscle could bear without further extension, while being stimulated to further contraction. (Schwann's method and results were stated in detail by Müller, 1833–1840, Vol. 2, p. 59ff.) Wundt attributed the lack of response to the book to a conspiracy of silence for which he held Du Bois responsible. After waiting in vain for something more than the original polite note of acknowledgment from his mentor, to whom the book was dedicated, Wundt concluded that Du Bois had probably never read past the introduction, which might have offended him by pointing to the need for something more than atomistic mechanism in dealing with the problems of living organisms. That the bitterness lingered is clear from Wundt's statement that despite this incident, he had friendly relations with many members of the Du Bois school in later years. We shall see later that this was not a general rule.

It is indeed possible to look upon the introduction as possibly the first fruit of Wundt's new outlook on life. It has short opening and closing passages that give a concise statement of the problem he had undertaken and the method he would follow, wholly within the spirit of the new "exact" physiology. Between those passages, set off by horizontal lines, lies an irrelevant discussion of the larger methodological problems of the life sciences generally, the tenor of which may be judged from this passage, to which Du Bois would indeed have taken exception:

> All conceivable atomic movements are, so far as experience shows, reducible to the fundamental laws of mechanics; but such formative forces as have been postulated for organic science would no longer be judged according to mechanical principles. They would be subject to laws the precise formulation of which is still to be discovered. It can by no means be asserted in advance that this is not possible, and therefore this view is not totally unjustified. (1858b, p. 10.)

Wundt said that he learned two important lessons from this experience: first, always to give maximum freedom to his students, and second, never to permit himself to become head of a school. These rules, he said, he ever afterward observed! Here we can only repeat what Titchener (1921a) said in a different context: "Whatever else Wundt learned in the course of his long life he had not learned to know himself" (p. 575). It seems clear that Wundt had entertained exaggerated hopes for recognition—both by Du Bois-Reymond personally and by the scientific community generally—of what was in fact a mediocre if not a trivial contribution. In addition, he had allowed his ambition to carry him into generalizations that were not justified by the context and that quite predictably irritated Du Bois. No "conspiracy of silence" was needed to explain the cool reception to his book at a time when memorable advances were being made by the application of "atomistic" methods to the problems of neuromuscular physiology.

Controversy with Hermann Munk

Wundt did not at once forsake this field of work to pursue other interests. In the following year, he published an article (Wundt, 1859) in which he claimed to have discovered a hitherto unreported effect on peripheral nerve of repeated electrical stimulation. He described an increased irritability, which he labeled "secondary modification" to distinguish it from a contrary effect that was known as *Ritter modification* and that Wundt proposed to call *primary modification*. At this time, Hermann Munk was studying the propagation of nerve currents, and he would not have wanted to overlook such a phenomenon. To put the matter in perspective, we should note that Munk was still far from the distinction we now associate with his name; he was, in fact, seven years younger than Wundt, and in 1859, he had just received his degree at Berlin at the age of 20. He was to spend his entire professional career there, being one of the "two ambitious young Jews" mentioned by William James, in a letter of 1867, as giving lectures "almost as instructive" as those of Du Bois-Reymond himself (James, 1920, Vol. 1, p. 121). (The other was Julius Rosenthal, who graduated the same year and became assistant to Du Bois.)

Munk (1861) analyzed Wundt's claim and concluded that what he had described was simply a change that takes place in nerve just after it is excised and that had already been reported by Pflüger, by Heidenhain, and by Rosenthal. Wundt had failed to consider the possibility that what he had observed was a time-dependent phenomenon rather than an effect of stimulation.

Munk's criticism was certainly valid. However, our chief interest is not in whether Wundt was mistaken but in how he conducted himself in this, his first professional controversy: he excused his inadequate data by saying that a full report would be published in a forthcoming textbook of electrophysiology; he resorted to digressions and countercharges; and he committed the sort of ambiguous shifts of meaning that were to exasperate his opponents in other controversies throughout his career. Since most readers will find it difficult to accept this statement without illustration, I include here Wundt's original definition of secondary modification and the one he used in a reply to Munk, without any hint of alteration:

> Secondary modification consists in the fact that after a short application of electrical current, irritability for current of that direction is heightened; after somewhat longer application, this modification passes through an inter-

mediate stage into the commonly observed primary modification. (1859, p. 537)

This aftereffect consists first in a reduction of irritability to current of the direction used (primary, negative modification), but it then passes over into a heightened irritability for current of this direction (secondary, positive modification). (1861a, p. 782)

How does one conduct a scientific discussion with such an opponent? Wundt's final sally closed with this insulting paragraph:

Herewith I regard the controversy between Herr Munk and myself as over and done with. I leave unnoticed many details of his article which are irrelevant to the matter and amount to mere verbal fencing. Still less need I waste words over "the greatest possible exactitude and conscientious care" on which my opponent prides himself. Who would be so cruel as to disturb the sweet and innocent pleasure of self-adulation? How lovely it is to wrap oneself in the mantle of an exact researcher . . . and how much more imposing are grandly eloquent phrases than sound proofs, aside from the fact that they are also more convenient! (Wundt, 1862f, p. 507)

Munk, who had already declared the controversy over and done with on his part, was provoked not only to the "concession," as he called it, that if Wundt's "carelessness" led to any more verbal shifts, he was capable of explaining that a healthy man was ready for the madhouse, but also to a detailed critique of Wundt's procedure and a suggestion that Wundt would be well advised to omit "secondary modification" from his promised textbook. In fact, the textbook of electrophysiology never materialized.

Assistant to Helmholtz

By pursuing this revealing controversy to its end, we have broken the chronological thread of our account. Let us go back to 1858. In that eventful year, Wundt not only published his first book but also became assistant to Helmholtz and initiated his career as a psychologist with the first article (1858a) of a series that would lead to his second book (1862a). We shall take up first the history of the assistantship, which has been the subject of a different sort of controversy.

The reader will recall that in 1852, Friedrich Arnold became Heidelberg's professor of anatomy and physiology—two disciplines that, at that time, rarely had separate chairs. Spurred, no doubt, by an awareness that one man could no longer do justice to both disciplines, he persuaded the ministry to establish a separate chair of physiology. With Bunsen acting as intermediary, this chair was offered to Helmholtz (then at Bonn), who accepted after a year's delay, largely to free himself from the need to profess anatomy as well as physiology (Stübler, 1926). At 37, Helmholtz had already published his epoch-making paper on the conservation of energy, measured the speed of the nervous impulse, invented the ophthalmoscope, and published the first part of the *Physiological Optics*. It is worth noting that his approach to each research problem was essentially mathematical and that this continued to be true throughout his life. The post of assistant to such a distinguished and universally respected scientist should have been a golden opportunity, and yet for Wundt, it turned into a blind alley. Wundt wrote that Helmholtz was so reticent as to be almost unapproachable, and since neither of them had any clear idea at the outset of what the duties of an assistant should be, those duties developed haphazardly, with Helmholtz suggesting at first that Wundt instruct the medical students in microscope technique and later that he assume the direction of a state-mandated course to acquaint all medical candidates with experimental laboratory procedures. After five years (four by his own account), Wundt resigned the post in order to have more time for other things.

A letter that Helmholtz wrote to Wundt, dated May 8, 1858, gives a somewhat different picture. Helmholtz wrote that matters regarding the proposed new Physiological Institute were at last sufficiently defined so that he could offer Wundt the assistantship for which he had entered his application in February. The stipend would be only 300 gulden, because the duties were such as might be assumed by a recent graduate who would regard the experience itself, and access to the facilities of the institute, as constituting a part of his recompense. The appointment would be for only one or two years at a time, but Helmholtz pointed out that it would be to his advantage not to have frequent changes. The duties would include the supervision of student exercises in the physiological laboratory, including microscopic and chemical techniques, as well as demonstrating vivisections and other time-consuming experiments not suited for lecture-hall demonstration. The assistant would also have to be present each day for the several hours when the institute would be open, to give help as needed to those doing research there, although Helmholtz would himself pass through from time to time to discuss projects with individual researchers. It would also be appropriate that the assistant should lecture on microscopic anatomy. (Full text in Schlotte, 1956, p. 335ff.)

These stipulations were intended to help Wundt decide if he really wanted the poorly paid position. Stated five months before Helmholtz came to Heidelberg, they cannot be considered vague, and they did rather accurately describe Wundt's future duties. In particular, Wundt's course offerings did include "Microscopic Anatomy with Demonstrations" in the first two semesters of his assistantship, and "Study of Tissues, with Microscopic Demonstrations" in four of the last six semesters (E. Wundt, 1927, p. 67).

On the subject of Helmholtz's reticence and Wundt's activities in the institute as distinct from the student laboratory, at least in the early period of his assistantship, we have an unusually trustworthy witness. Ivan Sechenov worked under Helmholtz for two semesters, starting in the spring of 1859, that is, in Wundt's second semester as an assistant. He described the laboratory as small, with a separate room for Helmholtz but not for Wundt, who shared one room with himself, another Russian named Junge, and two Germans, one an ophthalmologist and another who was busy with the myograph. Of Wundt he wrote:

> Wundt sat the whole year unfailingly at some books in his own corner, not paying attention to anyone and not saying a word to anyone. I did not once hear his voice. (Sechenov, 1945/1952, p. 39)

Equally unfailingly, Helmholtz spoke briefly to each of the four experimenters every morning to inquire about their progress and their difficulties, before disappearing into his own room. (Neither Wundt nor Sechenov mentioned that Helmholtz's first wife died very shortly after he arrived in Heidelberg.)

What Helmholtz modestly omitted from his letter to Wundt was that the major recompense to be taken into account by anyone hiring on as assistant to a distinguished scientist was the opportunity not simply to use the facilities of the institute for research but to benefit from the guidance of its director. This opportunity was one of which Wundt seems never to have availed himself. He prosecuted his research with characteristic proud independence, in that style of "solitary" dedication to his tasks that he himself saw as one of the outcomes of his early habits of study, which had expressed itself at Tübingen in a "surrender to a solitary life" and at Heidelberg, quite dramatically, in the almost secretive manner in which he prepared his entry for the prize competition in his mother's kitchen. All of Wundt's experimental work at Heidelberg seems to have been carried out in his own home, following a pattern that had once been common but was rapidly being eliminated by the establishment of scientific institutes at the leading universities. (However, Wundt [1862a, p. 202n] acknowledged that it was Helmholtz who suggested that he use projected afterimages to study eye movements and the horopter.) It may be said on Wundt's behalf that the projects in which he engaged came more and more to have a psychological dimension, so that it would not have been possible to carry them out in the same room in which some of the other workers were perhaps performing vivisections on frogs or rabbits. The question that remains is why under these circumstances he continued as assistant for five years. If the pay was poor and the hours long, and if the relationship with Helmholtz lacked any compensating recompense, why did he not resign earlier? Once the question is posed in this form, the answer that suggests itself is that Wundt hoped for some recompense that he never received. This hope need not have been explicit in awareness, but one recalls his need for a father surrogate in boyhood, as well as his disappointing relationship with Du Bois-Reymond, which came to its bitter ending just before Wundt started working for Helmholtz.

Wundt himself said that one reason for the lack of closeness between himself and Helmholtz lay in the fact that their research interests were so similar. We shall reexamine this question later, when we consider the controversy that Hall (1912) started as to whether Helmholtz dismissed Wundt because of his inadequate knowledge of mathematics. However, Wundt seems at times to have been deliberately challenging Helmholtz by choosing to work on problems that Helmholtz already had in hand and then thrusting his own unripe solutions forward as if to declare: "Look at me! Acknowledge me as your equal!" We will see instances of this as we look at Wundt's various publications during the five-year term of his assistantship. For however burdensome his duties may have been, they do not seem to have limited his productiveness.

The Beiträge

Wundt's second book (1862a) consisted of six articles on sense perception plus the famous programmatic introduction, which enunciated the need for an experimental psychology. The first article, written apparently during the period of convalescence from his illness, harked back to his hospital experience of several years earlier, which had convinced him that Weber's anatomical explanation of tactile localization was mistaken.

Instead of dealing with this limited problem, Wundt, in characteristic fashion, set it in the much larger framework of perception generally. To this larger question, he propounded a solution combining three elements: Waitz's (1849) Herbartian thesis that space results from our need to organize simultaneous competing ideas into a single experience, Lotze's (1852) theory of local signs, and finally, a Berkeleian reliance on associations cued to eye sensations. But how are these elements used to create the perception of space? He answered:

> This process is unconscious, and we can infer it only from those elements
> which enter into consciousness. But when we translate it into conscious terms,
> it takes the form of an *inference*. The *unconscious inference* is the process that
> joins itself to sensation, giving rise to perception. (1862a, p. 65)

The article contains no intimation that three years earlier Helmholtz (1855/1896) had used the concept of unconscious inference, though not that exact phrase, in discussing the nature of visual illusions. This was no way for an assistant to establish good relations with his new chief. They apparently never spoke together about this subject. After leaving the assistantship, Wundt at least three times asserted his priority to the concept: in his *Textbook of Human Physiology* (1865), in a review of Helmholtz's *Physiological Optics* (Wundt, 1867d), and in a survey article that deals at length with spatial perception (1867b). Without mentioning Wundt, Helmholtz (1868/1896) then asserted his own claim. Later, Wundt (1880, in reply to Erdmann, 1879) said that in 1858 he had not known about Helmholtz's earlier address, but that does not explain how he could have remained ignorant of it for so long afterward. Even if an honest mistake, Wundt's initial use of the concept without acknowledging Helmholtz's priority certainly cast a shadow across their relationship.

In any case, Wundt, in that first chapter, laid the basis for a psychological theory of space perception, not only by asserting the experiential foundations of tactile localization but by insisting that an unconscious logic was needed to make use of the empirical cues. Chapter 2 gave a history of theories of vision. Unimportant in itself, it is notable as Wundt's first historical exercise, the forerunner of the numerous historical interludes that constitute an enduringly valuable feature of the *Principles of Physiological Psychology* in all its editions. Chapter 3, on monocular vision, emphasizes the importance of sensations arising from the muscles of accommodation, and it goes on to say that although accommodation is at first an involuntary act, it becomes largely voluntary in adults, as shown by the fact that it is influenced more by attentional factors than by the physical characteristics of objects in the visual field. (Such "empirical" proofs, without experimental verification, abound.) He also argued that since directional movement of the eyes is clearly voluntary and is accompanied by conscious sensation, it must be the key to the psychological construction of space. In support of this view, he asserted (quite mistakenly) that we can discriminate "almost infinitesimal differences in degrees of contraction" of the eye muscles (p. 151). Elsewhere, he said that the relative simplicity of the eye muscles offers the best opportunity "to arrive at general laws about the mechanism of voluntary movements" in general, as well as being "the key to an understanding of visual perception, insofar as it rests on a physiological basis" (1862d, p. 11).

Wundt's interest in eye movements, to which he attributed such great significance, is one instance in which he apparently followed the lead of Helmholtz in selecting a problem for investigation. In the *Physiological Optics*, one may read this statement by Helmholtz:

> Professor Junge, of St. Petersburg, working in my laboratory, has endeavoured to determine the centre of rotation of the eye, by observing how much the luminous reflexes in the corneas of the two eyes approached each other when the visual axes were converged from parallelism to a definite angle of convergence. (Helmholtz, 1866/1925, Vol. 3, p. 38)

The reader will recall that Sechenov named Junge as the other Russian present in Helmholtz's laboratory in 1859. Wundt not only picked up the problem but, in his usual style, proceeded at once to use it as the base for an untenable theoretical structure. (Between 1859 and 1862, Wundt read a number of papers on eye movements, chiefly before the Heidelberg Scientific-Medical Association. The titles were given by E. Wundt, 1927. It appears that the substance of these is contained in the discussion of binocular vision in the *Beiträge*.) Instead of working under Helmholtz, accepting a junior position, Wundt chose to pursue the problem independently, and as we shall see, he arrived at mistaken conclusions.

Chapters 4 and 5 of the *Beiträge* deal with binocular vision. They reject the hypothesis of "identity" between corresponding points on the two retinas and offer a new solution to the horopter problem. (See below, under "Controversy with Ewald Hering.") They also describe experiments on such phenomena of binocular vision as contrast effects and stereoscopic fusion, which were not in themselves novel, but about which Wundt argued that they are explicable only if we assume unconscious reasoning. In Chapter 6, Wundt rejected the Herbartian principle that rival ideas exist in consciousness simultaneously and maintained

instead that whatever is present in consciousness at a given instant must
first have been formed unconsciously into a single percept, as happens in
stereoscopic fusion and in the construction of space. We will meet this
idea again when we examine Wundt's early experiments and theories on
the temporal characteristics of the thinking process, with which he was
busy at the same time.

Before closing, Wundt again emphasized the importance of unconscious inference as the basis not only of perceptual processes but of all
mental life, including the very fact of consciousness, as arising from a
logical differentiation between subject and object. He declared that the
elementary laws of logic must play the same leading role in psychology
that the concept of the cell plays in our study of the physical organism,
and he concluded on an almost ecstatic note that

> psychology is in the fortunate position of being able to guide its research not by
> an hypothesis but by an empirical fact, and this empirical fact is that the mind
> is an entity which independently acts and develops in accordance with logical
> laws. (p. 451)

Thus, the appeal to unconscious thinking does not in any degree lessen
the exclusively intellectualistic emphasis of the book as a whole and in no
sense represents an incipient stage of Wundt's future voluntarism.

The Introduction on Method

The six chapters we have been discussing had previously been published as a series of journal articles. In presenting them as a book, Wundt
added an introduction that rejected metaphysics as a basis for psychology
and asserted the need to go beyond the study of consciousness by using
genetic, comparative, statistical, historical, and, above all, experimental
method. The stated reason was that only in this way is it possible to
discover how conscious phenomena arise as "complex products of the
unconscious mind" (p. xvi). He called it a "prejudice" to suppose that
experiment cannot deal with the "higher mental activities" (p. xxvii), and
he intimated that still unpublished but recently completed experiments
clearly demonstrate the psychological law of the unity of ideational content (p. xxviii), which was of course basic to his theory of sense perception. Other experiments had demonstrated two important laws of mental
life: (1) that one mental process is dependent on another—this being
Wundt's "psychological" restatement of Fechner's "psychophysical"

law; and (2) that mental functions develop in accordance with logical principles—this being a generalization based on his theory of perception.

In future years, Wundt would reverse his position on most of these points. He would see experiment not as an essential supplement to introspective method but as a device to control it. He would himself emphatically reject the possibility of its application to higher mental processes, which he would seek to study only through the social history of their products. He would propound an anti-intellectualistic, "voluntaristic" psychology in which logic would not regulate mental development but would arise as a developmental product of more basic psychic processes. Only his assessment of Fechner's findings—an assessment that is demonstrably false in the light of present-day neurophysiology—would remain constant. His possible motivation in this merits some comment.

Wundt was a young man who had recently met frustration in a bold quest for recognition in one field of physiological research and had intensified his efforts in another. He was convinced that by his emphasis on psychological factors in perception he had an important message to deliver. There is no question that he was ambitious, there is much to suggest that he still indulged in daydreams of glory, and there is no fault attaching to either of these traits. On the other hand, his controversy with Munk, which took place in the period between the appearance of Fechner's *Psychophysics* (1860) and his own *Beiträge* (1862a), exhibited a testiness that, to put it mildly, was not altogether admirable. It is apparent that to such a young man, Fechner's great work would appear as a hostile invasion of territory that he had been mapping out for himself. It was not his temperament (as we see from his relations with both Du Bois-Reymond and Helmholtz) to enlist under the banner of another general. While some others questioned the psychological significance of Fechner's findings, Wundt sought to make them conform to his own direction of emphasis by declaring that they had *only* psychological significance; that Fechner had not discovered a *psychophysical* law but had merely given a fresh demonstration of something long recognized, how one psychological process varies under the influence of another. He illustrated this position to his own satisfaction by stating that "everyone has had the experience that the slightest annoyance, which would not be noticed when one is already depressed, is able to totally disrupt a cheerful frame of mind" (p. xxx). To restate this sample of "empirical psychology" in what is at least a framework of "thought experiment," readers may ask themselves whether they would respond with greater irritation to being jostled in a crowd, or to missing a local bus, when in an expansive or a depressed frame of mind, and then try to understand the makeup of a man whose cheery frame of mind can be "totally disrupted" (*gründlich zerstörrt*) by such a minor annoyance. Then, consider further that if this argument was to support Wundt's thesis, what he described must be a universal phenomenon, not an individual oddity or an occasional occurrence.

Controversy with Ewald Hering

Wundt thought that his solution to the horopter problem, on which Helmholtz had been working over a considerable time, merited a separate publication (1862a). This article involved him in a controversy with another young physiologist whose name is now known to all psychologists. Hering (1863) pointed to certain mathematical and conceptual errors in Wundt's article and also questioned the validity of some experimental observations that Wundt had advanced in support of his theory and that Hering found he could not reproduce. Leaving matters of observation aside, although history has shown Hering's acuteness of observation to be quite extraordinary, there could be no question about the errors in mathematics. Wundt had no choice but to concede them, but in retaliation, he seized on what he thought was another such error by Hering. He declared that Hering's solution (to the problem formulated by Wundt) was "unconditionally false" and gave his own correction instead. He then delivered the following jibe:

> If in the future Herr Hering wishes again to devote himself to the praiseworthy business of searching out the errors of calculation in the work of others, it is to be hoped that he will not on those occasions make even coarser errors than those which he wishes to correct. (Wundt, 1863, p. 174)

Hering (1864) replied that Wundt had indeed reached a correct solution by a fortuitous combination of false premises and wrong calculations but that he had failed to reduce his final equation to its simplest terms. If he had known how to do so, he would have recognized that his solution was in fact identical with the one that he called "unconditionally false."

Wundt (1863) also tried to sidestep the original point at issue by declaring it moot because Helmholtz meanwhile had reached a definitive solution to the horopter problem. This vicarious claim was premature. In the end, Helmholtz wrote: "The problem was solved by myself and Mr. E. Hering practically about the same time" (1866/1925, p. 484). Wundt was playing in the wrong league.

The Swiftest Thought

Again, we backtrack a little, to pick up the beginning of another and more interesting aspect of Wundt's experimental and theoretical work in this period. In 1861, German scientists met in congress at Speyer, not 40 kilometers by rail from Heidelberg, and Wundt took the opportunity to present two papers, one on eye movements and the other on what the astronomer Bessel had long before called "the personal equation." The latter paper (read September 18, 1861) was reported in the proceedings of the congress in these few lines:

> Dr. Wundt of Heidelberg spoke on the personal difference between visual and auditory observation. He regards this as an absolute magnitude, which is positive or negative because different persons either see first and then hear or the other way around, and from this the speaker explained the difference between Bessel's observations and those of others who, unlike him, would have heard first and then seen. (Quoted, in the original German, by Titchener, 1923.)

It happened that Bessel's former assistant, the astronomer Argelander, was present, and he protested that he, too, "saw first and then heard."

This refutation of an overhasty hypothesis only spurred Wundt to one that was even more ambitious and that was first stated in a family magazine in an article on "The Speed of Thought" (1862b). After summarizing findings on the relative slowness of nervous impulses compared to our intuitive notions of the speed of thought, and after discussing the implications of these data for the thinking process, the article states:

> For each person there must be a certain speed of thinking, which he can never exceed with his given mental constitution. But just as one steam engine can go faster than another, so this speed of thought will probably not be the same in all persons. (p. 264)

But how, it goes on, can we measure the speed of thought in different individuals? Wundt then described a method that anyone can use with the help of a large pendulum clock. (See Figure 1.) Attach a metal crosspiece to the shaft of the pendulum, a knitting needle perhaps, and hang a bell where this crosspiece will strike it as the pendulum swings. This device is labeled a *Gedankenmesser* or *thought meter*. (It may well have been

Figure 1. The "thought meter." (Wundt, 1862b, p. 264.)

suggested by the pendulum myograph in Helmholtz's laboratory, in which the smoked glass plate on which the tracing was made formed a part of the pendulum, the movement of which triggered switches placed at precisely determined points in the arc of movement in order to open and close the electrical circuit as desired.) If we desire to observe the exact position of the pendulum at the moment when the bell rings, said Wundt, we can never do this with complete accuracy. For himself, he found an error of about one-eighth of a second, and he took this to represent the time of his swiftest thought, that is, the shortest time intervening between two successive perceptions. No result was given for any other subject, nor was there any indication that there had ever been another subject. Nevertheless, Wundt stated that the experiment thus provided an important measure of individual differences. In addition, it gave a definitive answer to the age-old question that had puzzled even Aristotle, to wit, whether it is possible to think of two things at the same time. If we could do so, then we would also be able to see the pendulum's position when the bell sounds: "But consciousness holds only a single thought, a single perception. When it appears as if we have several percepts simultaneously, we are deceived by their quick succession" (p. 265).

This account in a popular magazine is the first published account of the complication experiment, which had been the basis for the hypothesis advanced at Speyer, that some persons tend to see first and others to hear first. It was also the basis for the claim subsequently advanced in the *Beiträge* that Wundt had found an experimental proof of the unity of perceptual content. The statement that what we believe to be a single experience consists of confused successive perceptions was suggested by Waitz's discussion of "general feeling" (*Gemeingefühl*). Not so obvious is the source of the notion that the "swiftest thought" is "the natural unit of time," as Wundt would soon be saying. However, it is possible to identify the source of this concept with a degree of probability that approaches certainty.

Starting in 1859, Wundt each year offered a course of lectures on anthropology, defined as "the natural history of man" (E. Wundt, 1927). In the introduction to the *Beiträge*, Wundt had specifically mentioned natural history as an important source of data for a scientific psychology. It is therefore safe to assume that he did not neglect to read that part of Buffon's *Natural History* that is specifically titled "The Natural History of Man." It includes a discussion intended to refute the then-popular fear that the pain experienced even in an instantaneous death may seem to last for a very long time and thus may constitute a sort of infinite torture. Here is a part of that discussion as it was translated by William Smellie, first editor of the *Encyclopaedia Britannica* and a contemporary of Buffon:

> The succession of our ideas is the only natural measure of time, and we conceive it to be shorter or longer in proportion to the uniformity or irregularity of their motions. But in this measure, there is a unit or fixed point, which is neither arbitrary nor indefinite, but is determined by Nature, and corresponds with the particular organization of individuals.
>
> Two ideas which succeed each other must necessarily be separated by an

interval; one thought, however rapid, must require some portion of time
before it can be followed by another. . . . This interval between our thoughts
and sensations is the unit or fixed point formerly mentioned; and it can be
neither extremely long nor extremely short, but must be nearly equal in
duration; because it depends on the nature of the mind and the organization of
the body, the movements of which must have a determined degree of celerity.
(Buffon, 1749–1767/1791, Vol. 2, p. 490)

It is all there: the swiftest thought, as measured by the interval between
thoughts, is the natural unit of time, and it varies with the individual
constitution. It is clear that Buffon deserves a place in the history of the
reaction time concept. Incidentally, *Encyclopaedia Britannica* (11th ed.) says
of Buffon, not of Wundt, that "he was given to excessive and hasty
generalization, so that his hypotheses, however seemingly brilliant, are
often destitute of any sufficient basis in observed facts."

Wundt's "Fireside Conversations"

By this time, Wundt had begun to play an active part in the movement for workers' education. He and several other young members of the
Heidelberg faculty gave popular lectures to branches of the Workers'
Educational League not only in Heidelberg but in other cities as well.
Wundt tells anecdotes about occasions when he lectured on the conservation of *"Kraft"* (he was surprised to find the auditorium filled with elderly
men and women) and on the theory of evolution (because women were
present, he was not permitted to show pictures of human and ape
embryos). It is likely that other popular lectures are reflected in three
articles that appeared in a magazine called *Fireside Conversations (Unterhaltungen am häuslichen Herd)*. This magazine had a distinctly liberal orientation, and its editor was Karl von Gutzkow, the author of *Die Ritter vom
Geiste,* the sensational novel that had so intrigued Wundt a dozen years
earlier. Wundt's style in these articles sometimes reminds us of Fechner's
essays published under the pseudonym Dr. Mises, and they show that
Wundt had the skill to present the topics of his own research in a manner
that would attract popular interest.

One article is an essay "On Time," in which Wundt deplored the fact
that we are slaves to artificial time and then wrote:

The first clock was the first policeman, a policeman that thought set up over
itself, and which brought with it all those limitations of personal freedom that
were to follow. . . . A natural instinct leads people to struggle against any

> power that tends to repress their independence. We can love everything—
> people, animals, flowers, stones—but nobody loves the police! We are also
> engaged, some more, some less, in never-ending conflict with the clock. . . .
> [But] through all this I totally forget that I am time; that it is I who sometimes
> flies with the wings of a bird and sometimes creeps like a snail, and that when I
> think I am killing time, I am really killing myself. (1862f, p. 591ff.)

Wundt can rarely have been guilty of that kind of self-destruction.

The other two "fireside conversations" are called "physiognomic studies," and they are especially worth noting because, like his article on the speed of thought, they show Wundt as interested at this time in problems of individuality, which are absent from his later psychology. One (1861b) was based on his work on eye movements, in which he observed that when our glance moves from one object to another, the eye follows a straight line if the second object is directly over or under, or directly to the right or left of the first object. But if the required displacement includes both vertical and horizontal components, the eye follows not a diagonal but an arc. Wundt classified persons according to whether the concave or the convex face of this arc was turned toward the object sought—a criterion that I find difficult to comprehend. Less ambiguous is the statement that the convex glance begins energetically and then slows down, while the concave glance starts slowly and then increases in energy. These movements, he claimed, reveal how the persons who make them perform every sort of mental and physical task!

The other essay (1862c) began with a discussion of the importance of tastes and smells in our lives. This is reflected in the figurative meanings that we give to words like *sweet* and *bitter*. Forming the mouth into the expression that is ordinarily induced by one of these taste experiences, even when nothing is being tasted, will, wrote Wundt, bring the actual sensation to consciousness. Just as the eye movements inform us about how volitional acts will be performed, the mouth reveals the person's deeper inclinations and disinclinations.

Early Political Activity

The league was also a forum for political discussion, and Wundt, as chairperson of the Heidelberg branch, became more and more involved in political matters. He represented the branch, and sometimes branches in other nearby cities, in regional conferences, and at one of these he had the good fortune to meet Friedrich Lange, who about ten years later would recommend him for the chair of inductive philosophy at Zurich. (Wundt erred in saying that Lange then occupied that chair; in fact, Lange did not teach at Zurich until 1869). In 1866, Wundt was elected to represent a Heidelberg district in the Baden diet. Although Wundt said that his service in that body lasted for about four years, this is certainly an error. The occasion for his election was a vacancy caused by the death early that year of his friend Eduard Pickford, an economist at Heidelberg. Petersen (1925) said that the election took place on April 26, and Wundt received 45 of the 51 votes cast. Wundt himself stated (1920, p. 234) that he entered the diet almost immediately after finishing a book published that year (Wundt, 1866a), and that he remembered writing the preface, which is dated September 1866, in the diet chamber. He also stated (1920, p. 30) that his political life ended more or less with the death of Karl Mathy (then president of the cabinet), which occurred February 3, 1868. It thus appears that his intense involvement in government affairs did not last more than 18 months, and there is general agreement that he resigned later that year.

Wundt stated in the autobiography (and also in a letter of 1872 to his fiancée [Schlotte, 1856]) that he resigned because he realized that politics could not be an avocation but required a total commitment that was incompatible with his scientific work. It is worth noting, however, that meanwhile, the Workers' Educational Leagues had become more radicalized, having become absorbed into the Allgemeiner Deutscher Arbeiterverein, which in 1868 became affiliated with the International Working Men's Association. This adherence of the league to a philosophy of class conflict led to Wundt's resignation from it and may have influenced his decision to retire from an active political life.

As a member of the diet, Wundt was affiliated with the dominant Progressive Party. His affiliation with the university made it natural that he should be charged with responsibilities in the field of education, and Wundt did in fact introduce measures dealing both with the secularization of the lower schools and with the abolition of the special legal immunities that students enjoyed, as a result of which, for example, dueling by students was a disciplinary matter for the university although it was a criminal offense for the population at large. His enthusiasm for eventual unity of the German states won him a place on the Peace Commission following the War of 1866 between Prussia and Austria. He referred to these activities in his autobiography, but more interesting to us are the arguments he advanced on certain specific issues.

Krueger (1922) gave the main points of a speech that Wundt made to the Heidelberg branch of the Workers' Educational League in the period just before the seizure of Schleswig-Holstein from Denmark in 1864, by the combined action of Prussia and Austria. Krueger's account is based on an outline of the speech found among Wundt's papers. Wundt stated that the goal of the entire working-class movement was the freedom and independence of the working class and its salvation from mechanization, but that this goal was indissolubly linked to German unity and freedom. German workers must therefore rise above their class interests, to fight with a sense of duty for the honor of the nation. Strength in warfare and soundness of character are independent of privilege, Wundt said, and they have more value than gold and possessions.

Petersen (1925) wrote of arguments that Wundt advanced, in an article in the *Heidelberger Journal* (1866, No. 15), against the agitation of the German Workers Union for universal suffrage. (Note that this article appeared just a week or two prior to his election to the diet, on April 26, by 45 of the 51 votes cast, in an election in which 57 were eligible to vote.) Wundt argued that universal suffrage was acceptable only under conditions of real equality, but that so long as soldiers, servants, and other persons in dependent positions, or those heavily in debt, could be commanded how to cast their votes, the effect would be to give greater advantage to those in control. So long as there was a standing army, it would serve to put these votes at the disposal of the government.

Lectures on Psychology

At the time when Wundt published the popular articles we mentioned previously, and presumably also delivered popular lectures in the same vein, he also for the first time offered a lecture course with the word *psychology* in its title. It should be recognized that prior to 1862, the possibility of giving such a course did not really exist for him. The chair of philosophy at Heidelberg was until that year occupied by the Baron von Reichlin-Meldegg, whom Wundt ridiculed for his superficiality (1920, p. 239ff.), pointing to this course title as evidence: "Psychology, including Somatology and the Study of Mental Disease." On the other hand, it should be noted that since 1856, psychology and psychiatry had been required courses for medical students (Stübler, 1926). Reichlin-Meldegg had in fact shown a pioneering interest in this field by writing many years earlier a two-volume work (1837–1838) with the same title, which was described by Ueberweg (1866/1898, p. 331) as having made "special use of the results of physiological investigations." When Eduard Zeller, whose interest was primarily historical, was named to the chair of philosophy, it became possible for Wundt to lecture on psychology. In the 25 semesters remaining before Wundt left Heidelberg, he lectured on psychology 12 times in all, as follows:

Psychology from the Standpoint of Natural Science
    Summer semesters of 1862, 1863, 1864; winter semesters of 1864–
    1865, 1865–1866, 1866–1867
Physiological Psychology
    Winter, 1867–1868, 1872–1873
Psychology, including the Study of Mental Disease
    Summer, 1868; winter, 1868–1869
Psychology
    Winters, 1869–1870, 1870–1871

The reader will notice that the two offerings of "Physiological Psychology" came five years apart. The occasion for each will be discussed later. The second offering of that course—which was never again repeated in Wundt's lifetime!—was the only course in psychology that Wundt taught during his last seven semesters at Heidelberg. (Data based on E. Wundt, 1927.)

Wundt could never be guilty of writing "too little and too late." His first course in psychology gave birth almost at once to a massive two-volume work, *Lectures on the Human and Animal Mind* (1863–1864). Twice in later years Wundt referred to this work as a "youthful indiscretion"— once in the preface to the drastically revised and much shortened second edition (1892), and again in his autobiography. On the first occasion, he attributed its failings to his inadequate experience at the time in the area of psychological experimentation, while on the second occasion, he regretted chiefly his premature efforts in the direction of ethnic psychology at a time when the necessary materials were not yet available. He also confessed that the treatment of animals was quite superficial and that they were included in the title only because of the current interest in Darwinism.

We shall look at this book first through the eyes of an anonymous contemporary reviewer (*Literarisches Centralblatt*, 1863, 1864). With only the first volume in hand, the work was recommended to laymen as giving a rich, clear, and interesting account of the physiological conditions underlying sensation and perception, although at times, particularly in the areas of optics and acoustics, the author stressed his own work where he might have used the work of others. The author's conclusions are called less clear than these expositions of fact. For example, the statement that "The physical movement in the nerves does not arouse sensation, but is itself sensation" (p. 134) is at odds with the statement that "different sensations are changes in the state of the mind" (p. 298). One is confused, also, by such statements as (1) "Thought is time and time is thought, because the thinking person measures it and thought is the only instrument which measures itself"; (2) "Space is experience and experience is space"; and (3) the implication elsewhere that time and space are identical. Statements about the duration of "the swiftest thought" (in Chapter 3) are found to be inconsistent with others in the discussion of the "personal difference" (in Chapter 23).

Later, the same reviewer summed up the content of the second volume concisely: the author

> deals successively with sensual, aesthetic, intellectual and religious feelings; in the discussion of desire, a few chapters are included on the instinctive behavior of animals and humans and . . . the origin of speech; he then turns to will and the question of free will, and ends with a consideration of the dependence of will and consciousness on the brain.

In fact, the greater part of the volume represents an attempt to write an ethnic psychology, reflecting the influence of Lazarus and Steinthal, who together founded the *Zeitschrift für Völkerpsychologie und Sprachwissenschaft* in 1859. However, the reviewer expressed skepticism about Wundt's confidence that ethnology can inform us better about psychological processes than can the study of individual consciousness. The reviewer also expressed the opinion that "it is convenient, but not very profound, to hide our ignorance about the causes of differences [in mental phenomena] and the laws of their varied formations behind the words *development* and *unfolding*." (Here we may remark that Hans Volkelt, 1922, on the other hand, has seen Wundt's early disposition toward developmental analysis of mental processes as the primary influence that gave rise to his interest in ethnic psychology.) Readers are told that although they will find much that is entertaining in this volume, anyone who wishes to assess the net gain for psychology should read Drobisch's critique of the first volume.

We turn, therefore, to Drobisch (1864). As the dean of Herbartian psychologists, writing in a Herbartian journal, he began by demonstrating Wundt's ignorance of Herbartian psychology. One example of many: Wundt stated that for Herbart the sum of the strength of all ideas into consciousness is a constant, and that this supposition can be experimentally disproved. In fact, that sum, for Herbart, included the strength of unconscious ideas. (Drobisch pointed out that Wundt should not have overlooked this fact, after discussing how the principle of conservation of energy applies to sensations. In later years, Wundt would say that conservation of energy does not apply to psychic causation.) Drobisch then roundly criticized Wundt for his sweeping generalizations based on trivial data, as when he estimated the time of the "swiftest thought" from observations based on only two sense modalities, while neglecting (1) the other senses; (2) successive perceptions involving only one sense; (3) other factors in the complex experimental situation in which the stimuli were presented; and (4) the problem of thought sequences that are not governed by immediate external stimulation. Some other criticisms were that Wundt failed to appreciate the true significance of Fechner's findings and that he was led into absurdities by his fascination with "identity philosophy." One fresh example is Wundt's statement that "mechanical and logical necessity are not essentially different [because] mechanism and logic are identical." Drobisch's final judgment, that Wundt's attempt to reform psychology was "hasty and premature," was one in which Wundt himself ultimately concurred.

Three Nonpsychological Books

In 1864 (not 1863, as the autobiography states), Wundt relinquished his assistantship (Schlotte, 1956). Whether Helmholtz had requested the resignation is a controversial question that is best examined after we have become acquainted with the work of Wundt's successor in that post. Wundt wrote that he resigned in order to have more time for his own work, but he was also under compulsion to make up somehow for the loss of the small stipend he had been receiving, and the three books that he wrote during the next three years were not of a psychological nature. He was granted the title of assistant professor at this time, but it was an empty title without monetary recompense. (However, the fact that he could list himself on the title pages of these books as "professor" at the prestigious University of Heidelberg did not hurt their sale, and it certainly helped his pride. That he did so without including the modifying word *assistant* [*ausserordentlicher*, literally, "extraordinary"] was a breach of the usual custom.)

Wundt's three earlier books (1858b, 1862a, 1863–1864), each with a different publisher, had all sold very poorly, and for his fourth book, he had to turn to a fourth publisher. The *Textbook of Human Physiology* was indeed a success. The first edition was soon translated into Dutch and Russian, the second (1868) was followed by translations into Hungarian and French, and the fourth and last (1878) by a translation into Italian (E. Wundt, 1927). Perhaps the most distinctive feature of the book was its frequent use of the first-person-singular pronoun, as in "I was the first to. . . ." This phrase occurs so often that an unknowing reader would assume that Wundt was, along with Helmholtz, Du Bois-Reymond, Brücke, and Ludwig, one of the handful of workers who had given shape to the new physiology.

His next book was a venture into philosophy: *The Physical Axioms and Their Relation to the Principle of Causality* (1866a). An anonymous review (*Literarisches Centralblatt*, 1867) was entirely favorable and summarized the book's content as follows:

> First the [six] axioms are defined and it is shown . . . how in the course of time quite contrary views have been held regarding each of them, according to whether the conceptual development was based on empirical or speculative grounds. In a special section, these opposed views are more sharply stated as ontological antinomies. The following chapter shows that the roots of these contradictions lie in different conceptions of causality . . . and (finally) that they are to be regarded altogether as laws derived from ripened experience.

The success of this book surely helped Wundt to obtain a chair in philosophy eight years later.

A third book, the *Handbook of Medical Physics* (1867a), was directed toward medical students who had inadequate preparation in the natural sciences. The idea for it came from the more advanced, pioneering work by A. Fick, which Wundt (1866c) reviewed. In fact, starting in 1866 Wundt became very active as a reviewer of books in physiology and the related sciences, probably chiefly to supplement his income and perhaps because it was the sort of work he could conveniently do in "idle" moments at Karlsruhe, where the diet met. Although these reviews were for the most part short and unsigned, two lengthy signed review articles, one dealing with a work by Helmholtz and the other with a work by Haeckel, deserve our special attention. We shall return to them shortly.

The Complication Pendulum

In the midst of all Wundt's writing, teaching, public lectures, and political activity in the early 1860s, he somehow still found time to continue experimental work with the complication pendulum, the apparatus that he designed to replace the pendulum clock that was his original "thought meter." Although he had made several summary statements about the nature of his work on the speed of thought, no reasonably complete description of it, and no data more precise than that vague "one-eighth of a second," had ever been published. Near the end of the first volume of the Lectures, a supplementary note to Chapter 3 promised that the second volume would contain such a report along with a description of an improved apparatus that would make more exact measurements of the speed of ideation possible. But the preface to the second volume ended with a statement that he had decided instead to publish it in a journal article, presumably because of its technical nature. No such article was ever published.

Meanwhile, the astronomer Hirsch had published two reports on experiments using the Hipp chronoscope to measure what he called "physiological time." He explained that his purpose was to provide absolute correction for individual errors in astronomical observations, instead of merely an adjustment based on the "personal difference" between observers, as had been the custom. His first report (Hirsch, 1861–1863; the paper was read in 1862) was based on experiments begun not more than a month after the date of Wundt's paper at Speyer, but there is no evidence that it was in any way stimulated by that paper. Hirsch's paper reported differences in time for manual response (1) to auditory, visual, and tactile stimulation; (2) between observers; (3) in Hirsch's own results when fresh and when fatigued; (4) according to the locus of tactile stimulation and the hand used for response; and (5) according to whether the stimulus was expected or unexpected. A sophisticated procedure for the calibration of the chronoscope is described, and for each series of observations, there is a calculation of the probable error of the mean and the probable error of individual observations. This work was interrupted because Hipp had loaned the chronoscopes to Hirsch for a limited period of time.

The second report (Hirsch, 1863) described an ingenious procedure in which a pendulum moved a simulated star across the meridian of an astronomical telescope, and the time measured was that between the instant of "passage" and the observer's manual response. One finding was that when the "star" moved more slowly, the response time was longer. We cannot but wonder whether the publication of this superb series of experiments did not occasion the delays in Wundt's promised report on his own work.

It was not till several years later that Wundt (1866d) acknowledged that contrary to his earlier views, further experimentation had shown that when a stimulus of one modality, such as sound or touch, occurs during an ongoing series of stimuli of another modality, such as vision (recall Drobisch's comment about Wundt's having neglected other features of the experimental situation!), it will combine with one or another element of that series depending on the tempo of the series, the observer's state of fatigue, and other experimental variables. It is no longer a matter, therefore, of whether a given person "sees first and then hears" or "hears first and then sees" but of which experimental variables favor one result or the other. No data were given. The "natural unit of time" was thus tacitly abandoned and was never mentioned thereafter.

The very brief description of the apparatus used to obtain these results is entirely compatible with the figure of the complication pendulum that was to appear in the first and all the subsequent editions of the *Principles of Physiological Psychology*. The *series* of visual stimuli results, of course, from the movement of the swinging pointer in front of the subdivisions of the scale. The speed of the pendulum's swing is regulated by a movable bob. The pendulum can not only ring a bell at a precise predetermined moment, but it can also produce a tactile stimulus by rotating a small platform on which the subject's finger rests.

Later that year, Wundt published a "popular lecture" on mental measurement (1866c). Pythagoras was honored for discovering the law of relativity in our sensations, and therefore no mention of Weber or Fechner was necessary, but Wundt took personal credit for opening a more important avenue to mental measurement by his discovery that the act of perception consumes more time than that required for nervous conduction between the sense organ and the reacting muscles. It is, he said, as if consciousness needs time to prepare itself to receive the impressions that are brought to it. He called this required time *Auffassungsdauer* or "apprehension time"—not yet apperception time. However, he acknowledged that the method had its limitations because of the fact that not all

mental processes take place in consciousness. In closing, Wundt used a
simile borrowed from Goethe:

> It is denied us to look behind the loom and see directly how thought is woven
> from a thousand threads, but we must nevertheless make the attempt to
> separate the finished tissue from the threads from which it was formed.
> (p. 412)

Neither article mentions Hirsch's work.

Judgments on Haeckel and Helmholtz

Haeckel's *General Morphology* appeared in 1866. The year before, at
31, he took a chair of zoology especially created for him at Jena. This
two-volume work has been called "a landmark in the history of biological
doctrine in the 19th century" (*Encyclopaedia Britannica*, 11th ed., article on
Haeckel). Haeckel himself would characterize it later (1899, p. 7) as the
work in which he drew attention to the fact that the biogenetic law applies
to humans as well as to animals and emphasized the logical bond between
the transformation of species and the doctrine of anthropogenesis, so that
if the former is valid the latter must be so as well, as a special deduction
from it. Wundt's critique (1867c) is of particular interest because of the
light it throws on his views on Darwin's theory of evolution at this time.
He judged that the factual parts of Haeckel's work were more valuable
than the theoretical parts, and he chided Haeckel for being less cautious
than Darwin in his exclusive emphasis on adaptation as the driving force
of evolution. He rejected Haeckel's claim to having shown that morphology could be an explanatory as well as a descriptive discipline. He also
rejected Haeckel's antiteleological position and characterized the book as
consisting of "random remarks, loose analogies and unfounded hypotheses, in which nothing can be found of principle, or consequence, or
thoughtfulness" (p. 17).

It is not irrelevant to draw the reader's attention at this point to the
fact that although one often meets quotations from Wundt's later works
in which he expressed great appreciation of Darwin's achievement, when
these are read in context it will be found that they are always followed by a
rejection of the basic concept of Darwinian evolution (which is development in response to blindly operating forces) and by insistence on a view

of evolution consistent with German idealistic philosophy and therefore directed primarily by teleological rather than accidental forces.

The year 1866 also saw the completion of Helmholtz's *Treatise on Physiological Optics* with the publication of its third part. This part dealt with the visual perceptions of space, precisely that subject on which Wundt had expended so much of his own effort. It is worth repeating here the paragraph, very nearly the last words in the volume, in which Helmholtz defined the conflict between his own views and those of Wundt:

> In its main features the above presentation of the subject is the same as that which I gave in a popular lecture published in 1855. [This quietly replies to Wundt's repeated claims of priority with respect to unconscious conclusions. One wonders how Wundt could go on after this still ignoring the 1855 address.] It differs in some ways from the more recent works which have been also based on an empirical theory of vision. Thus with reference to the measurement not only of the space-relations on the visual globe but also of the distance of the observed objects, I have not put so much stress on the muscular feeling as Wundt does, because, for the reasons which I have given, I think they must be regarded as quite inaccurate and variable. On the contrary, my method consisted in obtaining the main measurements on the visual globe by making different images fall on the same parts of the retina. Wundt, in particular, has made a very exhaustive study of the relevant psychic phenomena, for which we are much indebted to him. I have called attention to some special observations of his where I differ from him. (Helmholtz, 1866/1925, Vol. 3, p. 558)

The major part of Wundt's review (1867d) was nevertheless devoted to reasserting his claim to priority both for the concept of unconscious conclusions and for the role of muscular sensation in space perception and to insisting on the superiority of his own theories over those of Helmholtz. He wrote that "much as [he] appreciated" the approval that his theory of unconscious conclusions received from its adoption by Helmholtz, he had to disagree with the manner of its application, because Helmholtz used it only to explain visual illusions, whereas he himself had demonstrated that it was essential for a psychological explanation of space perception generally. With respect to the part played by muscle sensations, Wundt conceded that judgments based on these alone are variable, but he nevertheless maintained that the degree of correspondence between the capacity for differentiation between the extent of eye movements and Fechner's findings on differentiation of the magnitude of visual objects constituted convincing proof (*"triftiger Beweis"*) of their close relationship.

"Physiological Psychology" Arrives

In 1867, Max Leidesdorf and Theodor Meynert launched a quarterly journal of psychiatry that aimed to show "its connections with the morphology and pathology of the central nervous system, physiological psychology, statistics and forensic medicine." The plan was conceived in the spirit of the somatological emphasis that was then dominant in German psychiatry generally, and the use of the phrase "physiological psychology" in its subtitle was not innovative, as we can see from its previous use by Dunn (1858) and Piderit (1863). Wundt was invited to prepare an article on "Recent Advances in the Field of Physiological Psychology" (1867b), and thus, this phrase entered his writing for the first time. It was probably a reading of this article that led William James, who was then attending courses in physiology at the University of Berlin, to write in a letter that at Heidelberg, Hermann Helmholtz (whose name, indeed, was known worldwide) and "a man named Wundt" were working at the beginnings of psychology as a science (James, 1920, Vol. 1, p. 119).

Wundt devoted his review chiefly to the areas in which he could claim significant contributions for himself: visual space perception and measurement of the time required for mental operations. However, because of the nature of the assignment he also made extensive mention of the contributions of other workers. With respect to visual space perception, there are references to the work of Aubert, Classen, Delboeuf, Fick, Funke, Helmholtz, Hering, Mach, Panum, Volkmann, and Wittich. With respect to the time of mental operations, there are references to Cammerer, Hirsch, Höring (a student of Vierordt), de Jaager (a student of Donders), and Mach. Except for that of Panum, all of the work cited was published between 1863 and 1866. Physiological psychology was obviously a very lively area of research.

Wundt found his task so congenial that he said he would "perhaps" take a later opportunity to make a more complete exposition, and thus, in a sense, this article is the seed from which the *Physiological Psychology* was to grow. Meanwhile, it was doubtless as a direct outgrowth of this article that Wundt lectured on "physiological psychology" in the winter semester of 1867–1868. He was to use this course title only one other time in his entire career: five years later, at the time when he was engaged in writing the book that proclaimed this area to be "a new domain of science."

Research in Neurophysiology

However, something else first had to be cleared from Wundt's agenda. The publication of his *Researches on the Mechanics of the Nerves and Nerve Centers* (1871a, 1876c) shows that he had not given up hope of making a fundamental contribution to the field of neurophysiology, and the rising prestige of the natural sciences at Heidelberg, due to the achievements not only of Helmholtz but also of Kirchhoff and Bunsen, co-developers of spectral analysis, may have helped turn Wundt's mind and efforts again to experiments with nerves and muscles.

Wundt's principal tool in this research was the myograph (Figure 2), and his surprising statement that no other available method could reveal so much about the functions of the nervous system perhaps only betrays an awareness that his methods were antiquated before he was ready to

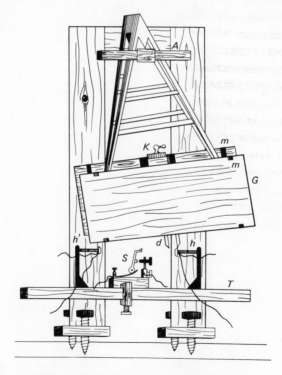

Figure 2. Wundt's pendulum myograph. (Wundt, 1871b, Fig. 1.)

publish the results of his protracted research. The actual results are of
little consequence and cannot be summed up in a small space; this
discussion is therefore limited to the theoretical structure that Wundt
(1876c) built upon these results. To do him justice, one must remember
that Waldeyer's neuron theory would not be stated until 1891 and that no
one had conceived that central nerve fibers might terminate outside nerve
cells rather than within them.

Wundt made three assumptions: (1) that the cells, unlike the fibers,
offer resistance to conduction, and that this resistance is greater in one
region of each cell than in another; for purposes of convenience, he
designated these regions "central" and "peripheral"; (2) that one end of
each fiber terminates near the periphery of a cell and that the other end
terminates more centrally in another cell; and (3) that these "mechanical"
relationships follow different patterns in the sensory and motor tracts.
The consequence is something that may be thought of as akin to the
physiological gradient hypothesis that Child (1924) advanced half a
century later. Child's gradients depend on relative levels of excitation; Wundt's gradients depend on relative strengths of resistance to
conduction.

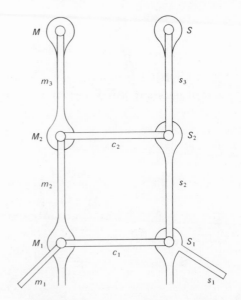

Figure 3. Wundt's schema of central nervous
conduction. (Wundt, 1876c, Fig. 41.) See text
for explanation.

Hall (1912, p. 324ff.) said of this work that it

deserves to be ranked as the boldest and most interesting hypothesis ever
offered to explain quite a large group of facts in a domain where we still have
no adequate theory, for Sherrington's conjectures [cf. Sherrington, 1906] are
less comprehensive.

But Hall added that "perhaps his rating with contemporary physiologists
has not been improved by this work." This theory is stated in the first
edition of the Physiological Psychology under the running head "Theory of
Central Innervation" (pp. 265–271), and even in 1908, in the sixth edition,
at a time when the neuron theory was being widely accepted, Wundt said
that he thought his hypothesis more plausible (Figure 3).

This research was the basis for the greater part (but not the final
section) of Wundt's first publication in English (1876a), where, however,
the theory stated above is only intimated (pp. 172–174). The reader who
turns to that article can see an example of Wundt's typical hastiness in the
related "finding" (p. 167, par. 2), which was acknowledged as an error in
the German publication that same year (1876c, p. 18).

Hall, Wundt, and Bernstein

This ambitious hypothesis, based as Wundt said on fourteen years of
intermittent labor in the laboratory, forms an appropriate backdrop to a
discussion of Wundt's relationship both to Helmholtz and to his own
successor in the post of assistant, Julius Bernstein. Hall (1912, p. 311) wrote
that Wundt "became for a time assistant to Helmholtz, who later desiring
a helper more accomplished in mathematics and physics, sought another
in his place." Wundt (1915) published a "correction" to the effect that his
duties did not involve such matters. His autobiography added that an
unnamed mathematician friend was amused by the idea that Helmholtz
would want such "assistance" (1920, p. 155n). These self-serving statements cannot be taken as refutations. More to the point would be evidence of Helmholtz's satisfaction or dissatisfaction with the manner in
which the assistant's instructional duties, which we have seen were not
inconsiderable, were carried out at a time when increasing emphasis was
being placed on the quantitative aspects of physiology.

We have seen that Wundt got off on the wrong foot with Helmholtz
by failing, for whatever reason, to acknowledge the latter's priority in the
matter of "unconscious inference," and that this circumstance long

hung as a cloud between them. We have seen that Wundt blundered in mathematics. We have read Sechenov's testimony that it was more difficult to communicate with Wundt than with Helmholtz. Now let us go on.

Wundt left the assistantship in 1864, although he wrote that he did so in 1863. The error may have some basis in fact. In 1863, the Physiological Institute moved from the cramped quarters described by Sechenov to more ample rooms (Hinz, 1961), suggesting the possibility that Helmholtz requested Wundt's resignation during that year because the expansion brought with it greater responsibilities for an assistant. Wundt's replacement, Julius Bernstein, was recommended by Du Bois-Reymond, a circumstance that at once suggests how Hall might have heard the story. Wundt himself said of Du Bois that "he did not hesitate to entrust to his young students things which were at best suitable for the ears of his academic colleagues" (1920, p. 109). It is therefore likely that whatever Helmholtz confided to his friend Du Bois, when he asked him to recommend an assistant, would later have been passed on by Du Bois to his assistants. In the semester before Hall went to Leipzig, he collaborated at Berlin with Du Bois's assistant, Hugo Kronecker, and so close was their relationship that he wrote to William James, "I have stood in much the same terms of intimacy and recipiency as last year to you, and [to him] I am likely to own a scarcely smaller debt of gratitude" (Ross, 1972, p. 81). If Kronecker had any juicy gossip about Wundt, Hall would have heard it before he went to Leipzig.

From these probabilities, we turn to a certainty: that Bernstein was both a better mathematician and a better physiologist than Wundt. Wundt said that one source of difficulty for himself was the coincidence of his research interests with those of Helmholtz. Bernstein's interests were in the same areas: the human senses and neurophysiology. While he served as Helmholtz's assistant, Bernstein (1868a), using the galvanometer that Wundt scorned, established the polarized membrane theory of nerve conduction that lies "at the core of modern theory" (Brazier, 1959, p. 22). He also demonstrated (mathematically!) that if we assume that cortical irradiation of sensory input is limited by local inhibitory processes, and that these are mobilized in direct proportion to the strength of that input, the extent of irradiation will correspond exactly to Fechner's law (Bernstein, 1968b). Wundt dismissed these assumptions as arbitrary. Today, the first is a firmly established fact, and the second must at least be accorded a high probability. Finally, Bernstein (1871) (Figure 4) also

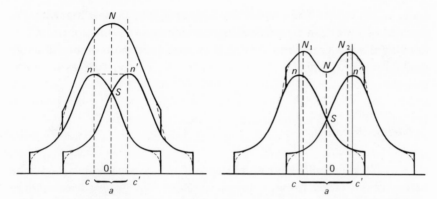

Figure 4. Bernstein's hypothesis relating cortical irradiation and inhibition to two-point tactile discrimination. After Bernstein (1871, Figs. 27 and 28).

applied his theory of irradiation to Weber's two-point threshold, pointing out that the summation of the irradiation fields from two points of the sensory cortex, when they are close together, is unimodal, just as if only one point were stimulated, but that when the two points are sufficiently far apart, the summation becomes bimodal, providing a basis for discrimination. It is clear that Helmholtz had found himself a mathematically adept assistant to replace Wundt and that the coincidence of their research interests did not impede Bernstein's progress. The demonstration that a purely physiological explanation of Weber's findings on spatial discrimination is indeed possible could not have made pleasant reading for Wundt, whose career as a psychologist started from the conviction that such an explanation was not possible.

Bernstein's book on nervous excitation (1871) came out at almost the same time as the first part of Wundt's work on "nerve mechanics" (1871b). Wundt reviewed it anonymously (1871a). After a nonevaluative résumé of Bernstein's experimental findings, the review closed with this passage:

> We shall not enter into the largely theoretical considerations in which the author deals with Weber's touch-circles of irradiation, the psychophysical law, etc., because the factual grounds on which the author seeks to explain the most important laws of the general physiology of the nerves and the senses seem to us inadequate. The hypotheses which he sets up regarding irradiation and sensation-circles can be reduced essentially to those originally assumed by Plateau and by Weber, which, we believe, have been refuted by the modern physiology of the senses.

For quite different judgments on Bernstein's hypotheses regarding Fechner's law and the two-point threshold, see Ward (1876) and Ladd and

Woodworth (1911). The account by Boring (1942), in keeping with the practice of American psychologists from about 1910 until about 1960 of denying the reality of cortical inhibition, makes no mention of the active inhibition of irradiation, without which Bernstein's hypotheses are unintelligible.

Academic Mobility

In 1871, Helmholtz left Heidelberg for Berlin to become at last what he had always wished to be, a physicist. Bernstein declined an offer to remain at Heidelberg as assistant professor and the next year, he received the chair that Goltz vacated at Halle. Willy Kühne, another former student of Du Bois, replaced Helmholtz, dashing Wundt's hopes in that regard. However, Wundt was at last assigned specific areas of instruction (anthropology and medical psychology), for which he would receive a guaranteed emolument (Bringmann, 1975). Though modest, it was sufficient to permit his marriage in 1872 to Sophie Mau (1844–1912).

At 40, Wundt had achieved scant professional recognition. He could, and doubtless did, ruefully compare his status with that of his younger cousin Julius Arnold, who in 1870 had been named full professor and director of the Institute of Pathology. Wundt had published seven books, yet no university sought him as a physiologist. He was considered for a chair in philosophy at Jena in 1872, and at Marburg in 1873, but despite supporting letters from Helmholtz (see Schlotte, 1956), he was not offered either post. Lange, who had gone from Zurich to Marburg in 1872, recommended Wundt for the chair in "inductive philosophy" that was still vacant at Zurich, but it is clear that this proposal did not arouse unanimous enthusiasm, since "about a year" passed between the time when Wundt was asked if he would accept such a call and the actual offer (1920, p. 242).

On "a hot summer morning" in 1874, Wundt was house-hunting in Zurich (p. 243). On Whitsunday, 1875, he was in Leipzig on the same errand (Schlotte, 1956, p. 338). It was gratifying mobility for one who had probably never given up hoping to escape from Heidelberg. In 1874, there were 68 medical students at Heidelberg, "more than 200" at Zurich, and 394 at Leipzig (Decaisne, 1876). Equally gratifying was the fact that he had earned recognition as a philosopher and could look forward to forgetting the frustrations of his own career in physiology.

However, before we leave Wundt settled at Leipzig, we must ask what it was about the *Principles of Physiological Psychology* that made the book so successful. I have previously stated my belief that this book benefited from Wundt's reading of Bain's *Senses and the Intellect* (1864), the first psychology book to open with a chapter about the nervous system (Diamond, 1974). Wundt read this book in its second (1864) edition, hence after publication of his own *Lectures* (1863–1864). Also, as mentioned above, his article on "recent advances" in physiological psychology had been an exercise in which he learned to discuss the work of others without necessarily emphasizing his own related achievements and goals. Finally, it is reasonable to suppose that his marriage in 1872 was an even more effectual tranquilizer than his brush with death fifteen years earlier and made it possible for him to drop the role of angry young man. These were some of the factors that enabled Wundt to write a book in which he appeared less as the advocate of his own theories than as spokesman for a broad movement. As Ebbinghaus (1908) later put it, Wundt was the first to graft all the nineteenth-century sproutings of the new psychology (sense physiology, personal equation, psychophysics, brain localization) onto the old, partially withered stock and thus revivify it.

The rapid advancement that came to its author following the publication of the *Physiological Psychology* is the best proof of how ready the world was to receive its message. In the course of time, Wundt substantially modified that message (see Chapter 6). Our concern now, however, is only with the original edition and how it was perceived at the time. For this purpose, we shall summarize what was said about it by the anonymous reviewer in the *Literarisches Centralblatt* as well as by William James, James Sully, and Friedrich Lange.

What the Reviewers Said

The review in the *Literarisches Centralblatt* (1874) summarized the book's purpose in a paragraph consisting largely of numerous short quotations from its opening pages (see pages 157–159 in this volume). It then went on to say that the book

> corresponds exactly to the need created by recent developments in physiology and psychology and the [consequent] lively demand for a *specialized* scientific treatment of the actual relations between body and consciousness.

Final judgment was reserved (in the first part of the review) because the treatment of important issues, and particularly the matter of relationships between consciousness and the organism, would be found only in the second part of the work, which was not yet published. The only specific issue discussed at some length was Wundt's argument against the doctrine of specific energies, and in this connection, attention was drawn to Wundt's failure to acknowledge that much the same argument had been put forward by Horwicz (1872). (Wundt excused himself in the preface to the completed work by saying that Horwicz's book had not come to his attention in time. His unhappiness over this incident may explain the bitterness of the polemic he conducted against an even more significant contribution [Horwicz, 1878], which he might have been expected to greet with some show of hospitality, as in line with his own thinking.)

After seeing the completed work, the reviewer made a judgment that history has confirmed: that by his thorough, scholarly treatment of all the new materials available, Wundt had "defined the scope and tasks of physiological psychology for a long time to come" and that his book would be influential in directing the work of many younger psychologists who shared the same objective. Nevertheless, strong reservations were expressed regarding the final, metaphysical chapter, in which Wundt characterized the mind as "the inner being of the same unity which we apprehend externally as its body." (See pp. 172–177 for the full text of that final chapter.) The reviewer also expressed disappointment that greater use had not been made of Darwin's theory of evolution. On the other hand, Wundt's critique of Herbart was seen as useful because it showed the danger inherent in any predominantly philosophical theory of consciousness.

All in all, Wundt was commended for very effectively meeting a current need, providing system where there had been scattered findings, and pointing to profitable lines for further advance. A noncommittal attitude was taken toward Wundt's many theoretical formulations of specific problems. The emphasis on the experimental nature of physiological psychology was seen as part of the program for progress "from the outside in."

James (1875) welcomed the *Physiological Psychology* as representative of that "serious revival of philosophical inquiry" coming from "men engaged in the physical sciences," whose "habits of patience and fairness, their willingness to advance by small steps at a time," gave promise of "results of the highest importance" (p. 195). In view of Wundt's prior record of rushing into print with ill-founded hypotheses, it is ironic that James should refer to him as "perhaps [the] paragon" of "these new prism, pendulum and galvanometer philosophers" (p. 196). The work, he said, "certainly fills a lacuna. . . . If, through a large part of it, the reader finds that physiology and psychology lie side by side without combining, it is more the fault of the science than of the author" (p. 197). "Wundt's book has many shortcomings, but they only prove how confused and rudimentary the science of psycho-physics still is." It is, nevertheless, "indispensable for study and reference" (p. 201).

James made no mention of Wundt's claim that he was defining the limits of a new field of science. The general tone of the review is to welcome not merely this book in itself but the broad movement it represented, a movement of cooperative endeavor between physiologists and psychologists that would surely, in time, provide the data needed as a basis for sound philosophy.

Sully (1876) did accept Wundt's claim to having "defined the boundaries of a new department of research in Germany," and he saw the work as "putting into systematic form the results of a number of more or less isolated inquiries" that "have as their common aim the determination of the exact physiological conditions of a certain group of mental phenomena" as well as the "common presupposition . . . that conscious activity goes on at every point hand in hand with nervous activity" (p. 21). He recalled the historical antecedents of physiological psychology in Germany, designating as early "builders of the edifice of physiological psychology" (p. 26) not only the sense physiologists who were early contemporaries of Wundt but such now-almost-forgotten names as Ritter (who discovered that flexors and adductors respond to stimulation too weak to excite response in extensors and abductors [Gotch, 1900]) and Ehrenberg (presumably mentioned for his early work on the acuity of vision). Sully contrasted the phrase "physiological psychology" with "mental physiology," which was current with English writers, and said that it "seems to lay stress on the fact that a certain portion of the mind is to be built up by an extension of the proper methods of physiological inquiry" (p. 27).

Lange, we know, was so favorably impressed that he recommended Wundt for the chair of inductive philosophy at Zurich. In the first edition of his *History of Materialism* (1866), Lange had coined the phrase "a psychology without a soul," which is now often mistakenly attributed to Wundt. The second edition [1873–1875] made a number of references to the *Physiological Psychology*, particularly in the chapters on "Mind and the Brain" and "Scientific Psychology." These references always come in the course of discussions of physiological matter, in the narrow sense of that word. To illustrate, I shall outline the discussion in which occurs the fullest reference to Wundt's work. The quotations are from the published English translation (Lange, 1881). We begin with a "position statement" by Lange:

> It will always be of service, in order to avoid a relapse into the old psychological ideas and to assist the right view to come to the front, if it is shown how even the complex psychical images can be explained from those simple beginnings with which exact research is now concerning itself. (Vol. 3, p. 152)

On the next page, Wundt is brought in to support this position:

> We possess now, too, at length, in Wundt's admirable "Principles of Physiological Psychology," a work which has already made the new and only fruitful views the basis of a comprehensive treatment of the psychological sphere.

Then, after direct quotation of a dozen lines stressing that "we must necessarily assume that elementary [nervous] forms are also capable of elementary performances only" (Wundt, 1873, p. 226), Lange paraphrased Wundt as follows:

> Everything, observes Wundt farther on, that we call Will and Intelligence resolves itself, as soon as it is traced back to its physiological elements, into nothing but sentient impressions transforming themselves into movements. (p. 154)

Lange was in fact restating the following passage in the *Physiological Psychology*:

> It is clear that the forebrain, in which the most significant functions of the cerebral cortex are concentrated, transforms sensory stimuli into extraordinarily complex movements of many forms. . . . Everything which we call Will and Intelligence resolves itself, as soon as it is traced back to its elementary physiological phenomena, into *nothing but* such transformations. (Wundt, 1873, p. 228—italics added)

In the final paragraph of the chapter, Lange summed up:

> This co-operation of very many, and, individually considered, extraordinarily feeble nerve impulses, must give us the key to the physiological understanding of thinking. (p. 161)

Thus, what Lange found "admirable" in Wundt's presentation was his use of elementary *physiological* facts to explain complex behavior—for to Lange, psychology was not limited to the study of consciousness. His other citations of Wundt's work fit the same pattern.

To summarize: these four expert reviewers agreed that Wundt's work grew out of an existing movement to find physiological foundations for all forms of mental activity, and that the term *physiological psychology* as used by him referred to just such use of physiological findings. This attitude is one that Wundt later characterized as a "widespread misunderstanding" about the nature of the new discipline (1920, p. 197). Did all four writers misperceive Wundt's intention? If so, their reviews demonstrate only so much more conclusively that the great impact of Wundt's book was due to the readiness of readers at the time to welcome a fundamentally physiological approach to psychological problems. However, it is difficult to believe that Wundt would have made his meaning so obscure.

The Inaugurations and Beyond

In his inaugural address at Zurich (1874; I have had access only to the French translation, 1875), Wundt left no doubt that a philosopher, not a physiologist, had come to fill the chair of inductive philosophy. The names of Aristotle, Leibnitz, and Locke occurred once each; Fichte twice, Hegel 4 times, Schopenhauer 5, Herbart 8, and Kant 21 times. Those who expected to hear that physiological research on the brain and the senses had significance for epistemology, or that the principle of conservation had a bearing on cosmology, or that Darwinism must modify our notions of man's place in the universe, were surely puzzled by the failure of this "inductive philosopher" to mention the name or work of a single scientist. The door was not slammed shut on such influence, but neither was it opened more than a crack. What was said with assurance was that "all experience is first of all inner experience" and that therefore, the monistic system that modern science requires "can only be idealism" (1875, p. 120). Furthermore, it must be an idealism along the lines initiated by Fichte, holding to the "idea of the necessary development of inner thought" (p. 125). This leaves little room for an "inductive" philosophy.

The inaugural address at Leipzig (1876) had a similar message:

> The more we are inclined today, and rightly, to demand that experience shall have an influence on philosophy, so much the more is it in place to emphasize that precisely in our time philosophy must assert its old influence among the empirical sciences. . . . Nothing can be more mistaken than the widespread opinion that these [empirical and materialistic] views emerged from the development of natural science itself. The standpoint of modern empiricism got

its foundation from philosophers. . . . Perhaps the time will not be far distant
when the metaphysics which is now so scorned by empirical investigators will
again be held in some measure of honor. (1876b, pp. 6, 23, 26)

Thus did Wundt enter on the second half of his life span, during which,
through a chain of circumstances that he had helped to set in motion but
over which he had largely lost control, he soon became "an important
rallying point for the generation of young men who saw experimental
psychology as a new avenue to man's self-understanding" (Diamond,
1976, p. 528).

Since the occasions for these two inaugural addresses are certainly to
be counted among the "high points" of Wundt's life, we must ask if the
addresses were inspired by political motives. They were so, in the most
literal sense. The call for adherence to a distinctively Germanic idealism
was in line with the wave of nationalist fervor that swept the universities
in the period following the Franco-Prussian War, when a united Germany arose under Prussian hegemony. One effect was a relative decline
of enrollment in the natural sciences and a rise in the popularity of the
Geisteswissenschaften or mental sciences. Wundt could enter into this
movement wholeheartedly, for it harmonized with the political program
that he had advocated ten years earlier.

Summary

We have reviewed the first half of Wundt's long life. In his professional work, we have seen evidence of motives incompatible with
genuine scientific dedication. His actions were often directed by personal
ambition. He magnified his own achievements, placed extravagant values on his own hypotheses, depreciated or disregarded the work of those
whom he regarded as his competitors, and bitterly resented all correction.
The enormous effort he sometimes expended on fruitless efforts to provide experimental support for overhasty generalizations shows that he
placed more faith in the validity of his speculations than in the force of
empirical evidence. These behaviors are more eloquent than protesta-
tions, and perhaps this is the real meaning of the priority he gave to
"inner" as against "outer" experience and to "will" over intellect.

Since behavior is a function of the situation as well as of the behaver,
new facets of his character might well have appeared following what
Titchener calls his "rapid rise to a position that may almost be called

pontifical" (1921a, p. 171n). It is not surprising that he should behave with kindly paternalism toward the students who revered his authority, or seemed to do so. At the same time, the fierce pride that arose as his compensation for early feelings of inferiority continued to make it impossible for him to deal with professional colleagues as equals. Hall's statement in this regard may be taken as the formulation of hypotheses for testing in an historical study of the later Wundt:

> Perhpas no one ever criticized so many of others' views or was more impatient of criticism or apparently so jealous of those who advanced along his own lines as he. . . . It almost seems as though no one was so generally right in criticizing those who preceded or were contemporaneous with him or so generally wrong in criticizing his own critics and his more independent pupils. He . . . almost seems to wish to be the last in fields where he was the first, instead of taking pleasure in seeing successors arise who advance his lines still further. (1912, p. 419)

If these statements are true, or approximately true, Wundt's actions must often have impeded the progress of experimental psychology. The whole question of his place and his importance in the history of modern psychology, of the relative weight of the beneficial and detrimental effects stemming from his actions, cannot be adequately dealt with simply by expounding his views and comparing them with subsequent developments, as is so often done. It is necessary to face the realities of his character and to ask how they influenced his conduct toward his contemporaries as well as their conduct toward him. That task remains to be done.

References

Bain, A. *The senses and the intellect* (2nd ed.). London, 1864.

Bernstein, J. Ueber den zeitlichen Verlauf der negativen Schwankung des nervenstroms. *Archiv für die gesammte Physiologie,* 1868, *1,* 173–207. (Reprinted in Bernstein, 1871.) (a)

Bernstein, J. Zur Theorie des Fechner'schen Gesetzes der Empfindung. *Archiv für Anatomie, Physiologie and wissenschaftliche Medicin,* 1868, 388–393. (b)

Bernstein, J. *Untersuchungen über den Erregungsvorgang im Nerven- und Muskelsysteme.* Heidelberg, 1871.

Boring, E. G. *Sensation and perception in the history of experimental psychology.* New York, 1942.

Boring, E. G. *A history of experimental psychology* (2nd ed.). New York, 1950.

Brazier, M. The historical development of neurophysiology. In H. W. Magoun (Ed.), *Handbook of Physiology, Section 1: Neurophysiology* (Vol. 1). Washington, D.C., 1959.

Bringmann, W. G. Wundt in Heidelberg 1845–1874. *Canadian Psychological Review,* 1975, *16,* 124–129.

Bringmann, W. G., Balance, W. D. G., and Evans, R. B. Wilhelm Wundt 1832–1920: A brief biographical sketch. *Journal of the History of the Behavioral Sciences*, 1975, 11, 287–297.

Buffon. [*Natural history, general and particular*] (William Smellie, trans.). 9 vols. London, 1791. (Originally published, 1749–1767.)

Child, C. M. *Physiological foundations of behavior*. New York: Holt, 1924.

Decaisne, G. Les universités de l'Europe en 1876. *Révue scientifique de France et de l'étrangère*, 1876, 17, 266–270, 369–375.

Diamond, S. The greatness of Alexander Bain. Unpublished invited address, Sixth Annual Meeting of Cheiron, International Society for History of Social and Behavioral Sciences, University of New Hampshire, June 2, 1974.

Diamond, S. Wilhelm Wundt. In *Dictionary of Scientific Biography* (Vol. 14). New York, 1976.

Drobisch, M. W. Ueber den neuesten Versuch die Psychologie naturwissenschaftlich zu begründen. *Zeitschrift für exacte Philosophie*, 1864, 4, 313–348.

Du Bois-Reymond, E. *Untersuchungen über thierische Elektricität*. Berlin, 1848.

Dunn, R. *An essay on physiological psychology*. London, 1858.

Ebbinghaus, H. *Abriss der Psychologie*. Leipzig, 1908.

Erdmann, B. Zur zeitgenössischen Psychologie in Deutschland. *Zeitschrift für wissenschaftliche Philosophie*, 1879, 3, 377–407.

Eschler, E. Ueber die sozial-philosophische Seite im Schaffen Wilhelm Wundts. *Wissenschaftliche Zeitschrift der Karl-Marx-Universität Leipzig*, 1962, 11, 737–761.

Fechner, G. T. Elemente der Psychophysik (2 vols.). Leipzig: Breitkopf und Härtel, 1860.

Fürbringer, M. Friedrich Arnold. In F. Scholl (Ed.), *Heidelberger Professoren aus dem 19. Jahrhundert*, Vol. 2. Heidelberg, 1903.

Gotch, F. Nerve. In E. A. Schäfer (Ed.), *Text-book of Physiology*, Vol. 2. Edinburgh, 1900.

Haeckel, E. *Ueber unsere gegenwärtige Kenntniss vom Ursprung des Menschen*. Bonn, 1899.

Hall, G. S. *Founders of modern psychology*. New York, 1912.

Helmholtz, H. Ueber das Sehen des Menschen [Leipzig, 1855]. In *Vorträge und Reden* (4th ed.), Vol. 1. Braunschweig, 1896.

Helmholtz, H. [*Treatise on physiological optics*, Vol. 3.] (Ed. by J. P. C. Southall.) Optical Society of America, 1925. (Originally published, 1866.)

Helmholtz, H. Die neueren Fortschritte in der Theorie des Sehens. *Preussischer Jahrbücher*, 1868, 21, 149–170, 261–289, 403–444. Reprinted in Helmholtz, *Vorträge und Reden*. 4th ed. Vol. 1. Braunschweig: Vieweg und Sohn, 1896.

Hering, E. Ueber W. Wundt's Theorie des binocularen Sehens. *Annalen der Physik und Chemie*, 1863, 119, 115–130.

Hering, E. Zur Kritik der Wundt'schen Theorie des binocularen Sehens. *Annalen der Physik und Chemie*, 1864, 122, 476–481.

Hinz, G. (Ed.). *Aus der Geschichte der Universität Heidelberg und ihre Facultäten*. Heidelberg: Ruperto-Carola (Sonderband), 1961.

Hirsch, A. Expériences chronoscopiques sur la vitesse des différentes sensations et de la transmission nerveuse. *Bulletin de la Societé* [Neuchâteloise] *des Sciences Naturelles*, 1861–1863, 6, 100–114.

Hirsch, A. Ueber persönliche Gleichung und Correction bei chronographischen Durchgangs-Beobachtungen. *Untersuchungen zur Naturlehre des Menschen und der Thiere*, 1863, 9, 200–208.

Horwicz, A. *Psychologische Analysen auf physiologischer Grundlage*, Vol. 1. Halle, 1872.

Horwicz, A. *Psychologischer Analysen auf physiologischer Grundlage*, Vol. 2, 2. *Die Analyse der qualitativen Gefühle*. Magdeburg, 1878.

James, H. (Ed.). *The letters of William James* (2 vols.). Boston, 1920.

[James, W.] (Unsigned review of W. Wundt, *Grundzüge der physiologische Psychologie.*) *North American Review*, 1875, 121, 195–201.

Kossakowski, A. Wilhelm Wundt und sein wissenschaftliches Erbe. *Wissenschaftliche Zeitschrift der Karl-Marx-Universität Leipzig*, 1966, 15, 717–726.

Krueger, F. Wilhelm Wundt als deutscher Denker. In A. Hoffman (Ed.), *Wilhelm Wundt: Eine Würdigung.* Erfurt, 1922. (*Beiträge zur Philosophie des deutschen Idealismus, II*, 3/4.)

Kurz, H. and Wedel, M. *Deutsche Literaturgeschichte.* Berlin, 1927.

Ladd, G. T., and Woodworth, R. S. *Elements of physiological psychology* (rev. ed.). New York, 1911.

Lange, F. A. *Geschichte des Materialismus.* Iserlohn, 1866.

Lange, F. A. [*History of materialism* (2nd ed.)] (E. C. Thomas, trans.). 3 vols. Boston, 1881. (Originally published, 1873–1875.)

Literarisches Centralblatt für Deutschland, 1858, 9, 395. (Unsigned review of Wundt, *Die Lehre von der Muskelbewegung.*)

Literarisches Centralblatt für Deutschland, 1863, 14, 773–774. (Unsigned review of Wundt, *Vorlesungen über die Menschen- und Thierseele, I.*)

Literarisches Centralblatt für Deutschland, 1864, 15, 964–966. (Unsigned review of Wundt, *Vorlesungen über die Menschen- und Thierseele, II.*)

Literarisches Centralblatt für Deutschland, 1867, 18, 1400. (Unsigned review of Wundt, *Die physikalischen Axiome und ihre Bezeihung zum Causalprincip.*)

Literarisches Centralblatt für Deutschland, 1874, 25, 225–228, 1481–1482. (Unsigned review of Wundt, *Grundzüge der physiologische Psychologie.*)

Lotze, R. H. *Medicinische Psychologie oder Physiologie der Seele.* Leipzig, 1852.

Ludwig, C. *Lehrbuch der Physiologie des Menschen* (2 vols., 2nd rev. ed.). Heidelberg: Winter, 1858–1861.

MacLeod, R. B. (Ed.). *William James: Unfinished business.* Washington, D.C.: American Psychological Association, 1969.

McKendrick, J. G. *Hermann von Helmholtz.* London, 1899.

Müller, J. *Handbuch der Physiologie des Menschen.* Coblenz: Hölscher, 1833–1840.

Munk, H. Ueber die Leitung der Erregung im Nerven, II. *Archiv für Anatomie, Physiologie und wissenschaftliche Medicin*, 1861, 425–490.

Munk, H. Ueber Dr. Wundt's "Bemerkung u.s.w." *Archiv für Anatomie, Physiologie und wissenschaftliche Medicin*, 1862, 145–148. (a)

Munk, H. Ueber Herrn Dr. Wundt's Replik. *Archiv für Anatomie, Physiologie und wissenschaftliche Medicin*, 1862, 654–660. (b)

[Peirce, C. S.] (Unsigned review of Wundt, *Principles of physiological psychology*, Vol. 1, 1904; trans. by E. B. Titchener). *The Nation*, 1905, 81, 56–57.

Peirce, C. S. *Collected Papers*, Vols. 7–8. Cambridge, Mass.: Harvard University Press, 1966.

Perry, R. B. *The thought and character of William James.* (2 vols.). Boston: Little, Brown, 1935.

Petersen, P. *Wilhelm Wundt und seine Zeit.* Stuttgart, 1925.

Piderit, T. *Gehirn und Geist: Entwurf einer physiologischen Psychologie für denkende Leser aller Stände.* Leipzig, 1863.

Ross, D. G. *Stanley Hall: The psychologist as prophet.* Chicago, 1972.

Schlotte, F. Beiträge zur Lebensbild Wilhelm Wundts aus seinem Briefwechsel. *Wissenschaftliche Zeitschrift der Karl-Marx-Universität Leipzig*, 19[55]–56, 5, 333–349.

Sechenov, I. M. [*Autobiographical Notes.*] Moscow, 1952. (Originally published, 1945.)

Spranger, E. *Geisteswissenschaftliche Psychologie und Ethik der Persönlichkeit* (5. Ausg.). Halle, 1925. Translated as *Types of men. The psychology and ethics of personality.* Halle, 1928.

Stübler, E. *Geschichte der medizinischen Fakultät der Universität Heidelberg 1386–1925*. Heidelberg, 1926.

Sully, J. Physiological psychology in Germany. *Mind*, 1876, 1, 20–43.

T[itchener], E. B. *American Journal of Psychology*, 1921, 32, 575–580. (Review of Wundt, *Erlebtes und Erkanntes*.) (a)

Titchener, E. B. Wilhelm Wundt. *American Journal of Psychology*, 1921, 32, 161–177. (b)

T[itchener], E. B. Wundt's address at Speyer. *American Journal of Psychology*, 1923, 34, 311.

Ueberweg, F. [*History of philosophy*, Vol. 2] (Trans. by G. S. Morris, from the 4th German ed.) New York, 1898. (Originally published 1866, the 4th edition in 1871.)

Villa, G. *Contemporary psychology*. New York, 1903.

Volkelt, H. Die Völkerpsychologie in Wundt's Entwicklungsgang. In A. Hoffman (Ed.), *Wilhelm Wundt: Eine Würdigung*. Erfurt, 1922. (*Beiträge zur Philosophie des deutschen Idealismus, II, 3/4*).

Waitz, T. *Lehrbuch der Psychologie als Naturwissenschaft*. Braunschweig, 1849.

Ward, J. An attempt to interpret Fechner's Law. *Mind*, 1876, 1, 452–466.

Weber, E. Muskelbewegung. In R. Wagner (Ed.), *Handwörterbuch der Physiologie* (Bd. 3, Abt. 2). Braunschweig, 1846.

Weber, E. H. Der Tastsinn und das Gemeingefühl. In R. Wagner (Ed.), *Handwörterbuch der Physiologie* (Bd. 3, Abt. 2). Braunschweig, 1846.

Wundt, E. *Wilhelm Wundts Werk. Ein Verzeichniss seiner sämtlichen Schriften*. Munich, 1927.

Wundt, E. Wilhelm Wundt. *Deutsches biographisches Jahrbuch*, II: 1917–1920. Stuttgart, 1928.

Wundt, W. Ueber den Kochsalzgehalt des Harns. *Journal für practische Chemie*, 1853, 59, 354–363. (Not seen by me.)

Wundt, W. Versuche über den Einfluss der Durchschneidung des Lungenmagennerven auf die Respirationsorgane. *Archiv für Anatomie, Physiologie und wissenschaftliche Medicin*, 1855, 269–313.

Wundt, W. Ueber die Elasticität feuchter organischer Gewebe. *Archiv für Anatomie, Physiologie und wissenschaftliche Medicin*, 1857, 298–308.

Wundt, W. Beiträge zur Theorie der Sinneswahrnehmung. I. :Ueber den Gefühlssinn mit besonderer Rücksicht auf dessen räumliche Wahrnehmungen. *Zeitschrift für rationelle Medicin*, 1858, 4 (3. Reihe), 229–293. (a)

Wundt, W. *Die Lehre von der Muskelbewegung. Nach eigenen Untersuchungen bearbeitet*. Braunschweig, 1858. (b)

Wundt, W. Ueber secondäre Modification der Nerven. *Archiv für Anatomie, Physiologie, und wissenschaftliche Medicin*, 1859, 537–548.

Wundt, W. Bemerkung zu den Aufsatz des Herrn Dr. H. Munk "Ueber die Leitung der Erregung im Nerven, II. *Archiv für Anatomie, Physiologie und wissenschaftliche Medicin*, 1861, 781–783. (a)

Wundt, W. Der Blick. Eine physiognomische Studie. *Unterhaltungen am häuslichen Herd*, 1861, 1 (3. Folge), 1028–1033. (b)

Wundt, W. *Beiträge zur Theorie der Sinneswahrnehmung*. Leipzig, 1862. (a)

Wundt, W. Die Geschwindigkeit des Gedankens. *Gartenlaube*, 1862, 263–265. (b)

Wundt, W. Der Mund. Physiognomische Studie. *Unterhaltungen am häuslichen Herd*, 1862, 2 (3. Folge), 503–510. (c)

Wundt, W. Ueber die Bewegung des Auges. *Archiv für Ophthalmologie*, 1862, 8, 1–87. (d)

Wundt, W. Ueber binokulares Sehen. *Annalen der Physik und Chemie*, 1862, 116, 617–626. (e)

Wundt, W. Die Zeit. *Unterhaltungen am häuslichen Herd*, 1862, 2 (3. Folge), 590–593. (f)

Wundt, W. Zur "secondären Modification." *Archiv für Anatomie, Physiologie und wissenschaftliche Medicin*, 1862, 498–507. (g)

Wundt, W. Ueber Dr. E. Hering's Kritik meiner Theorie des Binokularsehens. *Annalen der Physik und Chemie*, 1863, 120, 172–176.

Wundt, W. *Vorlesungen über die Menschen- und Thierseele* (2 vols.). Leipzig, 1863–1864.

Wundt, W. *Lehrbuch der Physiologie des Menschen.* Erlangen, 18[64]–1865.

Wundt, W. *Die physikalischen Axiome und ihre Beziehung zum Causalprincip. Einer Capitel aus einer Philosophie der Naturwissenschaften.* Erlangen, 1866. (a)

Wundt, W. (Review of A. Fick, *Die medicinische Physik.*) *Kritische Blätter für wissenschaftliche und praktische Medicin,* 1866, 201–202. (b)

Wundt, W. Ueber das psychische Maass. Ein populärer Vortrag. *Deutsche Klinik,* 1866, 18, 401–403, 409–412. (c)

Wundt, W. Ueber einige Zeitverhältnisse des Wechsels der Sinnesvorstellungen. Vorläufige Mittheilung. *Deutsche Klinik,* 1866, 18, 77–78. (d)

Wundt, W. *Handbuch der medicinischen Physik.* Erlangen, 1867. (a)

Wundt, W. Neuere Leistungen auf dem Gebiete der physiologischen Psychologie. *Vierteljahrsschrift für Psychiatrie in ihren Beziehungen zur Morphologie und Pathologie des Central-Nerven-Systems, der physiologischen Psychologie, Statistik und gerichtlichen Medicin,* 1867, 1, 23–56. (b)

Wundt, W. (Review of Haeckel, *Generelle Morphologie der Organismen.*) *Kritische Blätter für wissenschaftliche und praktische Medicin,* 1867, 13–17, 41–45. (c)

Wundt, W. (Review of Helmholtz, *Handbuch der physiologischen Optik.*) *Deutsche Klinik,* 1867, 19, 326–328. (d)

Wundt, W. Ueber die Entstehung räumlicher Gesichtswahrnehmungen. *Philosophische Monatshefte,* 1869, 3, 225–247.

[Wundt, W.] (Unsigned review of Bernstein, *Untersuchungen über den Erregungsvorgang im Nerven- und Muskelsysteme.*) *Literarisches Centralblatt für Deutschland,* 1871, 22, 1107. (a)

Wundt, W. *Untersuchungen zur Mechanik der Nerven und Nervencentren. 1. Abtheilung: Ueber Verlauf und Wesen der Nervenerregung.* Erlangen, 1871. (b)

Wundt, W. *Grundzüge der physiologische Psychologie.* (Introduction. Parts 1 and 2.) Leipzig, 1873.

Wundt, W. *Grundzüge der physiologischen Psychologie.* (Parts 3, 4 and 5.) Leipzig, 1874. (a)

Wundt, W. *Ueber die Aufgabe der Philosophie in der Gegenwart. Akademische Antrittsrede in Zürich.* Leipzig, 1874. (b)

(I have had access only to the French translation. See the following item.—S.D.)

Wundt, W. [Mission de la philosophie dans le temps présent.] *Révue philosophique de la France et de l'étrangère,* 1875, 1, 113–124. (See preceding item for original publication.)

Wundt, W. Central innervation and consciousness. *Mind,* 1876, 1, 161–178. (a)

Wundt, W. *Ueber den Einfluss der Philosophie auf die Erfahrungswissenschaften.* Leipzig, 1876. (b)

Wundt, W. *Untersuchungen zur Mechanik der Nerven und Nervencentren. 2. Abtheilung: Ueber den Reflexvorgang und das Wesen der centralen Innervation.* Stuttgart, 1876. (c)

Wundt, W. Berichtigende Bemerkung zu dem Aufsatze des Herrn B. Erdmann, "Zur zeitgenössischen Psychologie im Deutschland." *Vierteljahrsschrift für wissenschaftliche Philosophie,* 1880, 4, 135–136.

Wundt, W. *Hypnotismus und Suggestion.* Leipzig, 1892. (a)

Wundt, W. *Vorlesungen über die Menschen- und Thierseele* (2nd ed.). Hamburg and Leipzig, 1892. (b)

Wundt, W. Eine Berichtigung. *Literarisches Centralblatt für Deutschland,* 1915, 66, 1080.

Wundt, W. *Erlebtes und Erkanntes.* Stuttgart, 1920. (Posthumous.)

Standard Reference Works

Numerous factual details have been culled from the following standard reference works. To avoid needlessly cluttering the text, specific references are not made except for quotations. The articles profitably consulted in each are indicated in parentheses.

Allgemeine deutsche Biographie. (Reichlin–Meldegg. Wundt.)

Baedeker, K. *Southern Germany* (13th rev. ed.). Leipzig, 1929.

Biographisches Lexicon der hervorragende Aerzte aller Zeiten und Völker. (Friedrich Arnold.)

Biographisches Lexicon der hervorragende Aerzte der letzten fünfzig Jahren [1880–1930]. (Bernstein. Julius Arnold.)

Deutsches biographisches Jahrbuch. (See E. Wundt, 1928.)

Encyclopaedia Britannica (11th ed.). (Robert Bunsen. Buffon. Karl Ludwig. Karl Mathy. William Smellie. Baden, history. Franco–Prussian War. Schleswig–Holstein Question. International [International Working Men's Association].)

Jewish Encyclopedia. (Bernstein. Munk. Rosenthal.)

Neue deutsche Biographie. (Arnold, ärzte.)

'INFLUENCE' AFTER LEIPZIG

Kurt Danziger

WUNDT AND THE TWO TRADITIONS OF PSYCHOLOGY

The North American psychologist who wants to put Wilhelm Wundt's singular achievement into a broader historical perspective faces a peculiar difficulty. He will not find it easy to arrive at a fair and accurate characterization of Wundt's position on any of the fundamental issues of psychology, for to do that he would have to cut through a veritable thicket of misleading information whose roots run very deep. Although some paths have recently been hewn through the thicket (Blumenthal, 1975; Mischel, 1970), a great deal of clearing remains to be done.

Much of the English-language literature pertaining to Wundt and his position in the history of psychology constitutes a fairly effective set of barriers to a true understanding of the issues. These barriers can be seen as a series of successive hurdles that have to be overcome in turn. The first line of hurdles is constituted by the brief Wundt caricatures to be found in contemporary psychological texts. Here, Wundt is likely to be placed firmly in the tradition of British empiricism, a German version of John Stuart Mill whose psychological wisdom did not go beyond the quaint notion of "mental chemistry." If the inquiring reader has any remaining curiosity, which is unlikely, he will find himself referred to more extensive treatments along the same lines, in particular, the chapter on Wundt in Boring's authoritative *History of Experimental Psychology* (1950), and beyond that, to Boring's teacher and Wundt's preeminent English-language disciple, Titchener, whose psychological ideas are supposed to be, in all essential respects, a faithful replica of those of the master.

If one were now to take the trouble to compare the psychological

system of Titchener with the bits and pieces of Wundt's own writings that
are available in English translation, one would at least be able to establish
that one was dealing with two quite distinct psychological systems, the
one calling itself structuralism, and the other voluntarism. But if one
wanted to pursue the matter further, one would be confronted by the next
barrier, namely, that the largest part of Wundt's psychologically relevant
writings was never translated into English and more important than this,
that the translation of his work was quite selective: by and large, it was
only his elementary texts and the works he wrote for popular consump-
tion that were translated, while his major systematic works and numerous theoretical papers that were directed at a more sophisticated audience
of scholars and specialists were the ones that were not translated. Even in
the case of Wundt's historically most famous work, the *Grundzüge der
physiologischen Psychologie*, Titchener's published translation covers only
the psychologically least interesting first part, which contains a great deal
of information about late-nineteenth-century neurophysiology but very
little information about Wundt's psychological system (Anderson, 1975).
Wundt's more popular and more elementary writings, generally the ones
available in English, have all the limitations one usually associates with
publications of this type. They oversimplify, they sacrifice depth to a clear
schema that aids exposition, and they are full of provisional solutions that
can only be identified as such when one knows the systematic work on
which they are based. They also contain ambiguities and contradictions
that can be clarified only by reference to the fuller discussion of the issues
to be found elsewhere.

Supposing ourselves to have penetrated beyond these barriers to the
major works that constitute Wundt's real contribution, we come up
against the final barrier to a historically accurate appraisal of his position.
Whereas the other barriers mentioned so far may be described as extrinsic, this final barrier is intrinsic to Wundt's work at its best. Anyone who
wants a definitive account of the precise meaning of some of the key
concepts in Wundt's thought is in for trouble. Here I am referring not to
the kind of conceptual wriggling in debate that was a source of annoyance
to some of his less sympathetic contemporaries, like William James (1920),
but to something that goes a little deeper. One source of difficulty lies in
Wundt's status as a system builder with the scope of an encyclopedist.
This means that the same underlying issue, the same basic approach,
could receive a somewhat different treatment depending on the context.

More importantly, however, Wundt's ideas never stood still; he continued to modify them productively throughout a very long life.

These sources of fluidity in Wundt's concepts were thoroughly exploited both by his critics and by those who wanted to bask in the reflected light of his considerable prestige. By careful selection of the context and of the stage in Wundt's intellectual development, either of these groups could usually find what they wanted in Wundt's work. However, when Wundt's psychological thought is regarded in its entirety, with account being taken of the modifications produced by time and by context, it becomes apparent that there is a strong underlying consistency that characterizes it quite unambiguously. In what follows, I will attempt to outline some of these consistent features of Wundt's approach to psychological problems. But given the traditional misconceptions in the North American literature, this goal can be achieved only through a critical confrontation between the Boring–Titchener version of Wundt's psychology and Wundt's own version.

The Sources of Wundt's Basic Concepts

The key to the prevalent misinterpretation of Wundt's psychological theories is to be found in the fact that his work and that of the bulk of his English-language interpreters is based on entirely different intellectual traditions. These are the tradition of German idealist philosophy on the one hand and that of British empiricism on the other. Wundt's immersion in the current of German idealism was so complete that it hardly requires any special documentation. It is not only that Wundt was himself the author of a complete system of idealist philosophy (Wundt, 1889), within which his psychology was assigned its own place, but that from the beginning, his psychological writings contain explicit acknowledgments of their indebtedness to certain major figures in the German philosophical tradition. In the preface to the first edition of the Grundzüge, Wundt said that Herbart was second only to Kant in terms of the debt owed for the development of his own views (Wundt, 1880). But beyond Herbart and Kant, there looms the influence of Leibniz, in whose shadow Wundt clearly felt himself to be working from the beginning. In the preface to his first psychological work, the Beiträge zur Theorie der Sinneswahrnehmung of 1862, Wundt declared that the principle that stood at the head of his

empirical investigation of sense perception was the well-known Leibnizian addition to Locke: "Nihil est in intellectu quod non fuerit in
sensu—nisi intellectus ipse" (Wundt, 1862). Wundt's psychological mag-
num opus, the *Grundzüge*, once more evokes the spirit of Leibniz in its
final statement: "Not as simple being (*Sein*), but as the developed product
(*das entwickelte Erzeugnis*) of countless elements, the mind is thus what
Leibniz said it was: a mirror of the world" (Wundt, 1880). Numerous other
references to Leibniz at key points in Wundt's more theoretical works
make it clear that he felt a special affinity with this philosopher.

At this point, it is necessary to turn from Wundt's own statement
about the intellectual ancestry of his ideas to the corresponding statements in the Titchenerian tradition that so decisively molded the North
American view of where Wundt fitted into the history of psychology.
Neither Boring nor Titchener mentioned Wundt's repeated references to
his debt to Leibniz. Titchener (1921a) inserted a brief footnote to the effect
that "Kant and Herbart were the influences against which Wundt had to
fight most continuously. They were accordingly the influences which
most strongly affected him" (p. 163). Typically, this is a partial truth,
which draws a veil over the other part, the very real positive indebtedness
mentioned by Wundt himself. Boring mentioned some of the links between Wundt's and Herbart's terminology, but the underlying significance of these links never emerges. Certainly, no one whose appreciation
of Wundt's historical position is based on the Boring–Titchener account
would ever guess at the way that Wundt himself described his intellectual
roots.

For the German philosophical roots of Wundt's psychological concepts, the Titchenerian tradition substitutes what can only be described as
a historical myth, namely, the myth of the British sources of Wundt's
approach to psychology. The most innocuous aspect of this myth takes
the form of Titchener's assertion (1921b, p. 164) that the very idea of an
experimental psychology that Wundt put forward in the famous
methodological introduction to the *Beiträge* of 1862 was simply derived
from J. S. Mill's *Logic* of 1843. This assertion is actually much more
interesting for what it tells us about Titchener than for anything it might
tell us about Wundt. The fact of the matter is that Titchener did not have a
shred of evidence for his assertion. In this methodological introduction to
his first major contribution to experimental psychology, Wundt made
copious references to the ideas of those who inspired his work. Those

who are mentioned repeatedly are Fechner, Herbart, and Leibniz; numerous others are mentioned in passing. But there is no reference whatever to John Stuart Mill or, for that matter, to any other British psychologist. Examining Titchener's method (1921b) of establishing the link between Mill and Wundt, one finds that it depends essentially on that well-known methodological principle: What I say three times is true. We are told first that "no one can read the introduction to the *Beiträge* without being reminded of the sixth book of John Mill's Logic"; second, that "no one can doubt" that Mill "gave the cue" for Wundt's methodological improvements; and third, that "I have no doubt of Wundt's indebtedness to Mill" (pp. 164–165). Why Wundt should have kept this indebtedness a dark secret when he so freely proclaimed his other intellectual debts is something that remains unexplained. Unfortunately, generations of American psychologists accepted Titchener's pronouncements on Wundt as gospel; Titchener's unsubstantiated personal conviction became a convenient substitute for the study of the historical originals.

Boring (1950), for instance, wrote that Wundt "drew so much upon English psychology" (p. 337). If this is true, he did it in a rather surreptitious manner, for direct references to English psychology are quite rare in Wundt's work. In fact, compared to the copious references to German philosophers and psychologists, the explicit attention that Wundt gave to the English psychological tradition can only be described as minimal. In the early editions of the *Grundzüge*, only a few sentences are devoted to this topic. From the third edition of 1887 onward, a few more sentences of criticism were added, but in total, there is little more than a page in a work of over a thousand pages. When one contrasts this kind of treatment with the extensive discussion that Wundt devoted to the British tradition in his book on ethics (1897) and with his careful criticism of J. S. Mill's ideas on induction in his *Logik* (1883b) and elsewhere, it is clear that Wundt paid relatively little attention to the British tradition specifically in psychology.

Wundt's Version of Mental Mechanics

When we turn from such relatively indirect evidence to the substance of the ideas that are under discussion, we find that there are two topics that are always used to illustrate the affinity between Wundt and the

British psychological tradition: one is the topic of associationism, and the other is the topic of so-called mental chemistry. Let us examine these in turn.

When one looks at Boring's own account (1950, p. 337) of Wundt's use of the principle of association, one is immediately struck by the fact that the concepts involved are all derived from Herbart and not from the British associationists. The concepts that supposedly illustrate Wundt's associationism are those of fusion, assimilation, and complication, which were introduced by Herbart and which presented a rather different model of mental process than the concepts of British associationism, which Wundt did not use. The most that could be claimed, therefore, for Wundt's relationship to British associationism is that it was mediated by Herbart. But that means that the relationship becomes extremely tenuous, for not only does Herbart's account of mental mechanics differ quite decisively from that of the British associationists, but Wundt in turn made major modifications in the concepts he inherited from Herbart.

The Herbartian view of mental mechanism differed from its British contemporary, the mental analysis of James Mill, in terms of three characteristics that had already served to distinguish the mental philosophy of Leibniz from that of Locke. First, the elements of the mind were conceived as units of activity, not as static contents; the *Vorstellungen* of Herbart were conceived as centers of force, which makes them something very different from the static *idea* units of the British empiricists. Second, the mind and all its elements were conceived by Herbart as loci of spontaneity, of self-activity, quite the opposite of the essentially reactive view of mental life that characterizes the British associationist tradition. Third, for Herbart, the elements of the mind must be regarded as expressions of its underlying unity, a view that led to the Herbartian concept of apperception, which of course does not exist in the theories of the Mills and their predecessors. Herbart's account of mental fusion or combination therefore differs from the classical associationist account in that it is based on the self-activity of an apperceiving unity and not on the coalescence of separate elementary reactions to external influence.

Many of the misunderstandings that have become so general in the English-language literature on Wundt may be traced to the failure to distinguish between the Herbartian tradition of mental mechanism, to which Wundt was heir, and the tradition of classical British associationism, from which Wundt explicitly dissociated himself. It is well known that Wundt criticized Herbart severely for his nonempirical approach and for his intellectualism, but on the other hand, there was the debt to Herbart of which Wundt spoke, and that debt is nowhere more evident than in his discussion of the relationship of mental elements to each other and to mental wholes. Wundt criticized Herbart also in this context, but characteristically, the criticism takes the form of accusing Herbart of still being too much of an associationist. For Herbart, said Wundt (1887), the process of apperception became a matter of forces of attraction between mental contents, which means reducing apperception to association, whereas in reality, it is an "act of consciousness as a whole [*Act des Gesammtbewusstseins*]" (p. 369). Wundt went on to emphasize that this act of apperception is necessary for association to occur:

> Thus association is only possible on the basis of this central unity of our consciousness . . . ideas become connected because the single acts of the representational activity itself, of apperception, are thoroughly interconnected (p. 380)

Wundt repeatedly stressed that simple elements never occur in experience, that they are abstractions or even "invented sensations" (Wundt, 1885), and that the compounds that do occur in experience are always the product of apperception (Wundt, 1887, pp. 364–365). The latter occurs in two forms, called *passive* and *active*. Both are forms of volitional activity, which led Wundt to calling his system of psychology *voluntarism*. The difference is that active apperception involves an act of choice, whereas passive apperception does not (Wundt, 1887, p. 381). Active apperception leads to the establishment of connections on the basis of intrinsic meaning, passive apperception to the establishment of extrinsic associations.

Wundt's relegation of association to a kind of inferior apperception produced angry protests from the defenders of the classical British tradition. Alexander Bain (1887) himself criticized Wundt for "the treatment of Association, as almost exclusively an affair of motives," by which he presumably meant Wundt's voluntarism. Naturally, Bain saw no need for the concept of apperception, believing it to be just another name for facts that classical associationism had long accounted for. Wundt (1887, p. 389) replied that he had obviously been completely misunderstood and that he had never come across any recognition of the crucial distinction between apperception and association in any English psychologist. The clash between Wundt and Bain was symptomatic of the intellectual incompatibility of the Leibnizian and the Lockean traditions in psychology, an incompatibility that has continued to create barriers to an adequate understanding of Wundt's psychology down to our own day. The myth of

Wundt's "mental chemistry" serves as a further illustration of these barriers.

"Mental Chemistry" and Wundt's Concept of Synthesis

It is not uncommon for the more elementary English-language references to Wundt to single out his supposed mental chemistry for special mention. Now, as a matter of fact, Wundt never used the term in reference to his own system. What, then, is the source of this myth? The set created by a false but unquestioned assimilation of Wundt's psychological ideas to those of the British associationists is undoubtedly the crucial underlying factor. Both Wundt and J. S. Mill spoke of mental synthesis; they were both associationists, so if Mill referred to this synthesis as mental chemistry, Wundt must have done so, too. Boring provided the authority for this kind of reasoning. He wrote of Wundt's principle of creative synthesis: "In this principle we have Wundt's 'mental chemistry.' It is not strikingly different from John Stuart Mill's" (1950, p. 336). There follows a discussion of the views of James and John Stuart Mill, but no further explanation of Wundt's creative synthesis. Boring's notes at the end of his Wundt chapter refer the reader interested in Wundt's doctrine of elements to one of the theoretical papers in the *Philosophische Studien*; but this paper, when we look it up, turns out to be Wundt's (1883a) treatment of the logic of chemistry, which is entirely devoted to that science and does not mention psychology in any way! It does not seem unreasonable to conclude that Boring's equation between creative synthesis and mental chemistry was based less on his own historical research than on the opinion of his teacher, Titchener, who was for him the ultimate authority on Wundt.

If we turn to Titchener's comments on Wundt, we certainly find an opinion expressed, but the basis of that opinion is quite another matter. All that Titchener (1921a) said is that unnamed "critics" have assimilated Wundt's "psychical synthesis" to Mill's "mental chemistry." Titchener wrote a paper whose title refers to "Wundt's Doctrine of Creative Synthesis" (1922), but the paper itself deals only with some of Wundt's early ideas before the publication of the *Grundzüge*. The doctrine of creative synthesis itself is not discussed. At the end of the paper, Titchener said merely that "we may find it the more significant that references to Mill occur in all six editions of the *Grundzüge*." There is an implication that Mill's doctrine was somehow responsible for Wundt's later views and that Wundt had no right to criticize Mill's concept so severely in the later editions of the *Grundzüge*.

Wundt himself was more explicit. His reference to Mill's "mental chemistry" (1887) gives it credit for providing a good picture or illustration of the fact that the perception of space involves new qualities not contained in its psychological antecedents; but he immediately pointed out that the account of visual perception given by the "English psychologists" was subject to serious objections (p. 205). After detailing the more specific objections, he dealt with the limitations of the chemical analogy: it is only a way of illustrating one aspect of the process, but in general, mental causality is quite different from physical causality because of its "creative" aspect, which makes it in principle impossible to predict from the nature of the parts to the properties of the whole, as one can do in the case of compounds in the physical world (Wundt, 1887, p. 41).

If we recall that for Wundt, the process of apperception constituted the basic form of all mental activity, we can appreciate the gulf that separates his views on mental synthesis from those of J. S. Mill, who always implied that the synthetic process was itself reducible to processes of association and reproduction. Eventually, Wundt's principle of "creative synthesis" became the conceptual focus of his emphasis on the fundamental difference between synthetic processes in the physical and in the mental world. It became the primary example of his central psychological concept, the concept of *psychic causality*.

But it would be wrong to see in these later developments anything but a working out of themes that had been emphasized by Wundt from the beginning. The works of the 1880s quite ambiguously make apperception basic and emphasize the special character of psychic synthesis. Moreover, concern with the active synthetic aspect of psychological process is characteristic of Wundt's earliest contributions to psychology. While his two youthful works, the *Beiträge* of 1862 and the *Vorlesungen* of 1863, contain much secondary material and many concepts that he derived from others, what makes them different and identifiably Wundtian is not only their interest in the specifically psychological aspects of problems, but also their emphasis on the constructive activity of the mind. The latter is expressed in the concept of *synthesis*, which forms the crucial link in his theory of sense perception and of cognition. Already, at that time, he characterized synthesis as "the creative act in our process of cognition" (Wundt, 1863, p. 435) and as "that which is truly constructive in perception" (Wundt, 1862, p. 443).

At that time, Wundt conceived of the synthetic activity of the mind as a logical activity. The model that he constantly used to illustrate the process of mental construction was the logical judgment, either analytic or synthetic. This is where the influence of Kant becomes apparent. But while Wundt acknowledged this influence, he also took a characteristic and crucial step beyond Kant. He pointed out that the properties that Kant attributed to logical judgments in themselves were really attributes of the individual making the judgments (Wundt, 1863, p. 489). Thus, synthesis began its transformation from a purely logical into a psychological category. Wundt's early works provide the intermediate stage for this transformation: psychological construction is conceived of as logical construction. Subsequently, there occurred the crucial shift in Wundt's thinking, the recognition that psychological construction is not essentially a logical but a motivational—volitional process. But his early works remain as witnesses to Wundt's intellectual roots in the German idealist tradition. These roots put their unmistakable stamp on his first project for a new science of psychology, which, he said, was to investigate the mind as "a developing being acting out of itself according to logical laws" (Wundt, 1862, p. 451).

Wundt's Social Psychology

One further theme on which it is necessary to set the record straight concerns the role that social psychology played in Wundt's psychological system. Considering the enormous amount of time and energy that Wundt obviously devoted to the ten volumes of his *Völkerpsychologie*, one might imagine that this would be a redundant task. However, it is a fact that this aspect of Wundt's work has been ignored almost totally by American psychologists and that the result is a serious distortion of perspective on Wundt's psychology as a whole. It had been a highly characteristic feature of the British psychological tradition that it concerned itself solely with the psychology of the isolated individual. Its laws were timeless and ahistorical, and American psychology, not least American social psychology, has continued to follow this tradition. Wundt, however, was the product of different influences. German romanticism had firmly established the fact that sociocultural units had a life of their own, a historical life, whose laws must ultimately be relevant to the lives of the individuals who participated in these larger units. The lawfulness of cultural formations had been a very active area of research at the German universities during the period of Wundt's youth, and when he was working on his first textbook of psychology, the *Vorlesungen* (1863), the question of the relation of this research to psychology had just been raised very sharply in the pages of the *Zeitschrift für Völkerpsychologie*, which began publication in 1860. Wundt's book reflects this interest: it is as much concerned with psychological aspects of social and cultural formations as it is with psychological aspects of the physiology of sensation and perception. Moreover, in adopting a distinctly historicist position, Wundt's approach provided a corrective to the kind of social psychology that had been advocated by the Herbartians. At this time, we also get the first formulation of the characteristically Wundtian position that the experimental method is useful only for the investigation of a limited set of problems in psychology and that beyond these problems, historical methods must take over (Wundt, 1863, p. ix). It soon became clear that for Wundt, social psychology was a source of data and of principles that had to be taken into account by general psychology, whereas for the Herbartians social psychology had been simply an application of the principles of individual psychology (Volkelt, 1922). In this context, it is also worthy of note that Wundt explicitly placed his own approach to ethics in opposition to British utilitarianism by stressing that he looked for the origin of norms not in the psychology of the individual but in the psychology of groups, and for Wundt, the latter was not reducible to the former. Wundt's emphasis on the complementary relationship between individual and social psychology remained essentially the same throughout his long scholarly career, except that in the last 20 years of his life, he clearly regarded social psychology as the more important and the more promising element in this relationship (Wundt, 1908).

This stance was obviously a major source of embarrassment for Titchener, whose psychological system, by contrast, represented an extreme version of encapsulated subjectivism. His obituary (1921b) for Wundt in the *American Journal of Psychology* is remarkable for the fact that apart from the biographical details, it is very largely devoted to the argument that Wundt did not really mean what he said about social psychology. The argument is typical of Titchener's style, which was polemical and quasi-political rather than scholarly. Its flagrant misinterpretation of Wundt is easily revealed by comparing Titchener's assertions with Wundt's own statements in context, but it is doubtful that any of his readers bothered to do this. Quite apart from the problem of language, the topic of Wundt was of no interest to American psychology by the 1920s; in any case, Titchener was simply confirming the preexisting biases of his readers.

Wundt's American Interpreters

If we inquire into the reasons for the rise and the adoption of the Titchenerian image of Wundt among American psychologists, we have to take into account the interaction between the peculiarities of Titchener's special position and the relevant features of American psychology in general. In the preface to his first text, Titchener (1896) characterized his "general standpoint" as "that of the traditional English psychology." To that tradition he always remained faithful, attempting to give it a new lease on life by grafting onto it certain views of his own that had been stimulated by his acquaintance with Wundt's work. But while the stimulus of some of Wundt's ideas is detectable in Titchener's psychology, an enormous cultural and intellectual gulf separated the general approach of these two psychologists. The strange thing is that Titchener always tried to minimize this gulf, an attempt that sometimes involved rather bizarre intellectual acrobatics. If one were to speculate about the reasons for his behavior, one would have to take into account the fact that in the early part of Titchener's career, Wundt undoubtedly provided him with a certain amount of reflected prestige, but at the same time, one cannot read some of Titchener's comments on Wundt without realizing that there was a strong emotional involvement that was not simply utilitarian in character. One would also have to recognize the fact that Titchener's pronouncements were usually made, explicitly or implicitly, in the context of some polemic, where he was more concerned with scoring rhetorical points than with balance and objectivity (Danziger, 1980). Finally, one is struck by the very real difficulty that Titchener had in understanding and accepting concepts that differed fundamentally from his own. If one reads his attempts at interpreting what Brentano meant or what some of the Würzburgers meant, one finds that he is no more reliable than he is in the case of Wundt (Humphrey, 1951, p. 64). It seems that he genuinely could not think in terms of categories that differed fundamentally from the English positivist tradition.

Not that Titchener was very unusual in this respect. The legacy of Spencer and Mill ran extremely deep in the minds of most of the early American psychologists, even when specific, relatively superficial aspects of that legacy were explicitly rejected (Blumenthal, 1977). As far as Wundt's fundamental ideas were concerned, this usually meant that they were either dismissed as "metaphysical" or that they were reinterpreted within an alien intellectual framework that completely changed their meaning. It is apparent that James, Ladd, and Hall had little sympathy for or understanding of Wundt's psychological concepts. John Dewey was rather the exception among the early American psychologists for being thoroughly at home in German idealist philosophy. As early as 1887, we find him criticizing Ladd for misunderstanding Wundt's concept of apperception and therefore failing to appreciate the significance of Wundt's reaction time experiments. For Ladd and many others, Dewey (1969) observed, apperception was just a matter of clear and distinct perception,

> . . . while in the German use, introduced by Leibniz and continued in different aspects by Kant and Herbart, and made central by Wundt, it signifies . . . the influence of the organized mind upon the separate sensations which reach it.

For those who did not appreciate the underlying theory, Dewey continued, Wundt's reaction time experiments were just "a series of isolated measurements." Dewey's insights produced no lasting effects. A few years later, Titchener (1909, p. 367) repeated the standard positivist reduction of apperception to clarity of experience and soon declared this central facet of Wundt's psychology to be redundant.

John Dewey was by no means the only American interpreter who was able to appreciate the basic direction of Wundt's work. Presumably under Dewey's influence, G. H. Mead (1904) undertook a serious examination of Wundt's social psychology and subsequently made constructive use of Wundt's concept of the vocal gesture to develop some of his own social-psychological concepts. C. H. Judd (1897, 1932), a student of Wundt's and the translator of the Grundriss, gave a consistently accurate account of Wundt's position, an account that is, of course, sharply at variance with Titchenerian psychology. But these were men whose interests and philosophy did not coincide with those of the great majority of American psychologists and whose work was largely ignored by that majority. The fate of Wundtian psychology was sealed by the new wave of positivism that swept over experimental psychology, beginning in the closing years of the 19th century (Danziger, 1979). Eventually, this approach became identified with psychological orthodoxy, and in due course, it set its stamp on the way in which the discipline understood its own history. Boring's History (1929/1950) stands as a monument to these developments, in which Wundt's psychology was decidedly the loser.

This is a great pity, for in dismissing and misunderstanding Wundt, modern psychology not only deceived itself about an important part of its origins but also closed the door on a rich fund of ideas that might have rescued it from some of the sterility and some of the blind alleys that characterized it in the heyday of the psychological schools. Wundt's encyclopedic vision led to his lifelong attempt to integrate a variety of perspectives. He did not necessarily succeed, but his unique achievement bears witness to the fact that the tension among the different elements of his thought was a fertile tension.

While Wundt can be clearly situated in terms of the Lockean and Leibnizian traditions of psychology, there are other important influences that contributed to the complexity of his psychological system. The influence of Darwin, for example, was stressed by Wundt himself, though not always understood by some of his followers. The influence of some of the nineteenth-century German physiologists is obvious and has always received its due. But while many of Wundt's ideas were tied to the progress and also to the limitations of the science of his day, his vision for psychology was based on a broader perspective. There is no more succinct expression of that vision than the one he presents in his autobiography (1920):

> Whereas physiology believed it had to restrict itself to the strictly delimited area of sensation, it became my aim, on the contrary, to show, wherever possible, how the elementary processes of consciousness, sensations and associations, everywhere already reflected the mental life in its totality.

References

Anderson, R. J. The untranslated content of Wundt's Grundzüge der physiologischen Psychologie. Journal of the History of the Behavioral Sciences, 1975, 11, 381–386.

Bain, A. On association controversies. Mind, 1887, 12, 161–182.

Blumenthal, A. L. A reappraisal of Wilhelm Wundt. American Psychologist, 1975, 30, 1081–1088.

Blumenthal, A. L. Wilhelm Wundt and early American psychology: A clash of two cultures. *Annals of the New York Academy of Sciences*, 1977, *291*, 13–20.

Boring, E. G. *A history of experimental psychology*. New York: Appleton-Century-Crofts, 1950. (Originally published, 1929.)

Danziger, K. The positivist repudiation of Wundt. *Journal of the History of the Behavioral Sciences*, 1979, *15*, 205–230.

Danziger, K. The history of introspection reconsidered. *Journal of the History of the Behavioral Sciences*, in press.

Dewey, J. Review of Ladd's elements of physiological psychology. In *The early works of John Dewey*, Vol. 1. Carbondale: Southern Illinois University Press, 1969, p. 203.

Humphrey, G. *Thinking*. London : Methuen, 1951, p. 64.

James, H. (Ed.) *The letters of William James*, Vol. 1. Boston: Atlantic Monthly Press, 1920, p. 263.

Judd, C. H. Wundt's system of philosophy. *Philosophical Review*, 1897, *6*, 370–385.

Judd, C. H. In Carl Murchison (Ed.), *A history of psychology in autobiography*, Vol. 2. Worcester, Mass.: Clark University Press, 1932.

Mead, G. H. The relations of psychology and philology. *Psychological Bulletin*, 1904, *1*, 375–391.

Mischel, T. Wundt and the conceptual foundations of psychology. *Philosophy and Phenomenological Research*, 1970, *31*, 1–26.

Titchener, E. B. *An outline of psychology*. New York: Macmillan, 1896.

Titchener, E. B. *A textbook of psychology*. New York: Macmillan, 1909.

Titchener, E. B. Brentano and Wundt: Empirical and experimental psychology. *American Journal of Psychology*, 1921, *32*, 108–120. (a)

Titchener, E. B. Wilhelm Wundt. *American Journal of Psychology*, 1921, *32*, 161–177. (b)

Titchener, E. B. A note on Wundt's doctrine of creative synthesis. *American Journal of Psychology*, 1922, *33*, 351–360.

Volkelt, H. Die Völkerpsychologie in Wundts Entwicklungsgang. *Beiträge zur Philosophie des deutschen Idealismus*, 1922, *2*, 74–105.

Wundt, W. *Beiträge zur Theorie der Sinneswahrnehmung*. Leipzig: C. F. Winter, 1862.

Wundt, W. *Vorlesungen über die Menschen- und Thierseele*, Vol. 1. Leipzig: Voss, 1863.

Wundt, W. *Grundzüge der physiologischen Psychologie* (2nd ed.). Leipzig: Engelmann, 1880.

Wundt, W. Die Logik der Chemie. *Philosophische Studien*, 1883, *1*, 473–494. (a)

Wundt, W. *Logik*. Stuttgart: Enke, 1st ed., 1883; 3rd ed., 1908 (b)

Wundt, W. Erfundene Empfindungen. *Philosophische Studien*, 1885, *2*, 298–305.

Wundt, W. *Grundzüge der physiologischen Psychologie*, Vol. 2. (3rd ed.). Leipzig: Engelmann, 1887.

Wundt, W. *System der Philosophie*. Leipzig: Engelmann, 1889.

Wundt, W. *Ethics: An Investigation of the facts and laws of the moral life*, Vol. 2 (trans. E. B. Titchener, J. H. Gulliver, and M. F. Washburn). New York: Macmillan, 1897, pp. 53–83, 142–146, 151–159.

Wundt, W. *Erlebtes und Erkanntes*. Stuttgart: Kröner, 1920, p. 195.

3

Kurt Danziger

WUNDT'S THEORY OF BEHAVIOR AND VOLITION

During the past half century, it has become traditional to consider Wundt's theoretical contributions to psychology almost entirely in terms of problems of sensation and perception or, at most, in terms of general problems of cognition. This was a function of the historians' biases and interests rather than any reflection of Wundt's own position. For Boring (1942), who constituted the most influential source during this period, the area of sensation and perception was of supreme interest; it was the one area that merited a major historical text on the same level as the more general *History of Experimental Psychology*. However, this special concern with sensation and perception was not merely an expression of the particular research interests of one individual. More significantly, the concentration of historical interest on this area made it possible to use historical studies to project an image of psychology as an experimental discipline whose more recent historical development showed essentially the kind of cumulative linear progress that was accepted as the hallmark of the natural sciences (O'Donnell, 1979).

One consequence of this limited approach to the history of psychology was the relative neglect of a topic that was in fact the subject of considerable interest in the century preceding World War I: the explanation of human and animal movement and action. This neglect was no doubt also supported for a time by the belief of many psychologists that no one prior to J. B. Watson had anything relevant to say about behavior. Now, while it is true that behaviorism produced a change of terminology, this did not mean that the explanation of human and animal behavior was not a matter of profound importance to nineteenth-century psychology. The earlier part of the century had brought those physiological discoveries that firmly established the existence of a type of animal movement that depended only on identified sensorimotor arcs in the nervous system and did not involve the intervention of mind. This approach led to a sharp distinction between voluntary movement on the one hand and various types of involuntary movement on the other. The problems created by this stark dualism provided the instigation for much theoretical discussion and a considerable amount of laboratory work during the second half of the 19th century. These efforts were clearly directed at what in present-day language would be referred to as the explanation of behavior, but because of the historically given context, the issues were generally presented in terms of the topic of volition.

This is the period during which the concept of volition was increasingly discussed in naturalistic rather than moralistic terms. While ethical implications were still present, questions such as that of the relationship between voluntary and involuntary movement or that of the determinants of volitional processes were not in themselves ethical but psychological questions. In general, nineteenth-century psychologists tended to present the part of their theories that attempts to explain the active rather than the reactive or receptive aspect of psychological functions in terms of the concept of volition. That concept covers a great deal of what would later be discussed in terms of the psychology of drives and motives. As we will see, Wundt played a significant role in preparing this change.

Wundt's Opposition to the Theories of Lotze and Bain

In order to understand the nature of Wundt's contribution to this field, it is necessary to examine its relationship to the work of his predecessors. When Wundt began to concern himself with the explanation of human and animal movement, he had to come to terms with the solutions to the problems that had been proposed in the 1850s by two highly influential scholars: Lotze and Bain. Within three years of each other, these philosopher–psychologists had published accounts of the genesis of purposive behavior, which, though they bore the distinguishing marks of different intellectual traditions, had important common features. To some extent, this convergence was due to the fact that they were both clearly indebted to the earlier work of the physiologist Johannes Müller, who had been the first to attempt a reconciliation between traditional doctrines of the will and early nineteenth century discoveries in the neurophysiology of reflex action.

What was common to these mid-nineteenth century attempts to explain human and animal movement was the split between two levels of functioning, the voluntary and the involuntary. The latter depended on physiological mechanisms that did not involve subjective deliberation and choice. Several types of such involuntary movement were recognized at this time. In addition to simple or combined reflex movement instigated by a sensory stimulus, there was the "expressive" movement produced by the internal excitation characterizing emotional arousal. Finally, there was the kind of involuntary movement for which the term *ideomotor activity* later became popular, that is to say, a movement produced automatically by the representation or idea of that movement, as in hypnotic states or in spontaneous imitation. By this time, therefore, there had emerged a systematic appreciation of a range of human behavior that did not involve the operation of the will. While there had been earlier speculation in this area, there was now solid and systematic evidence that seemed to demand an essentially physiological account of the generation of these various kinds of involuntary movement.

But this development created a hiatus between one part of human behavior that was involuntary and another part that still involved the operation of subjective purpose and choice, in other words, of the will. How was this gap to be bridged? Lotze and Bain both adopted a genetic perspective in response to this problem: involuntary movement must exist prior to voluntary movement, and the latter must be regarded as an acquisition, the product of a process of learning. This proved to be one of the most important basic propositions in the history of psychology. Bain's (1855, 1859) account of this learning process contained the germs of much more modern formulations. He held that some of the purposeless spontaneous movements would accidentally lead to feelings of pleasure and some others to feelings of pain. If this process occurred repeatedly, these feelings would become associated with the movements that led up to them, so that the idea of pleasure would in future tend to produce movements that were previously followed by the experience of pleasure. As feelings become associated with certain situations, the basis exists for the production of appropriate movements that have previously led to pleasurable results in a particular situation. This process is the origin of voluntary activity, according to Bain.

Lotze's (1852, pp. 287–324) account is somewhat different. There is a bidirectional link between actual movements and the mental representation of these movements, so that while movements produce their mental representations, the latter can also produce the movements themselves. There is a complex apparatus of involuntary movements reflexly coordinated with a variety of physical stimuli. As these involuntary movements occur, they are subjectively represented, thus informing the mind of the possibilities of movement open to it. The mind thus learns to produce movements voluntarily by evoking the appropriate movement representations. While the views of Bain and Lotze entail different embryonic theories of motor learning, they clearly share a common perspective on the relationship of involuntary and voluntary activity: the latter arises on the basis of the former as a result of some kind of learning process.

It was precisely this supposition that Wundt refused to accept—first of all, because it seemed to him to imply a metaphysical dualism he would rather avoid. If movements originally run off without the intervention of the mind and mental processes only come to intervene causally in this mechanism at a later stage, then one is back at a Cartesian conception of physical and mental causes. However subtly the mental agency is introduced, it remains a mystery how it is able to intervene effectively in what has up to this point been a purely physical process (Wundt, 1885). Second, the Lotze–Bain notion of voluntary activity as a learned acquisition seemed to Wundt to conflict with everyday observations of the learning process. When a person acquires a new skill the process commonly observed is the reverse of that postulated by the view Wundt criticized. It is in the early stages of learning that the exercise of volition is at its height, only to subside when the skill has been learned and the acquired movements run off quite automatically. Wundt did not deny the existence of the opposite process, that is, the case where automatic movement patterns become integrated into complex voluntary movements; what he rejected was the exemplary or paradigmatic status of this case for the development of voluntary movement in general. The common case seemed to him to be rather the one where an initially voluntary activity becomes automatized as a result of practice (Wundt, 1883).

Wundt was able to make use of the much discussed experiments on the behavior of spinal frogs to strengthen the plausibility of his point of view. Pflüger (1853) had demonstrated that the behavior of such laboratory preparations showed peculiarly adapted characteristics. For example, the brainless frog makes wiping motions with its leg when the side of its body is stimulated with acid, but when the leg on the stimulated side is amputated, the frog attempts to reach the spot with the opposite leg. Pflüger felt that such apparently purposeful behavior required us to suppose that some form of mental activity must be involved even at the spinal level, which an earlier generation of physiologists had supposed to involve nothing but simple reflex arcs linking specific stimulus areas with specific responses. Lotze (1853) took issue with Pflüger's interpretation from his own point of view, which was based on the unity and indivisibility of the mind. For Lotze, there could be no spinal mind, and the apparent purposefulness in some of the behavior of spinal laboratory animals must simply be taken as evidence that the purely physical machinery of reflexes was more complex than previously supposed. Pflüger's experiments only served to reinforce Lotze's dualistic model, which envisioned a mind that learned to control a complex apparatus of involuntary activity. Any remaining doubts about the existence of mental processes at the spinal level were probably dispelled by the later experiments of Goltz (1869), which showed how completely nonresponsive and of course nonadaptive the behavior of spinal frogs could be if the physical conditions did not activate the machinery of their reflexes. Such animals would, for example, sit quietly while the temperature was gradually raised to the point at which their death occurred.

The Pflüger–Lotze controversy was an important landmark in the history of nineteenth-century attempts to explain behavior. It stimulated considerable research and discussion. Wundt grappled with its implications as early as his *Lectures on the Human and Animal Mind* (1863, Lecture 57), though he had revised his position by the time the *Grundzüge der physiologischen Psychologie* appeared. He did not accept the relative adaptiveness of reflex behavior at the spinal level as evidence of mental activity, but he did see it as evidence of a process of automatization of originally voluntary activity that must have taken place in the course of evolution. The very inconsistency of the adaptiveness of the behavior of the spinal animal, totally nonadaptive under some conditions though strangely adaptive under others, pointed to a phylogenetically earlier stage, bits and pieces of whose adaptive acquisitions had passed into the inherited organization of later generations. In the words of the English translation of the second edition of the *Lectures:* "The purposive character of the reflexes becomes then readily intelligible, if we regard them as resulting from the voluntary action of previous generations" (Wundt, 1894a, p. 227). In terms of phylogenetic development, the reflex level of activity is more plausibly regarded as the product of a less mechanical kind of purposive activity rather than as its precursor.

On the level of individual development, the situation is somewhat complicated by the fact that the individual does have a range of inherited reflex reactions in his repertoire. But Wundt did not believe that these mechanisms played any significant role in the development of adapted voluntary behavior. As the latter is clearly a later accomplishment, the question arises of what its precursors might be in the development of the individual. Wundt excluded reflexes, and he also excluded Bain's notion of "spontaneous" vital activity as including nothing that is not better represented by the more precise terms *reflex* or *automatic movement*, the latter being the product of central physiological excitation. For Wundt, the primitive antecedent of complex voluntary action must have two characteristics that all these automatic mechanisms do not have: consciousness and direction. If these characteristics were not already present at the most primitive level of behavior, their appearance in the course of development became an unresolvable mystery that Wundt refused to accept.

From Impulse to Choice: The Development of Volitional Activity

The psychological tradition to which he was heir provided Wundt with an alternative concept of primitive forms of activity: the concept of impulse or drive. He proceeded to accord it the status of *the* fundamental psychological phenomenon. Drives, as conceived by Wundt and the German psychological tradition, were a characteristic of human and animal organisms that simultaneously involved both mind and body, both direction and force. The German word is *Trieb*, which nowadays translates fairly readily as "drive," though that is only because during the present century the term has become more familiar to English-language psychology. Wundt's contemporaries translated it as "impulse," so we partly retain this usage in the present discussion. However, it should be noted that the lack of the concept in the British psychological tradition created problems for translators that they sometimes solved in ways that created confusions that the history of psychology has yet to sort out. How, for example, was the English-speaking reader to guess that the term *impulse* to be found in Wundt's translated work and the term *instinct* to be found in Freud's translated work are both versions of the identical German term, *Trieb*?

This term had been used by Reimarus (1760) in the eighteenth-century to refer to animal instinct, but it had also been given a metaphysical meaning by the philosopher Fichte (1817). For the Hegelian psychologist, it was the natural striving of the living subject for self-realization. By the middle of the nineteenth-century, most of the German philosopher–psychologists used the term, and for some, it was the basis of psychology. For example, at the time that Wundt was beginning to interest himself in psychology, the use of the drive concept as *the* basic explanatory category of psychology was being propagated by the now forgotten introspectionist, Fortlage, whom Wundt later credited with "some fine comments," although he disapproved of his methods (Wundt, 1888). For Fortlage and others, the drive concept referred to a specific union of four components: a feeling of pleasure or unpleasure (*Unlust*, the same term that Freud used); a striving toward or away from some condition; a temporal relationship between a present negative and a future positive state; and specific movements that tend to eliminate the negative or to achieve the positive state (Fortlage, 1855, Vol. 1, p. 301). Drives form the elementary units underlying the life of the mind and of the body. They constitute a union of mental and physiological events at the most basic level. For Fortlage, the role of drives was all-pervasive; there were unconscious drives and cognitive activity was seen as the product of drive inhibition.

Wundt (1879) did not accept these extreme views, but he did agree on the fundamental status of affect and impulse. His approach differed from that of his predecessors in that it was governed by a strong genetic perspective. In his view, drives provided the origin of a process of psychological development in the course of which differentiated psychological functions appeared. Thus, it was not reflexes that provide the foundation on which adapted voluntary behavior was based, but drives. At the time that Wundt developed his theory, Kussmaul's (1859) systematic studies of the behavior of neonates were well known. Wundt (1880) suggested that the neonatal responses described by Kussmaul were of three types: (1) "automatic movements," mostly of the limbs and trunk, produced by central physiological excitation; (2) true reflexes produced by specific sensory stimulation, as in the startle reaction and in the movement of the eyes in response to light; and (3) "impulsive movements" (*Triebbewegungen*), which included sucking movements and the responses to sweet and sour tastes. The last differed from the first two in that the response was more than simply a reaction to antecedent conditions: it included an aspect of "striving," that is, a directional component expressing either the acceptance or the rejection of the stimulus by the organism. It was these impulsive movements that constituted the basis for the development of complex voluntary activity, because only they involved the crucial component of "volition."

The concept of volition was so central to Wundt's thought that he came to identify his psychological system as *voluntarism*. But his use of these terms was somewhat idiosyncratic. Volition, in Wundt's sense, did not necessarily involve an act of conscious choice or decision. In fact, he criticized Lotze for limiting the operation of the will to such cases. For Wundt, the act of choice constituted only a special case of "volitional activity"; it was a product of a psychological development in which volition first appeared in simpler forms. The primitive manifestation of what Wundt called will occurs in the form of drives. This is the basis on which the later forms of volition (i.e., choice and decision) develop. For a contemporary understanding of Wundt's psychology, it is useful to bear in mind that what he meant by *voluntarism* was not something that referred to the act of will in the narrow sense but something that had a great deal in common with what were later to be referred to as *dynamic approaches* to psychology. In other words, Wundt's psychology was one that emphasized the primacy of affective–motivational processes and regarded them as the indispensable foundation for the explanation of psychological events.

Like most of his other theories, Wundt's views on volition were subject to periodic revision. However, once he had developed the independent position of his mature years, these revisions did not affect his fundamental views, and it is with these that we are concerned here. There is, however, a real structural difference between the revisions of his views during the period of intellectual gestation in his early years and the later revisions. In the early works, the main features of what was to become Wundt's characteristic approach are often only intuitively indicated together with much intellectual baggage that was dropped subsequently. Gradually, the main outline of his views was stated more clearly and explicitly, and after a certain point, the revisions affected only relatively specific aspects, leaving the framework largely intact. In the case of his theory of volitional activity, that point was clearly reached with the second edition of the *Grundzüge der physiologischen Psychologie* in 1880. In regard to this fundamental aspect of Wundt's thinking, the first edition of 1873–1874 was still a transitional work, and many of the major changes that Wundt made in the second edition concern the topic of volition. These changes also involved a completely new restatement of his fundamental ideas on psychology in the concluding section of the work. After 1880, he undertook no changes of comparable magnitude. Therefore, in order to avoid unnecessary confusion, we will take the second and the very similar third edition (1887) of the *Grundzüge* as the main basis for the following exposition of his views. These were the editions that coincided with the first flourishing of the program of experimental research on reaction times that was stimulated by Wundt's theories of volitional behavior, and they were also the editions that his most important critics and commentators generally referred to.

Wundt regarded all drives as being affective in nature. This affect imparts direction to the impulsive movement, manifesting itself either as a striving against or a striving for some state of affairs. Subjectively, this manifests itself in feelings of aversion or of desire produced by some instigating condition. These feelings exist before there is any knowledge of drive goals, that is, of the conditions that will satisfy the drive and alleviate the affect. Such knowledge, Wundt agreed, is the result of learning. But the basis for this learning does not lie in the setting up of associations between the two separate processes of movement on the one hand and feelings of pleasure or pain on the other. The original movements, being impulsive movements, are already accompanied by an affective component. It is only later that feelings gain a temporary and limited independence from the motor component by a process of differentiation set in motion by the inhibition of the movement component due to internal or external factors.

At this point, we reach a fundamental precept that runs through all of Wundt's psychological theorizing. It involves a derivation from his "actuality principle," which can be summed up in the rule that psychological categories, like sensation, feeling, and volition, should never be confused with the actual psychological process itself. Such categories are intellectual abstractions whose referents exist not as separate entities but only as components in a complex process that follows a course of development marked by changing interrelationships among the components. Thus, if we describe the genesis of voluntary out of involuntary activity in terms of the setting up of associations between sets of entities called feelings, sensations, ideas, and movements, we are committing the error of converting the concepts of the psychologist into neatly distinct sets of objects that then require yet another set of reified hypotheses to unite them again (Wundt, 1883). In reality, according to Wundt, the process of development is more like a process of differentiation in which the potentially identifiable components of an original unity achieve a certain degree of relative independence. The term that Wundt used to designate this original unity was *drive* or *impulse* (*Trieb*): "The course of both general [i.e., phylogenetic] and individual development shows that drives are the fundamental psychic phenomena from which all mental development originates" (Wundt, 1880, Vol. 2, p. 455). This is true also of the development of cognition:

> The psychic synthesis of sensations always involves the contributing factor of movement which is produced under the influence of sensory stimulation, originally as impulsive movement accompanying the sensation. The spatial and temporal order of ideas originates in this connection. The apperception of ideas is originally tied inseparably to movements corresponding to the ideas. Only gradually internal separates from external volitional activity through the temporary inhibition of the external component of impulsive activity, so that apperception remains as an activity that has become independent. Thus psychological development is essentially based on the separation of the initially joined parts of an impulsive activity. Once separated these components experience independent development, and when they are once again linked with movements, new, more complex forms of impulse emerge out of them. (Wundt, 1880, Vol. 2, p. 456)

Originally, then, sensation, affect, and movement are linked in an undifferentiated complex. When the movement component is inhibited (because physical or physiological conditions prevent its execution or, more generally, because incompatible movement tendencies are aroused), the sensory and affective components continue on their own and gain a degree of independence. This development provides the basis for the formation of new connections among the three components. Thus, what the older theories had regarded as a primitive fact—namely, the association between a movement and the mental idea of that movement—Wundt regarded as a relatively late product of psychological development. The formation of such movement images would have to involve a process of synthesis performed on more primitive movement sensations, and this process could take place only when developmental differentiation had gone some way. The setting up of links between movement images and the actual movements that corresponded to them would have to await these developments.

The result of the entire development process is the gradual transition from a state of affairs where a given set of stimulus conditions inevitably produces a particular kind of impulsive action to one where it arouses a multiplicity of response tendencies. Wundt referred to this as the transition from simply determined to multiply determined volitional activity. A final aspect of this development involves the association of movements with their external effects insofar as the effects become cognitively represented. This is a later development because at the level of pure impulsive movements, there is no anticipation of results. The simultaneous cognitive availability of a multiplicity of movement and effect images makes possible the characteristic feature of fully formed voluntary activity, the act of choice. While the intensity of the affective component would usually be reduced in the course of the development of volitional activity, that component never disappears. There was no such thing as a purely rational choice in Wundt's system.

Wundt's terminology reflects his distinction among different types of motivated behavior. Following the glossary of English equivalents appended to Judd's translation of the *Outlines of Psychology* (Wundt, 1897), which was prepared with Wundt's collaboration, we get the following classification: *volitional activity* refers to motivated behavior in general. This is subdivided into *impulsive acts*, which represent primitive drive activity; *voluntary acts*, which involve the simultaneous presence of several motives, among which one predominates; and *selective acts*, which are voluntary acts in which the predominance of one motive is preceded by a conscious act of deliberate choice. The effect of Wundt's scheme is to abolish the ancient opposition of will and impulse and to treat them as different developmental forms of the same basic process.

It should perhaps be emphasized that the act of choice was for Wundt a link in a network of causal determination and did not imply a freedom of the will in any absolute sense. Voluntary activity was always determined by psychological causes. Wundt did not believe that the will operated by fiat, though the network of determinants in which the act of volition was embedded was one of psychological rather than physical causes. While all volition depended on "the supply of innervation energy available in our nervous system" (Wundt, 1887, p. 483), the specific course of volition was a matter of a "psychic causality" in which the general dispositions developed in the course of the individual's life played a major role.

The development of voluntary action out of an original level of undifferentiated drive activity represents only one side of Wundt's treatment of the psychology of action and movement. In the discussion of his objections to the older theories of Bain and Lotze, it was mentioned that Wundt not only rejected the idea that reflexes or automatic movements generally formed the basis for the development of voluntary action, but that, on the contrary, he also maintained that such automatic behavior mechanisms were in fact the product of changes in activities that had started off by being volitional in nature. In the case of the innate reflexes, he regarded this process of change as having taken place in the course of phylogenetic development, as we have seen. But he applied the same analysis to the development of acquired automatic reactions in the course of individual development. The effect of repeated practice on a voluntary action is first to make it return to the level of a simply determined volitional activity; that is to say, a specific set of response tendencies comes to predominate, thus eliminating the element of choice. The process is therefore the reverse of that involved in the genesis of voluntary action. But the process of automatization can go further and result in the formation of completely automatized habits where the element of motivation or volitional activity has disappeared altogether. This last process may also occur when the starting point is not voluntary action but simple drive activity. The essential condition for this process of automatization is always the repeated exercise of the motor activity, and its explanation is entirely physiological: the repeated passage of a nerve impulse through particular pathways results in a relative lowering of thresholds, thus increasing the facility with which the impulse travels these pathways in the future (Wundt, 1880, Vol. 1, p. 269).

It is clear from all this that Wundt emerged with a theory of behavior change that provides for a duality of processes that move in opposite directions. In the later editions of the *Physiological Psychology* (1903, Vol. 3, p. 312) and also in the *Völkerpsychologie*, Wundt (1900, Vol. 1, p. 34) summed up his scheme of behavior change in a diagram that looks like this:

<pre>
Automatic movements   ← Drive   → Voluntary
    -----   -----
   and reflexes   ← movements ←   movements
                             ←
</pre>

The three bottom arrows represent the process of progressive automatization that usually begins with voluntary movements but that may also begin with drive movements as indicated by the top left arrow. The top right arrow represents the previously discussed differentiation process, in the course of which voluntary movement develops out of impulsive activity. In Wundt's view, therefore, behavioral change cannot be reduced to one type of process; but involves two entirely different processes that work in opposite directions. The one process results in simplification and automatization, the other in greater complexity and autonomy. The one is a process of training and habit formation, the other a process of psychological development.

Although the conception of these two diverging processes forms the core of Wundt's theorizing in the area of behavior change, it must be noted that he also admits a third process that is not represented in his diagram. As we have seen, his concept of impulsive movements involves the notion of an original union between affect and movement. Insofar as this union persists in the course of development, any conditions that come to arouse the affect will also tend to arouse the movement that is tied to it. It is not even necessary for the aroused affect to be identical to the original affect; it is necessary only that the two affective patterns have some similarity to each other. Wundt (1900, Vol. 1, p. 112) referred to this phenomenon as the "association of analogous feeling"; it is a process to which he assigned a key role in the development of a special class of movements, namely, expressive movements. In terms of his threefold division of movements into voluntary, automatic, and drive movements, the movements of emotional expression clearly fall into the last category, involving an original union of sensation, affect, and movement (automatic movements would lack the affective component). Insofar as movements of emotional expression become voluntary, no new principles are involved. But such movements are also involved in psychological developments that do not alter their status as drive activity. From being evoked by relatively simple sensory stimuli, they come to be evoked by complex situations and ideas. Wundt regarded this development as mediated by the affective component, which would have to be somewhat similar in the simple and the complex situation for a similar expressive movement to be evoked on both occasions. This is as close as Wundt ever came to a theory bearing some resemblance to the concept of conditioning.

Given Wundt's general position, it comes as no surprise to find that he frequently criticized the conception of human behavior that had emerged in Britain around the middle of the 19th century, the main contributors being Bain, Spencer, and Carpenter. This approach to the explanation of behavioral change was characterized by a heavy reliance on two principles: the principle of training or habit formation and the principle of utility. Neither of these found favor with Wundt, and insofar as Darwin (1872/1965) employed these same concepts—for instance, in his notion of "serviceable associated habits"—he, too, became the target of Wundt's criticism. As far as the concept of habit training was concerned, Wundt objected that it represented a preoccupation with external conditions while neglecting internal psychological conditions of behavior change. In any case, we have seen that for Wundt, behavior change was a matter of the differentiation or else the simplification of complexes rather than the combination of originally separate entities.

The questions raised by the principle of utility were even more far-reaching. According to the British school of thought, behavior changes as a result of a selection process that favors activities that have been useful to the individual; such activities may then continue to be reproduced by force of association even when their original usefulness is over. Wundt (1900, Vol. 1, p. 68 ff.) objected first of all to the tendency to apply this principle universally, suggesting rather that there are large areas of behavior where it is simply irrelevant. Second, he criticized the tendency of proponents of the utility principle to substitute their own perspective for that of the individual (or the organism or the culture) under study. The effects that were supposed to govern behavior change were generally the effects that were clear to the outside observer, but this did not mean that they functioned as motives for the individuals involved in the change. Third, Wundt saw in the utility theory a major example of what he referred to as "intellectualism," a type of psychological theorizing that never failed to evoke his disapproval. In general, "intellectualism" involved the tendency to explain mental life in terms of essentially cognitive processes, like the association of ideas, while neglecting the special character and underemphasizing the role of the affective and dynamic (volitional) processes that Wundt regarded as basic. More specifically, the utility theorists tended to explain adaptive behavior in terms of the individual's intellectual anticipation of the effects of his actions. Wundt, on the other hand, regarded actions that fitted this model as a relatively advanced product of a psychological development that depended essentially on the vagaries of affectively charged drives. While the utility theorists tended to equate motives with intellectually perceived ends, Wundt distinguished sharply between motives, which were the actual determinants of action, and anticipated effects, which might or might not become motives, depending on the affective situation.

In his later writings, Wundt increasingly conceptualized the individual–environment relationship in terms of his principle of the *heterogony of ends* (Wundt, 1903, Vol. 3, p. 787). This principle expressed, first, the fact that individual goals change as a result of action on the environment. Second, it attributed this change to the fact that the individual's actions on the environment generally have unintended consequences. Insofar as the effects produced differ from the effects intended, the latter would become modified. Wundt made it clear that this effect would also be produced when the discrepancy between subjective goal and objective result is quantitative rather than qualitative. (One is reminded of level-of-aspiration experiments when one reads some of Wundt's remarks on this point, though he was himself very far from suggesting anything as specific as that.) At other times, new goals would arise because of the unintended side effects of voluntary movements. Vague though it is, this principle is of interest for two reasons. First, it shows that Wundt regarded behavior change at the level of voluntary action as essentially a matter of motivational learning. Second, it illustrates Wundt's belief that at this level, it was not success that provided the essential condition for learning but the absence of success. What he presented was an incipient theory of behavior change that differs rather fundamentally from the traditional selection-by-utility model of the mid-nineteenth-century British psychologists.

The total pattern of Wundt's various discussions of the psychology of action and movement is clearly such as to exclude the concept of *behavior* in the abstract and hence to exclude the possibility of general laws of behavior change. Wundt's theories in this area presuppose the existence of various types of movement that differ not only in complexity but also in kind. The principles involved in the modification of movements vary with the nature of the movement. But the different categories of movement also develop out of each other, so that the theory also has to be concerned with the principles involved in these developments. In the course of replying to criticism, Wundt (1883) referred to his theory of volitional action as a "genetic" theory. Compared with most other theories of the time it certainly was that. The reason that it did not do much to advance genetic perspectives in psychology was that the empirical methods that Wundt advocated—at least, on the level of individual psychology—were totally unsuitable for throwing light on genetic hypotheses. Nevertheless, there were aspects of his theories that were relevant in an experimental context, and it is to these we must now turn.

The Apperception Concept and the Experimental Context

Apart from his more general genetic perspectives on behavior, Wundt also developed a more specific model of the psychological processes involved in the production of overt action patterns. His explanation was mentalistic in the sense that the operation of dynamic–volitional processes was described in categories that were taken from mental life rather than from biology or from some psychophysically neutral language that did not exist in his time. Thus, he described the functioning of the dynamic principle in human behavior in terms of the concept of *apperception*, which is essentially the focalization of some content in consciousness. Wundt's model of mental functioning is that of a field in which there is always a polarity between the central part (the *Blickpunkt*) and the periphery (the *Blickfeld*), that is, between the focal point and the rest of the field. This polarization is the product of the apperceptive process, which is a fundamental active principle that is responsible for the fact that all experience is structured. Apperception, however, was for Wundt the characteristic manifestation of volition. It was the dynamic principle that gave direction and structure both to experience and to movement.

Apperception is a central process that operates in two directions. On the one hand, it operates on sensory content producing the complex forms of perception and ultimately of ideation. This aspect of apperception is relatively well known. But for Wundt, this was only half the story. Apperception also operated on the motor apparatus. Just as the contents of the cognitive field were structured in terms of focus and periphery, so the field of skeletal movements involved some that were apperceived and others that were peripheral at any particular time. Just as the apperception of perceptual content imposed form and direction on perceived figures, so the apperception of movements of the individual's own body imposed patterning and direction. Neurophysiologically, this process involved the selective inhibition of motor centers (see the diagram in Wundt, 1904, p. 318). In Wundt's terms, an apperceived movement constituted a volitional action. In this case, he spoke of an "external" form of volitional activity, as contrasted with the "internal" form in which some ideational content is apperceived. In either case, apperception operates as a patterning principle. To appear clearly in consciousness, a mental content must be apperceived, and this means that we are never aware of simple sensation elements but only aware of compounds. Similarly, the role of apperception on the motor side means that actual movements, even impulsive movements, are not motor elements but are generally compound action patterns.

In the third edition of the *Grundzüge der physiologischen Psychologie*, Wundt (1887, Vol. 2, pp. 263, 472) introduced an important distinction between what he called "impulsive apperception" and "reproductive apperception." The former involves the motor direction of the apperception process, the latter a cognitive direction. In impulsive apperception, the central dynamic process affects the motor apparatus directly, so that the apperceived movement is actually carried out. In the course of the developmental process previously described, movement images are eventually formed by the differentiation and recombination of movement sensations. Subsequently, these movement images may be recalled in a process of reproductive apperception, where it is the idea of the movement rather than the movement itself that moves into focus. Thus, unlike impulsive apperception, reproductive apperception does not involve the actual carrying out of the movement but only the memory of the movement. In applying this distinction to the scheme of development, it is clear that the most primitive level of activity involves impulsive apperception, where the central excitation discharges directly into certain patterns of motor activity. This is what happens in what Wundt called "impulsive movements" (*Triebbewegungen*), as in the sucking of the infant. But such motor activity leads necessarily to the formation of motor images (no matter how rudimentary) which can then be recalled by reproductive apperception. This process makes possible the cognitive fusion, analysis, and recombination of motor images and creates new movement possibilities, which in turn may become the focus of impulsive apperception. Wundt thought that the simultaneous arousal of two or more motor patterns played an important role in the cognitive elaboration of movements leading to the development of increasingly complex patterns.

In terms of historically important consequences, what proved to be the most significant difference between Wundt's theory of volition and that of his predecessors was not directly a matter of the content of the theory but a matter of its practical results. Unlike others who theorized about the genesis of voluntary action at this time, Wundt derived conclusions from his theory that could be put to experimental test. In doing so, he initiated a development whose consequences went far beyond anything he had foreseen or intended. Wundt found the experimental vehicle for demonstrating certain implications of his theory in the reaction time studies that had been conducted in the 1860s and 1870s by Donders, Hirsch, Exner, and von Kries. What Wundt added to these studies was not so much a matter of technical innovation as a matter of theoretical orientation. The earlier studies had been conducted from a physiological perspective and published in physiological journals. By putting the reaction time experiment in the context of the theory of voluntary action, Wundt transformed it into a psychological experiment that was conducted in order to throw light on issues that were primarily psychological and not physiological. The reaction time studies conducted during the first few years of Wundt's laboratory constitute the first historical example of a coherent research program, explicitly directed toward psychological issues and involving a number of interlocking studies (Cattell, 1886; Friedrich, 1883, 1885; L. Lange, 1888; N. Lange, 1888; Merkel, 1885; Tischer, 1883; von Tschisch, 1885). It was Wundt's theory of volition that provided the conceptual cement that transformed what would otherwise have been a collection of isolated studies into a coherent program that demonstrated the practical possibility of systematic psychological research.

One of the first examples of the experimental implications of Wundt's theoretical schema was provided by the distinction between sensory and muscular reaction times. We have seen that Wundt's theory involved a bidirectional operation of apperception, either on sensory content or on the motor apparatus. If this theory is true, then it should have consequences for the speed with which a voluntary action is carried out. The fastest action would be expected to occur with the motor direction of apperception, while the direction of apperception on the sensory stimulus would be likely to delay the action somewhat, because the apperception of the movement would have to be interpolated before an actual movement could take place. Now, Wundt saw in voluntary attention a means of manipulating the apperceptive process experimentally. Thus, by instructing the subject to concentrate either on the stimulus or on the response, the two directions of apperception could be differentially strengthened. The expectation was that reaction times would be longer in the former case than in the latter, and this theory provided an explanation for the laboratory findings of some of Wundt's students that sensory reaction times were longer than muscular ones (L. Lange, 1888).

Prolonged practice with constant interstimulus intervals produced a tendency to react before the presentation of the stimulus or to react to stimuli other than the expected one, a finding that Wundt interpreted in terms of his theory of automatization, according to which involuntary reactions generally succeeded voluntary ones and not vice versa.

Wundt also conceived the idea of using the two kinds of reaction time as a way of studying experimentally some of the characteristics of the two directions of behavioral change that he had distinguished theoretically. In his view, the muscular type of reaction offered opportunitiess for studying the automatization process, while the sensory type made it possible to study the development of multiply determined voluntary actions out of simple ones (Wundt, 1897, p. 199 ff.). For instance, when the muscular reaction was subjected to conditions of prolonged practice with constant interstimulus intervals, the response latency could be reduced to zero or the reaction would even occur before the presentation of the stimulus or in response to an extraneous stimulus. These observations were taken as evidence of the automatization process. On the other side, variations in experimental conditions were used to complicate the cognitive task in the sensory type of reaction, requiring the subject to discriminate between stimuli, choose among alternative movements, and so on. For Wundt, this was a way of studying some of the factors involved in the transition from the simple to the complex type of voluntary activity, that is, the process that was opposite to automatization. When one compares successive formulations of Wundt's theories of volitional activity after 1880, it becomes apparent that his conceptualization was subject to considerable modification and sharpening in the light of experimental results. His earlier formulations provided a general impetus and direction for the experimental work rather than a set of specific hypotheses.

By the time the Leipzig laboratory was in its second decade, the accumulation of experimental data and a changing climate of opinion produced a gradual eclipse of Wundt's theoretical formulations (Danziger, 1979). But this eclipse should not lead us to underestimate their historical importance. It was Wundt's theory of volitional activity that provided the set of specifically psychological issues that transformed some rather pedestrian physiological studies into a research program with extraordinary implications. Employing the much abused term *paradigm* in the rather specific sense of "exemplar," one might say that the Wundtian reaction time experiment in the context of his apperception theory provided psychology with a first genuine experimental paradigm of its own. In Wundt's own estimation, the link between his experimental work and his theory of volitional activity was clear:

> Just as the introduction of the experimental method is the most obvious external criterion which distinguishes the new from the old psychology, so it might be said that, for the views which have emerged under the influence of this method, the concept of the will has become the central problem towards which all the other main problems of psychology are eventually oriented. (Wundt, 1906, p. 342)

Some Early Reactions to Wundt's Theories

Initial reactions to the theory of "volitional activity," which Wundt first formulated clearly in the second edition of the *Grundzüge der physiologischen Psychologie* (1880), were mixed. Philosophers of the old school did not like it, but among those who were interested in a naturalistic approach to psychology, there was a more positive response. Julius Baumann (1881) wrote an extremely long-winded philosophical critique of Wundt's ideas in this area, to which Wundt replied in his own journal, the *Philosophische Studien* (Wundt, 1883), to be followed by further comments on Baumann's part (Baumann, 1883). Apart from taking Wundt to task for his idiosyncratic use of the term *volition*, which was justified, Baumann objected to Wundt's "Darwinistic" way of treating the human will as part of a natural order that embraced reflex, impulsive, and voluntary action in a single continuum of development. Baumann took his stand on the philosophical tradition from Kant to Lotze, according to which human volition stood above nature. Wundt counterattacked by charging that metaphysical theories about *the* will as an independent entity were simply based on a reification of abstractions derived from a particular analysis of our behavior. His theory, Wundt explained, was meant to do justice to two basic sets of observations: that consciousness is always active and not merely a passive mechanism of registration, and that consciousness is always associated with movements in the physical world.

Wundt fared much better at the hands of G. H. Schneider, a follower of Häckel and an ardent champion of Darwinian naturalism. Schneider (1879, 1880) had been a pioneer of comparative psychology in Germany and subsequently (1882) attempted to show that human voluntary activity could be explained as an adaptive development without recourse to metaphysical concepts of will. In this attempt, he made considerable use of Wundt's formulations regarding the role of apperception and the developmental interrelationship of impulsive, reflexive, and voluntary activity. His disagreement with Wundt on one point is of some interest. Wundt had expressed the belief that "internal" apperception (i.e., the focalization of some psychic content) was primary and "external" (i.e., motor) apperception was secondary. Schneider (1882, p. 308 ff.) argued very convincingly that biologically, this relationship must be reversed, a motor direction of the central psychophysical apperceptive process being primary. Several years later, Wundt (1897, pp. 183–184) seems to have reversed his own position on this point. But at other times, he seems to have suggested that neither internal nor external volitional action may claim priority. Here, his notorious slipperiness becomes apparent. The philosopher Wundt and the scientist Wundt did not always speak with the same voice.

However, during the 1880s, it was Wundt the scientist who was at the height of his influence. His account of the interrelationships among the various types of movements carried all the more weight as the Leipzig reaction time experiments opened up prospects for the empirical investigation of issues that had hitherto been reserved solely for speculative treatment. The new style of psychology textbook usually took its cue from Wundt's *Physiological Psychology* in its relatively naturalistic treatment of the topic of "volition." One finds echoes of Wundt's theory of behavior in the work of Sully (1884) in England and to a lesser extent of Ladd (1887) in the United States.

But the reaction was not long in coming. In 1888, a young German scholar by the name of Hugo Münsterberg entered the psychological scene with a monograph on volitional action that was explicitly at variance with Wundt's view. The core of Münsterberg's position was the doctrine of sensationalism, the principle that all contents of consciousness were reducible to sensations. Ideas were complexes of sensations and feelings were qualities of sensation. This was simply a way of expressing a model of the mind as essentially a registering mechanism. There was no room here for the impulsive–affective aspect of mind that played so large a role in Wundt's theory. Another aspect of sensationalism that brought it into sharp conflict with Wundtian psychology was its peripheralism, that is, its emphasis on the peripheral rather than the central origin of psychological processes. From Münsterberg's point of view, all movement was ultimately reflex movement. In the course of individual development, these movements became adapted to securing beneficial effects for the organism, but this was a purely physiological process that did not involve any causal role for so-called impulsive or apperceptive mental processes. The mental aspect of movement was simply the sensation or idea of movement: the mind registered, but it did not activate. Münsterberg's position was unusual among German academics. Philosophically, he partly returned to the fold by a peculiar dualism that had room for a world of "eternal values," but in practice, this stance made no difference whatever to his psychology. In the course of his subsequent North American career, Münsterberg's ideas on the explanation of human and animal movement fell on fertile soil. But for Wundt, Münsterberg's theories came to function as a kind of "antipole," the opposition to which helped to define and clarify the essential features of his own approach to the explanation of behavior. The monographs of the 1890s (Wundt, 1891, 1894b) in which he reverted to issues in this area, as well the later editions of the *Physiological Psychology*, are extremely critical of the position adopted by Münsterberg. Wundt used these occasions to reaffirm the primacy of central impulsive processes for the explanation of behavior.

The young Münsterberg had found a powerful patron in the person of William James, who arranged for him to direct the Harvard Psychological Laboratory. Given James's intense irritation with Wundt and his style (James, 1894), Münsterberg's disagreements with the oracle of Leipzig certainly did not hurt his chances. But for us, the differences of substance that divided Wundt and James are more instructive than the incompatibility of their intellectual styles. As far as the explanation of behavior was concerned, the key to their differences probably lies in James's fervent commitment to a form of the doctrine of the freedom of the will and Wundt's thoroughgoing determinism.

For Wundt, and those influenced by him, central impulsive–affective processes formed a sufficient and entirely natural basis for the development of voluntary action. For James, the natural component of these processes was defined in terms of sensory feedback from the organic changes of emotion or from the kinesthetic stimulation produced by movement of the skeletal musculature. While sensations could reflexly produce movement, they could not choose among themselves. For choice, an additional mental function, the will, was necessary: "Will is a relation between the mind and its ideas" (James, 1890, Vol. 2, p. 559). For Wundt, on the other hand, will was a psychophysical process already

involved in an affective–motor discharge; it was not something added at
the level of choice among *ideas* of action, the latter being seen as a product
of psychological development. Wundt tried to argue for a continuity of
psychological processes from impulsive motor discharge to voluntary
selection among ideas; James tried to argue for discontinuity.

It is this fundamental divergence that makes their well-known difference about "feelings of innervation" intelligible. This was the question
of whether what James called "the mental determination of a voluntary
act" involved not only a kinesthetic memory image of the act but also an
awareness of outgoing motor impulses. When one examines their respec-
tive comments on the matter, it becomes very obvious that this issue was
far more important to James than it was to Wundt. There is a striking
discrepancy between James's lengthy and passionate discussion of the
matter and Wundt's relatively brief and rather noncommittal comments
(James, 1890, Vol. 2, pp. 492–521; Wundt, 1880, Vol. 1, pp. 372–378). What
is even more significant for an understanding of the underlying issues is
the fact that while for James, this was a key problem in the psychology of
volition, Wundt treated it solely as a problem in the psychology of *sensation*
(with implications for perception) and did not discuss it in the context of
volition. While in the context of the special problem of muscular sensation
Wundt was for a long time prepared to recognize the existence of feelings
of motor innervation *in addition to* kinesthetic sensations, this recognition
had no bearing on his theory of volition because the latter was for him a
question of *impulse* and not of sensation at all. His theory was that all
volitional activity had its basis in a central psychophysical process that
manifested itself subjectively as feeling and objectively as movement. The
nature of the experienced feeling would vary with the type of volitional
activity. For instance, the so-called feeling of activity (*Tätigkeitsgefühl*) was
characteristic of the highest level of volitional activity, namely, voluntary
activity, and simpler forms of volitional activity involved cruder affective
components. All these affective processes involved central neurophysio-
logical changes, but whether the outgoing motor impulse was part of
these was a highly specific question that seemed to Wundt to be devoid of
theoretical implications for his general position (Wundt, 1891).

What separated Wundt and James was the more general question of
whether "volitional" processes were present in all directed motor activity, as Wundt held, or whether they operated only on the level of a mental
choice among ideas, as James maintained. In order to support the latter
position, James had to show that the mental side of movement consisted

only of sensations or ideas of movement, for in the last analysis, the existence of an affective motor consciousness would have made voluntary choice a matter of conflict among competing impulses. Now, while the notion of a free choice among ideas was conceivable, the notion of a free choice among affects was not. If the will was to be free and moreover open to ethical considerations, it had to be conceived of as operating on the level of ideas rather than of affects. This difference between James and Wundt was far from being a merely philosophical squabble about words. It entailed diverging implications for any empirical research program in the area of volitional activity. The Jamesian model suggested that research efforts ought to concentrate on investigating the genesis of those sensorimotor mechanisms that provided the foundation on which the will performed its work. The Wundtian model, on the other hand, encouraged research on the affective aspects of volitional activity, a trend begun by Wundt in the 1890s and continued after his death by the so-called second Leipzig school.

While certain general features of Wundt's and James's explanations of human behavior continued to exert their influence on the development of psychology, the specifics of both their theories quickly fell victim to the powerful wave of positivism that swept over experimental psychology in the early years of the twentieth century (Danziger, 1979). However, in both cases, there were also internal reasons that would work against these theories in a research context. In Wundt's case, vagueness and inconsistency on crucial points often offended his critics. However, his theories were fruitful enough over a considerable period, and it is by no means obvious that they were any more vague or any less consistent than most of their replacements in the first half of the twentieth century.

But Wundt did create some rather substantial difficulties for himself. Not the least among these arose out of his absolutely unwavering insistence that those affective processes that played such a key role in his explanation of behavior had to be *conscious* processes. This meant that he was never prepared to consider the role that latent affective dispositions might play in behavior. The difficulty was compounded by his rigid views about the nature and scope of psychological experimentation (Danziger, 1980). As valid experimentation depended for him on the strictest objective control and/or monitoring of mental processes, the largest area of voluntary behavior was considered forever beyond the reach of laboratory methods (Wundt, 1907). In effect, Wundt painted himself into a corner. On the one hand, he proclaimed that the key to the explanation of purposive behavior lay in the processes of impulse and affect. But only the conscious aspects of these processes had psychological reality, and these were precisely the aspects that largely resisted experimental investigation. Wundt's only way out was to say that the problem could not be solved on the level of individual psychology but required a new approach altogether, that of *Völkerpsychologie*, or the psychological study of cultural products.

While the social psychological studies of Wundt's later years produced some interesting results, they had only limited relevance for the exploration of the dynamic causes of individual behavior and development. That unsolved problem that Wundt had bequeathed to later generations of psychologists could be confronted only by penetrating the frontiers that Wundt had attempted to set up for psychological method and theory. Nevertheless, his own work involved directions that pointed beyond those frontiers and sowed seeds that bore late fruit that would have seemed strange indeed to the old master.

References

Bain, A. *The senses and the intellect.* London: Longmans, Green, 1855.

Bain, A. *The emotions and the will.* London: Longmans, Green, 1859.

Baumann, J. Wundt's Lehre vom Willen und sein animistischer Monismus. *Philosophische Monatshefte,* 1881, 17, 558–602.

Baumann, J. Nochmals Wundt's Lehre vom Willen. *Philosophische Monatshefte,* 1883, 19, 354–374.

Boring, E. G. *Sensation and perception in the history of experimental psychology.* New York: Appleton-Century-Crofts, 1942.

Cattell, J. McK. Psychometrische Untersuchungen. *Philosophische Studien,* 1886, 3, 305–336, 452–492.

Danziger, K. The positivist repudiation of Wundt. *Journal of the History of the Behavioral Sciences,* 1979, 15(3), 205–230.

Danziger, K. The history of introspection reconsidered. *Journal of the History of the Behavioral Sciences,* 1980, 16, in press.

Darwin, C. *The expression of the emotions in man and animals.* Chicago: University of Chicago Press, 1965. (Originally published, 1872.)

Fichte, J. G. *Die Thatsachen des Bewusstseyns.* Stuttgart: Cotta, 1817.

Frotlage, K. *System der Psychologie.* Leipzig: Brockhaus, 1855.

Friedrich, M. Über die Apperceptionsdauer bei einfachen und zusammengesetzten Vorstellungen. *Philosophische Studien,* 1883, 1, 39–77.

Friedrich, M. Zur Methodik der Apperceptionsversuche. *Philosophische Studien,* 1885, 2, 66–72.

Goltz, F. L. *Beiträge zur Lehre von den Functionen der Nervencentren des Frosches.* Berlin: A. Hirschwald, 1869.

James, W. *The principles of psychology*. New York: Holt, 1890.

James, W. Professor Wundt and feelings of innervation. *Psychological Review*, 1894, 1, 70–73.

Külpe, O. Die Lehre vom Willen in der neueren Psychologie. *Philosophische Studien*, 1888–1889, 5, 179–244, 381–446.

Kussmaul, A. *Untersuchungen über das Seelenleben des neugeborenen Menschen*. Leipzig: Winter, 1859.

Ladd, G. T. *Elements of physiological psychology*. New York: Scribner, 1887.

Lange, L. Neue Experimente über den Vorgang der einfachen Reaction auf Sinneseindrücke. *Philosophische Studien*, 1888, 4, 479–510.

Lange, N. Beiträge zur Theorie der sinnlichen Aufmerksamkeit und der activen Apperception. *Philosophische Studien*, 1888, 4, 390–422.

Lotze, R. H. *Medicinische Psychologie oder Physiologie der Seele*. Leipzig: Widmann, 1852.

Lotze, R. H. Pflüger's Die sensoriellen Functionen etc. *Göttinger gelehrte Anzeigen*, 1853, 3, 1737–1776.

Merkel, J. Die zeitlichen Verhältnisse der Willenstätigkeit. *Philosophische Studien*, 1885, 2, 73–127.

Münsterberg, H. *Die Willenshandlung, ein Beitrag zur physiologischen Psychologie*. Freiburg: Mohr, 1888.

O'Donnell, J. M. The crisis of experimentalism in the 1920's. *American Psychologist*, 1979, 34, 289–295.

Pflüger, E. *Die sensorischen Functionen des Rückenmarks der Wirbelthiere nebst einer neuen Lehre über die Leitungsgesetze der Reflexionen*. Berlin: Hirschwald, 1853.

Reimarus, H. S. *Allgemeine Betrachtungen über die Triebe der Thiere, hauptsächlich über ihre Kunsttriebe*. Hamburg: Bohn, 1760.

Schneider, G. H. Zur Entwicklung der Willensäusserungen im Thierreiche. *Vierteljahrschrift für wissenschaftliche Philosophie*, 1879, 3, 176–205, 294–306.

Schneider, G. H. *Der thierische Wille*. Leipzig: Abel, 1880.

Schneider, G. H. *Der menschliche Wille*. Berlin: Dümmler, 1882.

Sully, J. *Outlines of Psychology*. London: Longmans, Green, 1884.

Tischer, E. Über die Unterscheidung von Schallstärken. *Philosophische Studien*, 1883, 1, 495–542.

von Tschisch, W. Über die Zeitverhältnisse der Apperception einfacher und zusammengesetzter Vorstellungen untersucht mit Hülfe der Complicationsmethode. *Philosophische Studien*, 1885, 2, 603–634.

Wundt, W. *Vorlesungen über die Menschen- und Thierseele*. Leipzig: Voss, 1863.

Wundt, W. Über das Verhältniss der Gefühle zu den Vorstellungen. *Vierteljahrschrift für wissenschaftliche Philosophie*, 1879, 3, 129–151.

Wundt, W. *Grundzüge der physiologischen Psychologie* (2nd ed.). Leipzig: Engelmann, 1880.

Wundt, W. Zur Lehre vom Willen. *Philosophische Studien*, 1883, 1, 337–378.

Wundt, W. Die Entwicklung des Willens, in *Essays*. Leipzig: Engelmann, 1885.

Wundt, W. *Grundzüge der physiologischen Psychologie* (3rd ed.) Leipzig: Engelmann, 1887.

Wundt, W. Selbstbeobachtung und inner Wahrnehmung. *Philosophische Studien*, 1888, 4, 292–309.

Wundt, W. Zur Lehre von dem Gemüthsbewegungen. *Philosophische Studien*, 1891, 6, 335–393.

Wundt, W. *Lectures on human and animal psychology* (2nd ed.) (trans. Creighton and Titchener). New York: Macmillan, 1894. (a)

Wundt, W. Über psychische Kausalität und das Princip des psychophysischen Parallelismus. *Philosophische Studien*, 1894, 10, 1–124. (b)

Wundt, W. *Outlines of psychology* (trans. Judd). Leipzig: Engelmann, 1897.

Wundt, W. *Völkerpsychologie*, Vol. 1. Leipzig: Engelmann, 1900.
Wundt, W. *Grundzüge der physiologischen Psychologie* (5th ed.). Leipzig: Engelmann, 1903.
Wundt, W. *Principles of physiological psychology* (trans. Titchener, Part 1 of 5th German ed.). New York: Macmillan, 1904.
Wundt, W. Die Entwicklung des Willens. In *Essays* (2nd. ed.) Leipzig: Engelmann, 1906.
Wundt, W. Über Ausfrageexperimente und über die Methoden zur Psychologie des Denkens. *Psychologische Studien*, 1907, *3*, 301–360.

4

Arthur L. Blumenthal

WILHELM WUNDT AND EARLY AMERICAN PSYCHOLOGY
A CLASH OF CULTURES*

Attempts to subsume mental processes under the types of laws found in the physical sciences will never be successful.

Wilhelm Wundt, 1866

Volitional activities are the type in terms of which all other psychological phenomena are to be construed.

Wilhelm Wundt, 1908

I must confess that to my mind there is something hideous in the glib Herbartian jargon about *Vorstellungsmassen* and their *Hemmungen* and *Hemmungssummen*, and *sinken* and *erheben* and *schweben*, and *Verschmelzungen* and *Complexionen*.

William James, 1890

There are many psychologists who have a predilection for the cortex; my own leaning is towards the sense organ.

Edward B. Titchener, 1908

We need a psychology that is usable, that is dietetic, efficient for thinking, living and working, and although Wundtian thoughts are now so successfully cultivated in academic gardens, they can never be acclimated here, as they are antipathetic to the American spirit and temper.

G. Stanley Hall, 1912

*A revised and extended version of a paper originally appearing in the *Annals of the New York Academy of Sciences*, 1977.

Historiography

Long after the prominence of Wilhelm Wundt as a psychological theorist had faded from the collective consciousness (or collective verbal behavior) of American psychologists, the most successful historian of psychology at mid-20th century, E. G. Boring (1929, 1942, 1950), summarized Wundt's work with the following dozen or so points: that Wundt's psychology began as physiological psychology (1950, p. 317); that Wundt claimed psychology as one of the natural sciences (p. 319); that to Wundt *scientific* meant "experimental" (p. 321); that Wundt made introspection the primary method of his laboratory (p. 328); that Wundt borrowed British associationism and was an elementalist (in the sense of mental chemistry) (p. 329); that Wundt was a mind–body dualist (p. 333); that Wundt opposed the implication of an active agent (p. 339); that Wundt's psychology was exceptional for its narrowness (p. 343); and that Wundt's life was withdrawn from the world of the affairs of common men (p. 344).

For some time afterwards, psychologists in English-speaking (and many other) countries paraphrased Boring whenever writing about Wundt. Eventually, however, a later generation of scholars gradually came to the reexamination of the original historical documents in the original language. And now, it has been shown several times that Boring is open to question on the above statements; that is, Wundt's views were either the opposite of or fundamentally different from each of the above descriptions (Mischel, 1970; Blumenthal, 1970, 1975, 1979; Klein, 1970; Bringmann, Balance, and Evans, 1975; Danziger, 1979; Leahey, 1979; Sabat, 1979; Rappard, 1979).

Understandably, initial reactions to this revisionist history have included disbelief. Psychologists who are untrained in the problems of historiography certainly might ask if the reporting of such history was not a rather straightforward task, and so how could such error possibly arise?

One answer has come from Samelson (1974) who has described how social scientists have the habit of creating "myths of origins" that evolve, consciously or unconsciously, in such ways as to serve the function of justifying their present position in the course of history. This habit may even result, I might add, in serious distortions in the translation of a body of literature from one language into another.

As students of history soon learn, this is an age-old problem in historiography in general, whether it be political history, intellectual history, or the history of psychology. So allow me to illustrate the problem further with a neutral example from another discipline—that of the history of British royalty—and then perhaps the parallel situation in psychology will seem more within the realm of possibility.

For centuries in Great Britain, children learned from folktale and nursery rhyme of the succession of English kings. One dramatic moment in those tales is where the reign of the Plantagenet kings came to an end, and the reign of the Tudors began. Richard III, last of the Plantagenets and considered a villain, was slain by the conquering forces of Henry VII, first of the Tudors. The death of Richard was rarely thought of as much of a loss, it seems, because he was described as both physically deformed and mentally deranged and, worse, a psychopath who had assassinated two nephews to fend off their threat to his rule. Such ugly recollections trace back to accounts written by the great Sir Thomas More—who came along too late ever to have known Richard, but who did, nevertheless, receive firsthand accounts from Henry, the conquering Tudor king.

Thomas More was a man of such respect and authority that it was considered bad manners to contradict him. And yet, the occasional historian working here and there in dusty corners of old monasteries, publishing in obscure academic journals, was able to show that Richard's nephews had, in fact, outlived him. Hence, he could not have been their assassin. Also, it was shown that Richard was not deformed in the ways shown in later caricatures and, further, that in his deeds as king he was a noteworthy humanitarian admired by his subjects.

The old legends of Richard's villainy, however, had developed a robust life of their own, and they survived admirably. They became the subject of one of Shakespeare's plays and were reported as fact in early editions of the Encyclopedia Britannica. In a word, these legends now served a cultural function in making one part of British history more intelligible. In particular, they made the succession of kings from Plantagenet to Tudor appear as an upward move in the advance of British civilization.

The lesson of this example is that history is often written by the momentary victors when the defeated are not around to argue their case.

Now, let us return to the history of psychology. Today, everyone could agree, I should think, that the traditionally received history of Wundtian psychology was not written by Wundtians. And in some quarters of American psychology, there arose such severe hostility toward Wundt that it may well have been felt that a history of the

Wundtian era written by a Wundtian would be *prima facie* inappropriate. That is, it would be like accepting histories of the Hitler period written by Nazis.

In any case, the history of the Wundtian era in psychology has often been cast in the form of legends about Wundt that, whether true or false, appear in textbooks largely as pedagogical devices for illustrating psychology's later progress in the American twentieth century. To the degree that that is true, the curiosity of the historical scholar might well be aroused. One might thus suspect that it could possibly be interesting to search out some summaries and interpretations of Wundt written by, say, German, Italian, Danish, Russian, or even English-speaking intellectual historians who were either quite close to or sympathetic to Wundt and who were not prompted by the later presentist motives (e.g., Passkönig, 1912; Hoffmann, 1924; Petersen, 1925; Kiesow, 1929; Sganzini, 1913; Villa, 1903; Höffding, 1915; or Goldenweiser, 1932). Or if truly ambitious, one might even turn to the serious study of Wundt's own writings in the original language.

There is, it is true, relatively little serious study of Wundtian thought that appears in English. Many more of Wundt's books, in fact, were translated into Russian—even into Spanish—than were ever translated into English. Moreover, the scattered English translations have, in most cases, a serious problem, which is indicated well by two influential translators themselves (Creighton and Titchener) writing in their preface to a brief edition of Wundt's *Vorlesungen* (1893) as follows, "we have aimed to furnish a literal, as distinguished from a verbal rendering of the German text" and "have attempted a precise use of words even at the cost of literary effect." That decision—a sad one indeed since the "precision" now appears doubtful—seems to have been the model for most of the few other translations. Although a dedicated reader might disentangle the awkward syntax of these translations, still the liberties that were taken to reshape Wundt's thoughts is another matter. Those distortions made it easier to give out-of-context quotations that were to help form some misreadings on the part of later historians. This is not the place to go into the technical details of translation errors. For a few examples, see Blumenthal (1975; 1979).

The remainder of this chapter is, for the most part, concerned with the sources, direct and indirect, of the distortions and the subsequent erasure of Wundtian psychology from the consciousness of the twentieth century. But first, we must reflect on the essence of that psychology.

Wundt's Psychology

The dominant school of psychological thought in mid-nineteenth-century Germany was that of the philosopher Herbart, whose theories were fundamentally mechanistic and associationistic, though tempered with some native German rationalism. Herbart's work was decidedly nonexperimental, for at heart he was a mathematician in his approach to psychology. It was in those days around mid-century, however, that the experimental method began to receive wide notice because of its successes in the hands of physiologists. The idea then came about quite naturally, and was frequently suggested in Germany, that these new methods—involving quantification, replicability, public data, and controlled tests—might be usefully applied to any and all problems of human knowledge. And in this way, the adjective *physiological* (*physiologischen*) came to mean "experimental." Thus, there was talk of "physiological linguistics," "physiological aesthetics," "physiological pedagogy," and "physiological psychology."

The young Wilhelm Wundt—then a laboratory assistant at Heidelberg—took up the challenge of these proposals. And as he did, his 60-year career as a scientific psychologist began one day in one of those moments of self-conscious insight. It happened at a time in his life when friends described him as an absentminded, daydreaming young scholar of Heidelberg. One of the notions that was then occupying the wandering thoughts of young Wundt was the old "personal equation" problem found in astronomers' writings. If you don't remember, there had been systematic differences between astronomers in their measures of the passage of stars across grid lines in telescopes. These slight differences in measured star transits depended on whether the astronomer first focused his attention on the star or on his timing device. Around 1860, after setting up some crude apparatus to simulate this situation and make some measurements, Wundt suddenly realized that he was measuring the speed of a central mental process, that for the first time, he thought, a self-conscious experimental psychology was taking place. The time it takes to switch attention voluntarily from one stimulus to another had been measured—it varied around a tenth of a second.

At this moment, the unfolding of Wundt's theoretical system began. For it was not the simple fact of the measured speed of selective attention that impressed him as much as it was the demonstration of a central, voluntary control process. From then on, a prominent theme in Wundtian psychology was the distinction between voluntary and involuntary actions. This theme seems clearly related to classical German philosophical traditions (which were strongly present in Wundt's thoughts) that is, the philosophies of Leibniz, Kant, Tetens, Fichte, and Schopenhauer. In Wundt's work the interest in central control processes is represented by the term *apperception*, which is a term that abounds in the German philosophical literature, though it is rarely incorporated into Anglo-American thought.

Wundt was so elated by his discovery that he rushed off to Speyer, Germany, to an annual convention of scientists. And standing there before a skeptical audience, the unknown young Wundt proudly announced the death of Herbartian psychology and the beginning of a new experimental psychology founded on his measurement of the central mental-control process. He argued against Herbart's mental mechanics with the counterclaim of the essential unity of consciousness, which was shown by the simple demonstration (Wundt's experiment) that we can apprehend only one thing at a time. We can only switch attention from single item to single item and at a rate no faster than one-tenth of a second per item.

The criticism of Herbart was to be extended to classical associations. It is not correct to conceive of laws of association as always operating automatically because, as Wundt claimed in his *Grundzüge*, they are always subject to the accommodation of attention. Wundt promised, in his early writings, that complex and often *ad hoc* associationist explanations of psychological phenomena would be supplemented by more powerful laws of attention (or "apperception").

Among his philosophical antecedents it seems to have been Schopenhauer's "philosophy of the will" that impressed Wundt at this time. It was apparently from Schopenhauer that Wundt derived his central theoretical tenet that "volition is the type of phenomenon in terms of which all other psychological phenomena should be construed" (1908). At roughly the same time that he arrived in his new professorship at Leipzig and began organizing the psychological laboratory there, he chose the word *voluntarism* (*Voluntarismus*) as the designation for his school of psychology. That word was actually suggested to him by a colleague at Leipzig, the historian Paulsen. It was not at all strange that Wundt should maintain close contact with historians, because before he ever lectured on psychology, he had lectured on history and cultural anthropology in his early years at Heidelberg (E. Wundt, 1927), where he had earned his living, however, as a physiologist and physician.

Schopenhauer's studies of volition were, of course, highly metaphysical. In that Wundt was an early experimentalist, he did not follow Schopenhauer in the metaphysical approach. Wundt thus named himself "the first empirical voluntarist" and thus began the long empirical search for those inner forces that are most fundamental in determining our experience.

Whenever a voluntarist philosophy appears, its immediate corollaries are purposivism and motivation. In Wundtian thought, these show up in the view that psychological processes are understandable only in terms of their goal orientations or consequences, which was not the case for the events of physics (Wundt, 1866). Thus, Wundt came to the fateful separation of physical and psychological causality—a trend in his thinking that was raised to the level of a "principle" in the early 1890s. It was this principle that kept Wundt forever at war with the positivist movement. That movement, in opposition to Wundt, called for the "unity of the sciences" and hence opposed this distinction of types of causality. And at times, it also called for the reduction of all sciences to physics. (See Danziger, 1979, in regard to the debates between the Wundtians and the positivists.)

"Physical causality," in Wundt's accounts, is classical mechanics. In "psychological causality," as Wundt claimed, new terms are introduced that are not found in physics, these being *purpose, value*, and *anticipations of the future*. The central mechanism of psychological causality was, of course, apperception, which in modern terms translates roughly as "selective attention." For Wundt, however, it was more than merely selective; it was more fundamentally constructive and creative. And with that capacity in mind, Wundt derived his first principle for the description of elemental psychological processes, the principle of "creative synthesis." It is the statement that all experiences are constructed internally under the control of the central volitional process. The mental constructions produce new qualities, forms, or values that cannot be wholly attributed to external stimuli or to more elemental events. The synthesis ensures that the events of immediate experience will be organized into coherent wholes.

A number of corollaries followed this first principle of synthesis. A second principle was titled "the principle of psychic relations." It states that the significance of any mental event is dependent upon its context. Each experience depends not only on integration and construction but also on the comparison and relation of that experience to its context. A third principle, of "psychological contrasts," concerned related opponent-process effects. Simply stated, antithetical experiences intensify each other. After a period of pain, a slight pleasure will loom large; a sweet substance tastes much sweeter if eaten after a sour substance; and so on.

Three more related principles concerned the extended development of psychological processes, whereas the above three are primarily concerned with the briefer development of immediate perceptions, cognitions, or memories. These further generalizations begin with "the principle of mental growth," which refers to the progressive integration or summation of experiences over longer intervals of time. Concept formation is the best example. Such formations are the basic mechanism of the continuity of experience and action. Without them, individual creative syntheses would remain separated from each other so that life would be disorganized and chaotic.

The second developmental principle is "the principle of heterogeneity of ends." It says that sequences of voluntary activity may be understood only in terms of the ends or goals toward which they are directed, but when those goals are attained, new and unforeseen results are always produced. That is, although we may be propelled by purposes and goals, we can never fully anticipate what the consequences of our actions will be.

The last of these Wundtian generalizations was titled "the principle of development toward opposites" and is an extension of the above principle of contrasts. It states that men's emotions, behaviors, and experiences, when viewed developmentally, fluctuate between opposing tendencies. A long period of one type of activity or experience builds up a pressure to seek some opposite form of experience or action. These fluctuations, Wundt observed, are found not only in the life and experience of the individual, but also in the pattern of human history. Moods, styles, and social systems all reflect such cyclic patterns.

It was the characteristic of Wundt's writing that he amassed so much material, ostensibly illustrating these six generalizations, that it seems few have ever been able to read through it all. Let me summarize it by quoting Charles Hubbard Judd, who may have read it all and who was certainly one of the least noticed among Wundt's American students.

Judd (1932) concluded that Wundt's psychology was "functional and synthetic, never atomistic and structural."

On the last page and in the last paragraph of his *Lectures on Human and Animal Psychology*, Wundt summarized the essence of his psychology, so I will present that statement here. The following is taken from the 1893 edition, which appeared at the midpoint of his career:

> Physical causality and psychological causality are polar opposites. The former always implies the postulate of a material substance; the latter never transcends the limits of what is immediately given in mental experience. "Substance" is a surplus metaphysical notion for which psychology has no use. And this accords with the fundamental character of mental life, which I would always have you keep in mind: It does not consist in the connection of unalterable objects and various states. In all its phases it is *process*; an *active*, not a passive, existence; *development*, not fixation. The understanding of the basic laws of this development is the primary goal of psychology.

Let us now return to the historical issues that form the primary focus of the present chapter.

The Leibnizian versus the Lockean Tradition

G. S. Brett, once considered the most erudite among historians of psychology, employed a productive historical distinction between two contesting views of man (Brett, 1912). One view is identified largely with German philosophical traditions which received a strong impulse from Gottfried Leibniz at the beginning of the eighteenth century. This impulse underwent various transformations through German rationalism and romanticism. The other viewpoint, associated most often with English philosophy, may be linked with the name of John Locke, who held a position in the English-speaking world analogous to that of Leibniz in the German world. The names of Locke and Leibniz stand as symbols if we are to understand the history of psychology. In recent times, it was Gordon Allport who in his influential book *Becoming* (1955) brought home to American students the importance of this distinction.

Wundt viewed his psychology as the modern representative of the Leibnizian tradition, including the works of Spinoza, Wolff, Tetens, Kant, Humboldt, Mendelsohn, Hegel, Schelling, Fichte, and Schopenhauer. These influences included Leibniz's notions of volition, levels of consciousness, and holistic orientations; Spinoza's assertion that volition, or desiring and striving, is the supreme human faculty; Wolff's analyses of the distinctions between empiricist and rationalist psychology; Mendelsohn's notions of feelings and emotions; Kant's notion of volitional apperception; Hegel's use of developmental laws; Schelling's and Tetens's writings on emotion and volition; and finally Fichte and Schopenhauer as more direct sources of Wundt's voluntarism. To say the least, Wundt was not unmindful of these historical antecedents. Most of his texts begin with a history-of-philosophy orientation.

Recall, now, the Lockean tradition. For those readers in the Anglo-American (and French) worlds, we have, because of our history and cultural forms, been most comfortable, or at least most instructed, in this tradition. Among the English thinkers, we regard Adam Smith, Hartley, Hume, and the Mills as our own. They are so familiar as to need little introduction. They, of course, showed many variations in their empiricist and materialist formulations. Closely related to this tradition were similar streams of thought in France carried forward by such thinkers as Diderot, Montesquieu, Condillac, and Condorcet.

Locke had taught that there is nothing in our mental processes but the product of sensation. This argument had prompted Leibniz to reply that there is nothing, of course, except the mental processes themselves. Leibniz thereby charged Locke with overlooking those central processes that, as Leibniz felt, are directive in the formation of experience. Among the intellectual descendants of these two philosophers, this difference of view has continued down to the present day.

Both Locke and Leibniz stood on the threshold of the burst of eighteenth-century intellectual activity known as the Enlightenment. The Anglo-French Enlightenment was, in particular, especially concerned with making a break with the mysticism and the hermetic thought that had been strong in the previous intellectual epoch (see Robinson, 1976). Inspired by Newton's physics, the English and French thinkers who followed consistently attempted to reorient philosophy on a basis of physical science. For psychology in the Lockean tradition, this approach often meant a picture of man as under strict environmental control, or it meant models of man based on machines or on analogies to Newtonian mechanics. While rejecting the past, there was a spirited futurism found among many of these thinkers, and it shows in their many programs and projects for utopian societies (see Becker, 1932). In contrast to that Enlightenment spirit, the German *Aufklärung* generally retained a strong historical orientation. Thus, when considering a better or more perfect world, the German thinker would be more likely to describe a return to some golden or classical age in the past.

The American Temper

Early American thought is an offshoot of the Anglo-French Enlightenment. Locke's philosophy had spread rapidly throughout the colonies and became gospel in American academic institutions and eventually in American politics (Roback, 1964). Locke's political philosophy spelled out the argument that should a king's rule become tyrannical and inimical to the welfare of his subjects, then those subjects would be justified in rebellion.

American society at its outset, however, was guided more by the practical necessities of survival. As a new society without a unique intellectual tradition of its own and remote from European educational centers, there is little wonder that this society would quite generally celebrate the yeoman's life and become suspicious of the obscurities of foreign philosophical systems. The pioneer's glorification of the ordinary man gave him special faculties that pedantic philosophers were thought to lack.

But there is one other example (besides that of Locke) of the acceptance of a European philosopher in America that is rather striking. The case I have in mind occurred later in the nineteenth century—that of Herbert Spencer, the self-made, self-educated, civil engineer turned philosopher. Some have described Spencer's work as having a rather homespun, cracker-barrel quality. But it was more than his particular style that brought him success in America. According to the historian Hofstadter (1944), of all nineteenth-century philosophers, Spencer was closest to the spirit of the earlier Anglo-French Enlightenment of the 18th century. Yet Spencer was also armed with visions for the practical application of the Darwinian theory of evolution.

Like his intellectual ancestors, Spencer had futurist utopian visions. He saw evolution marching forward toward the greatest perfection and the most complete happiness. But then we find that this final reward was offered in return for an acceptance of the miserable social and political conditions of the industrial society in which Spencer lived in England.

Spencer's sociological writings give arguments against all state aid to the poor, sanitary supervision, regulations on housing, and protection from medical quacks. As he explained, "The whole effort of nature is to get rid of the poor and unfit, to clear the world of them, and make room for the better" (Spencer, 1864).

Spencer made one celebrated visit to America in 1882, and it is likely that no other foreign intellectual has received a more welcoming reception here. Indeed, it was no less than Andrew Carnegie who greeted Spencer and entertained him lavishly. And some of Spencer's writings, which had not sold well in Europe, were serialized in popular American magazines.

Hofstadter (1944) described this period in American history, a time of rapid expansion and industrialization, as "a vast human caricature of the Darwinian struggle for existence and the survival of the fittest." Spencer furnished that society with its rationalizations in the form of social Darwinism. But as Hofstadter recounted, Spencer fell from American popularity as suddenly as he had arrived when it became obvious to influential Americans that a free social evolution was not proceeding in the desired directions. After Spencer's appeal had faded, in its place came *pragmatism*, a wholly American prescription that allowed that men should manipulate and reorient the environment according to their needs and desires. The psychological viewpoints that were then emerging from James, Dewey, Hall, Cattell, Thorndike, and many of their compatriots were, in Hall's words, "dietetic, efficient for living, working and thinking" (Hall, 1912).

One trend, of perhaps special interest to the intellectual historian, was the Englishman Titchener's influence in recasting Wundtian thought to render Wundt more compatible with British (Lockean) philosophical traditions (see Danziger, 1979). While at Cornell, Titchener cast himself successfully in the role of the primary representative of Wundtian psychology in America. (At the time, there was considerable competition for that role.) Yet, in Titchener's hands, Wundt's principles of apperception, his voluntarism, his purposivism, and his dominant interests in history were extremely muted or even fundamentally changed. Titchener's treatment of Wundt may be analogous in some respects to the British distortions of the viewpoints of the Viennese philosopher Wittgenstein, who had been transplanted to British soil early in this century (see Janik and Toulmin, 1973).

The Clash of Cultures

In the late nineteenth century, the practical necessities of American life included increasing needs for higher education. The German universities had, in that century, grown more rapidly than those elsewhere, and one could then find certain types of medical and scientific training only in Germany. Between the mid-nineteenth century and World War I, approximately 50,000 Americans sought higher degrees in German (and Austrian) universities. The medical degree was most often sought, for a German medical degree would allow one to charge higher fees after the return to an American medical practice. At one point, American medical students were so numerous in Vienna that they were able to dominate classes and demand that instruction be given in English. In spite of such linguistic reactions, American curiosity about things German was now growing. In the case of psychology at that time, this meant curiosity about Wilhelm Wundt, the one professor who had done more than anyone else to put that discipline on a scientific foundation.

William James was an early follower, and indeed an avid admirer of Wundt (James, 1875). But alas, scholarly relations between Wundt and James apparently had no chance of success, and the sarcastic comments they soon directed toward each other are still quoted in textbooks. It may have started with Wundt, who did not reciprocate James's early admiration. Wundt only acknowledged that James was a talented writer but apparently felt that James never bore any sophisticated or original views on psychology.

The antagonism, however, ran much deeper than this, and it ran much beyond these two men. There was clearly, as is reflected in James's writings, a bewilderment on the part of many Americans about the intricate and painstaking laboratory methods of German science. It was the same or a similar spirit that separated the two even more deeply in the realm of philosophy, where the intricacies and subtleties of language are so critical—the German linguistic forms seldom translating in any simple way into English. To James, the German-style scientific laboratory was a confusing "three-ring circus." To him, the language of German philosophy was simply "hideous." These and many similar comments by the highly influential James and several of his American contemporaries appealed to a growing American xenophobia that was mentioned in the previous section.

Later, it was mostly James's polemics against Wundt that were frequently remembered and quoted, but those statements were only a part of James's larger reaction. For example, James had acted as chairman of an international psychological congress in Paris in 1889. On his return, he described Herbert Spencer as "an ignoramus," G. E. Müller as "brutal," and Gustav Fechner as a man whose careful work in psychophysics would produce "just nothing."

Many American students who went to study in Wundt's laboratory had difficulties not unlike those suffered by James. The problems they faced are easy to understand. Imagine the 22-year-old American, with only a year or two of college German and an introductory philosophy course to prepare him, struggling to understand Wundt's lectures. Many of them survived, it seems, because although Wundt did not speak English, he understood it well enough so that the Americans were not compelled to answer in German. But at one point, according to Tawney (1921), Wundt had been on the verge of banning American students from his program because so many of them lacked sufficient facility in German.

Indeed, for all the American students who went abroad to attend Wundt's lectures, very little of Wundt's psychological system survived the return passage. It may be that Wundt was seldom well understood. It is extremely clear that what did come back with these young Americans was the laboratory apparatus and the floor plan of Wundt's Leipzig laboratory. These were the things, from Wundt, that seemed to have the greatest impact on early American psychology. Viewed superficially, the early laboratories at Johns Hopkins, Harvard, Cornell, Chicago, Clark, Berkeley, Stanford, and other places would have appeared to be a great monument to Wundt. The instrumentation from the Leipzig laboratory proliferated in its American setting. But then, when one reads the early American journals of psychology, one quickly realizes that Wundt was not truly honored in all this carpentry and shop work. That is, the tachistoscopes, timers, gauges, etc, were not used for the study of volition but were soon measuring the habits, sensations, and associations of the Lockean tradition.

Wundt's first American student, G. Stanley Hall, dropped out of Wundt's lectures after one semester to turn to more understandable lectures that concerned physiology. Many years later, Hall brought out a book titled *Founders of Modern Psychology* (1912), which was widely read and which contained a 150-page chapter on Wundt. It is largely an intellectual biography of Wundt, yet it contains a large amount of fabricated information about Wundt's life and work, and like several other American writings of the time, it reveals conflicted feelings toward Wundt. In Leipzig, the German translation of Hall's text was received with shock, and Wundt immediately published a frantic notice in a German literary magazine in which he said that Hall's account "is a fictitious biography which was invented from beginning to end" (Wundt, 1915a). Several later American textbooks cited Hall's chapter as a source and accepted uncritically its description of Wundt. And up to and including the present day, Hall's chapter remains the longest and the most detailed study of Wundt available in English.

Among the other early American students of Wundt, there was the highly energetic James McKeen Cattell, who unlike Hall, stuck it out in Leipzig and eventually, after some interruptions, received a Ph.D. from Wundt. But Cattell characterized himself as having no taste for philosophy, as being an apparatus man, and as having no interest in theorizing (Roback, 1964). It was Cattell whom Wundt singled out with that phrase so tirelessly repeated in American historical accounts, *"ganz Amerikanisch,"* or "typically American."

Recognizing certain obvious scientific accomplishments in Wundt's formative psychological laboratory, many early American psychologists reflected ambiguous feelings toward Wundt. For example, Knight Dunlap, an early American behaviorist, who once failed an attempt to learn German and who professed a dislike of German philosophy, included the following comment in his autobiography of 1932:

> The astonishing thing clearly seen in retrospect is that where we apparently have made our greatest breaks with the past, we have actually honored historical consistency the most. In casting overboard the most confusing accumulations of theory and interpretation (for which we may hold the Germans largely responsible), we have based our progress more solidly upon the methods and practical aims of the German laboratories. If we consider the long line of researches upon reaction-times, perception of space and time, memory and learning, and all the other studies of performance initiated a generation ago, we realize that our reconstructions and reformulations are but preparation for the more vigorous attack on these problems . . . we are but the more honoring the sturdy pioneers who filed the claims on the territories we now occupy.

Another strong feature of the activities of that early generation of Wundt-trained American psychologists was their immediate turn, in so many cases, to applied and commercial interests. Even the most application-oriented of the German psychologists, Hugo Münsterberg, ended up pursuing his career in America. And Cattell, Judd, Hall, Witmer, Scripture, and many others were all soon engaged in commercializing psychology in one form or another. Contrary to superficial accounts, Wundt did not oppose applied psychology as such. He did oppose the use of the graduate schools of science and philosophy and of the Ph.D. degree as the route to applied technologies. There were, in Germany, numerous technological institutes that could ostensibly serve this function. Moreover, Wundt felt that a loss of sensitivity to the distinction between pure and applied science could be harmful to both areas (Wundt, 1910).

With the approach of World War I, the schism between Wundt and many of his American counterparts grew to a hopeless breach. His former students in America were now embarrassed by Wundt's political actions. Along with 92 other German professors, in 1914 Wundt signed a manifesto appealing to the international community for understanding of the German position. Then came his book *Nations and Their Philosophies* (1914a), in which English and, by implication, American commercialism and morality is examined unfavorably. And finally, there appeared a pamphlet by Wundt titled *Concerning True War* (1914b), containing similar sentiments.

Let us look briefly at what Wundt said in these writings. The English and the Americans, he felt, view the existence of man as a sum of commercial transactions that everyone makes as favorable for himself as possible. So material values are wholly dominant in those societies, and all other aspects of life are subordinate. The primary goals of British and American science is, he claimed, useful inventions and physical comforts, rather than the deepening of man's understanding of himself and of nature.

In describing what he found to be the shallowness of British ethical theories (particularly Spencer's), and what he found to be a simplistic-naive realism in British and American philosophy, he used as epithets the words *egotistic utilitarianism, materialism, positivism,* and *pragmatism.* In regard to political freedom, he claimed that the Anglo-American societies had little to do with true individualism. Rather, they led only to a leveling of life and a lack of diversity, where small but powerful economic interests were the chief agents in the formation of public opinion.

Wundt, it seems, feared the trends in the mass democratic civilization of the West. But it was not the fear of a defender of an old aristocracy (indeed, Wundt had been involved in reform movements that went against the old German aristocracy). It was, rather, the fear of an intellectual fighting for a cultural heritage that he had dedicated his life to preserving and extending and that was now slipping away. His Leibnizian tradition, which he felt offered a higher view of man because of its emphasis on volition and intellect (Wundt, 1917), was now under severe threat from foreign forces and ideologies (cf. Ringer, 1969).

Among the reactions in Germany that followed on the loss of the war, there was a public clamor to abandon the older professors and to convert German universities into centers for applied subjects and practical training. The German psychological laboratories then went into decline under the pressure of this and other socioeconomic upheavals, although German psychology was not without some significant accomplishments during the period between the world wars. After Wundt's death, the old Leipzig laboratory became heavily concerned with "psychotechnics." Wundt was rarely read again in the English-speaking world.

It is one of the ironies of recent history that the anti-German attitudes of the American public were much greater during World War I than they were during World War II. The emotional rejections of German psychology (and science) that one reads in the literature of the World War I period may be interpreted in that light. At about the time of Wundt's death in 1920, caricatured accounts of him and of his psychology were beginning to appear, some from those writers who were eager to supersede him, some from those in America who were seeking additional justifications for divergent trends that were occupying the newer psychology in this country. These descriptions of Wundt were often not motivated by serious interest in accurate historical portrayal; rather they came from the usual presentist motives of elevating the status of one's own present-day work.

The particular description of Wundt that became the "official" and accepted description through the influence of E. G. Boring's 1950 history text may be seen today as the result of the many historical forces reviewed above. This comment is not meant to discredit Boring or his monumental work, for at the time of its writing Boring's description of Wundt was probably the most intelligible and most acceptable one for the great majority of American psychologists. For them, it served to crystallize an explanation of the history of psychology that, for its time, was satisfying and that justified the course of psychology's progress in the first half of the twentieth century.

References

Allport, G. *Becoming*. New Haven, Conn.: Yale University Press, 1955.
Becker, C. L. *The heavenly city of the eighteenth-century philosophers*. New Haven, Conn.: Yale University Press, 1932.
Blumenthal, A. L. *Language and psychology: Historical aspects of psycholinguistics*. New York: Wiley, 1970.
Blumenthal, A. L. A reappraisal of Wilhelm Wundt. *American Psychologist*, 1975, *30*, 1081–1086.
Blumenthal, A. L. The founding father we never knew. *Contemporary Psychology*, 1979, *24*, 449–453.
Boring, E. G. *A history of experimental psychology*. New York: Century, 1929.
Boring, E. G. *Sensation and perception in the history of experimental psychology*. New York: Appleton-Century-Crofts, 1942.
Boring, E. G. *A history of experimental psychology* (2nd ed.). New York: Appleton-Century-Crofts, 1950.
Brett, G. S. *A history of psychology*, Vol. 2. London: Allen, 1912.
Bringmann, W., Balance, W., and Evans, R. Wilhelm Wundt 1832–1920: A brief biographical sketch. *Journal of the History of the Behavioral Sciences*, 1975, *11*, 287–397.
Danziger, K. The positivist repudiation of Wundt. *Journal of the History of the Behavioral Sciences*, 1979, *15*, 205–230.
Dunlap, K. Autobiography. In C. Murchison (Ed.), *A history of psychology in autobiography*, Vol. 2, Worcester, Mass.: Clark University Press, 1932.
Goldenweiser, A. *History, psychology, and culture*. New York: Knopf, 1932.
Hall, G. S. *Founders of modern psychology*. New York: Appleton, 1912.
Höffding, H. *Modern philosophers*. London: Macmillan, 1915.
Hoffman, A. (Ed.). *Wilhelm Wundt, Eine Würdigung*. Erfurt: Stenger, 1924.
Hofstadter, R. *Social Darwinism in American thought*. Philadelphia: University of Pennsylvania Press, 1944.
James, W. Review of *Grundzüge der physiologischen Psychologie* by W. Wundt. *North American Review*, 1875.
James, W. *Principles of psychology*. New York: Holt, 1890.
Janik, A. and Toulmin, S. *Wittgenstein's Vienna*. New York: Simon and Schuster, 1973.
Judd, C. Autobiography. In C. Murchison (Ed.), *History of psychology in autobiography*, Vol. 2. Worcester, Mass.: Clark University Press, 1932.
Kiesow, F. Il principio della sintesi creatrice di G. Wundt e la teoria della forma. *Archivo italiano di Psicologia*, 1929, *7*, 61–79.
Klein, D. B. *A history of scientific psychology*. New York: Basic Books, 1970.
Leahey, T. Something old, something new: Attention in Wundt and modern cognitive psychology. *Journal of the History of the Behavioral Sciences*, 1979, *15*, 242–252.
Mischel, T. Wundt and the conceptual foundations of psychology. *Philosophical and Phenomenological Research*, 1970, *31*, 1–26.
Passkönig, O. *Die Psychologie W. Wundts*. Leipzig: Siegismund and Volkening, 1912.
Petersen, P. *Wilhelm Wundt und seine Zeit*. Stuttgart: Frommanns, 1925.
Rappard, H. *Psychology as self-knowledge: The development of the concept of the mind in German rationalistic psychology and its relevance today*. Assen, The Netherlands: Van Gorcum, 1979.
Ringer, R. *The decline of the German mandarins*. Cambridge, Mass.: Harvard University Press, 1969.

Roback, A. *A history of American psychology* (2nd ed.). New York: Colliers, 1964.

Robinson, D. *An intellectual history of psychology.* New York: Macmillan, 1976.

Sabat, S. Wundt's physiological psychology in retrospect. *American Psychologist,* 1979, *34,* 635–638.

Samelson, F. History, origin myth and ideology: "Discovery" of social psychology. *Journal for the Theory of Social Behavior,* 1974, *4,* 217–231.

Sganzini, C. *Die Fortschritte der Völkerpsychologie von Lazarus bis Wundt.* Berne: Francke, 1913.

Spencer, H. *Social Statics.* New York: Appleton, 1864.

Tawney, G. In memory of Wilhelm Wundt. *Psychological Review.* 1921, *28,* 178–181.

Titchener, E. B. Lectures on the elementary psychology of feeling and attention. New York: Macmillan, 1908.

Villa, G. *Contemporary psychology* (trans. from the Italian by H. Manacorda). London: Swan Sonnenschein, 1903.

Wundt, E. *Wilhelm Wundts Werke.* (Appendix: *Vorlesungen.*) Munich: Beck, 1927.

Wundt, W. *Die physicalischen Axiome und ihre Beziehung zum Causalprinzip.* Erlangen: Enke, 1866.

Wundt, W. *Grundzüge der physiologischen Psychologie.* Leipzig: Engelmann, 1874.

Wundt, W. *Logik,* Vol. III, Leipzig: Engelmann, 1908.

Wundt, W. *Vorlesungen über die Menschen- und Thierseele.* Hamburg: Voss, 1893.

Wundt, W. Über reine und angewandte Psychologie. *Psychologische Studien.* 1910, *5,* 1–47.

Wundt, W. *Die Nationen und ihre Philosophie.* Leipzig: Kröner, 1914. (a)

Wundt, W. *Über den wahrhaften Krieg.* Leipzig: Kröner, 1914. (b)

Wundt, W. Eine Berichtigung. (Gegen das Buch von Stanley Hall, Die Begrunder der modernen Psychologie.) *Literarisches Zentralblatt für Deutschland,* 1915, No. 84, 1080.

Wundt, W. *Leibnitz.* Leipzig: Kröner, 1917.

5

R. W. Rieber

WUNDT AND THE AMERICANS
FROM FLIRTATION TO ABANDONMENT

In 1920, no less than G. Stanley Hall had the following to say about Wilhelm Wundt:

> Wundt has had for decades the prestige of a most advantageous academic chair. He founded the first laboratory for experimental psychology, which attracted many of the most gifted and mature students from all lands. By his development of the doctrine of apperception he took psychology forever beyond the old associationism which had ceased to be fruitful. He also established the independence of psychology from physiology, and by his encyclopedic and always thronged lectures, to say nothing of his more or less esoteric seminary, he materially advanced every branch of natural sciences and extended its influence over the whole wide domain of folklore, mores, language, and primitive religion. His best texts will long constitute a thesaurus which every psychologist must know. (p. 6)

Following his marvelous tribute, Hall[1] reversed Hamlet's reproach to his mother by demonstrating that he must be kind only to be cruel. Hall

[1] In his book *Life and Confessions of a Psychologist* (1923) G. Stanley Hall listed several factors responsible for the decline of psychology during this period. The first of these factors Hall pointed out to be "the fact that Wundt for so long set the fashion here, served his apprenticeship in physics and physiology instead of biology (which would have been a better propaedeutic); hence his disciples have little use for evolution or the genetic aspects of psychic powers and activities." Much earlier in his academic career, especially when he was professor of psychology and pedagogy at Johns Hopkins University, Hall was much more sympathetic to Wundtian psychology and was responsible for the publication of and wrote an introduction to a book entitled *Habit and Its Importance in Education* (Redstock, 1886), an essay in pedagogical psychology translated from the German of Dr. Paul Redstock. This book is basically a summary of both Wundtian and other related theories and applications for teachers. Although it is rather doubtful that Wundt officially approved of this work, the book is nevertheless highly appreciative and influenced by the Wundtian psychology of the period and is equally well endorsed by G. Stanley Hall.

Figure 1. G. Stanley Hall.

went on in the next paragraph to contrast Wundt with Freud, demonstrating the gross limitations of Wundt's narrow approach to the understanding of the human mind. He proceeded to warn his readers with an almost foreboding prophecy of what is to come that "We cannot forebear to express the hope that Freud will not repeat Wundt's error in making too abrupt a break with his more advanced pupils like Adler or the Zurich group." And, of course, this warning did not unfortunately prevent this from becoming a reality (Green and Rieber, 1980).

The question arises as to why Hall and many others (e.g., Münsterberg,[2] Baldwin, and Cattell[3]) were unhappy about Wundt's influence on

[2]Hugo Münsterberg received his Ph.D. under Wundt at Leipzig in 1885. According to Boring (1957), Münsterberg, while still in Germany, had deviated from the Wundtian psychology of the time. This deviation resulted in some major disagreements and debates between Münsterberg and the Wundtians in Leipzig. William James admired Münsterberg's early separation from Wundtianism and called him to be in charge of Harvard's psychological laboratory in 1892. Münsterberg was one of the major forces that facilitated the Americanization of psychology during this period. He was the first psychologist to apply psychology to the law in his classic book *On the Witness Stand* (1908) and, thereafter, to industry, medicine, and education. The first textbook with the term *applied psychology* in the title was written by him in 1914 under the title *Psychology: General and Applied*. There is no mention of any tension between Münsterberg and Wundt in Margaret Münsterberg's book *Hugo*

American psychology. Some important clues are provided by Blumenthal in Chapter 4. Obviously, the full answer to this question would constitute more intensive investigation, and our intention is not to take on this task but simply to provide a short survey of Wundt's influence on the development of American psychology.

Our objective is to achieve this task in such a way as to demonstrate how Wundt and his ideas were both assimilated and dramatically transformed through a process that we shall refer to as the *Americanization of psychology.*

The Americanization Process

In order to aid an understanding of the meaning of the concept of Americanization, we provide a brief description of the groundwork for this process. The groundwork for psychology before the Civil War was largely shaped by the mental and moral philosophers and the religiously oriented colleges and universities in New England. Rieber (1980) provided a thorough discussion of this period and how such men as Thomas Upham and Francis Wayland contributed to this development. As a system rather than for its content, the mental and moral philosophy of the pre-Civil War period was new and different, containing the essence of the American dream as we know it even today. Tarnished though this dream

---

Münsterberg: His Life and Work (1922). Any reference that Mrs. Münsterberg made to the relationship between Wundt and Münsterberg was always couched in a positive vein. It is not clear as to whether this omission was a sensitive and tactful consideration on the part of Mrs. Münsterberg or a possible indication that the differences between Wundt and Münsterberg were so minor as not to interfere with an ongoing friendly relationship. (For more specific details regarding the differences between Münsterberg and Wundt as well as between William James and Wundt, see Chapter 3, by Kurt Danziger.) Nevertheless, it appears that Münsterberg's work in psychology—at least, during his American period— was more characteristic and compatible with American philosophic and psychological trends. Furthermore, it could be characterized as a variation on the theme of pragmatism and particularly applied psychology.

[3]In discussing a comparison of Wundt and Galton's influence on American psychology, Solomon Diamond (1980) regarded Galton's influence as having been greater, even though historians have given more recognition to Wundt. Diamond went on to make it clear that the early bearers of Galton's influence on Americans were Cattell and Jastrow, but the methods originated by Galton—including test batteries, word association, the questionnaire, twin comparison, classification based on the normal distribution, and especially correlation and regression techniques—have been prominent in the development of American psychology.

may have become, it has not been replaced, perhaps because nearly all belligerents in our psychosocial controversies still subscribe to its basic premises.

A brief definition of this dream is essential to our understanding of the groundwork for psychology in America. This groundwork included a belief in equal opportunity and the right of everyone to participate in the shaping of his own life and destiny. This belief was basically compatible with the democratic government of agrarian capitalism during the pre-Civil War period and with the industrial capitalism of the postwar period. All scientific discoveries were valued because they were seen as applied to the good of each and every individual and to the nation as a whole.

The second important part of the groundwork consisted of the belief that every individual had the capacity to change for the better in accordance with his needs and desires—the "do-it-yourself" philosophy embodied in the children's story of the little red hen. This aspect of America's character was seen not as some arbitrary and capricious activity but as a more serious behavior directed toward the benefit of all mankind. Therefore, any application of the science of the human mind was fundamental to the Americanization process. Education, of course, was a necessary and important instrument for the cultivation of both body and mind. The family as an institution played a key role in providing the discipline and moral training, and the knowledge and skill required by the growing society.

A third and important part of this groundwork was religious faith and lifestyle, extremely varied, but usually true to the ethnic origins of the founders. The Deity was to be appreciated not only through the study of the Scriptures but also through the accurate study of nature—the work of the Creator. This attitude provided for the connection between the belief in the value of the inner life of the individual and the importance of self-knowledge. All these beliefs were brought to America in their rudimentary forms by the Puritan Pilgrims and have remained alive, in some measure, to the present day.

The above-mentioned factors, however, were responsible for the easy assimilation and transformation of phrenology and mesmerism, Darwinism, Wundtian psychology, psychoanalysis, and many other related fads or movements. Wundtian psychology was shaped or Americanized to make it conform to this preexisting framework in a considerable measure.

The Functionalist–Structuralist Debate

The functionalist–structuralist debate in American psychology at the turn of the century has been written about by many scholars during the last few decades, for example, Krantz (1969), Boring (1969), and Rychlak (1977). Heidbreder (1969) gave a fine description of this controversy in the following manner:

> Functionalism *did* make its appearance as a psychology of protest. Its leaders *did* oppose the school that was then the establishment in American psychology: the classical experimentalists, essentially Wundtian in outlook, who saw as their basic and immediate scientific task the introspective analysis of conscious experiences under experimentally controlled conditions. These were its psychologists who, during the ensuing controversy, came to be called structuralists. And the functionalists *did* place more emphasis on the study of behavior than the classical experimentation has accorded it. Without denying introspection a legitimate and useful role, the functionalists in their own researches drew heavily on behavioral data. Influenced as they were by Darwinian theory, they undertook investigations that required that most, and in some cases all of the empirical data be obtained from the study of behavior—researched in developmental psychology, in educational and other forms of applied psychology, and in animal psychology, to mention a few examples. (p. 177)

Titchener's role is adequately covered elsewhere in this book (Danziger, Chapter 3; Blumenthal, Chapter 4) and therefore, we will not elaborate on it any further.

In relating to the functionalist–structuralist debate, Rychlak (1977) made some important points. For instance, William Caldwell prompted Titchener to write his famous 1898 paper entitled "The Postulates of a Structural Psychology," which appeared in the *Philosophical Review*. Titchener employed the functionalist–structuralist dichotomy in two ways. First and most importantly, he considered functionalism second-class and subordinate to structuralism. Second, he advocated a teleological description, thereby identifying all functionalists as teleologists. The basic assumptions of this structuralist position were that sensations and affections are elements of the mind and that they are incapable of being derived from one another. Moreover, they are subject to determination by the factors of intensity and quality. The temporal aspects of mental life were also very important to Titchener, because he was not willing to conceive of emotions and sensations as being free of some form of temporal order. Even though Caldwell and, to a certain extent, Mary Calkins were sympathetic with the early Titchenerian attempt to define structuralism, they were not at all happy with the way that Titchener developed this structural or content psychology during the early 1900s. As Rychlak (1977) pointed out, "They were humanists wanting to see a role for intentionality by way of self-direction in the psychology of their time."

Calkins (1906) even accused Angell of having defected to the structuralist position in his emphasis on the importance of the physical basis of behavior. However, Angell (1906) was quick to point out that the functionalists at Chicago were not at all sympathetic with the Wundtian methodology of a "direct observation of inner experience."

Another aspect of this tension between functionalism and structuralism concerned the Darwinian theory of evolution. Angell made it perfectly clear that the functionalists of the Chicago school wished to study the mind in its relationship to the biological foundations of the organism in terms of both phylogenetics and ontogenetics. The differences between Darwin and Wundt and their effect on the Americans are discussed later in this chapter along with the contributions of James Mark Baldwin.

Psychological functionalism was involved in what one might call a common-law marriage with biology and physiology and, therefore, could not see itself as an ally to Wundtian psychophysical parallelism. As Rychlak (1977) pointed out, the often-cited historical debate between functionalism and structuralism was "no confrontation at all in one aspect and a misfired polemic in another." Rychlak went on to say:

> It [the functionalist–structuralist debate] was begun by a humanist, who found the Newtonian interpretations of science brought to this country by Wundt's students lacking in something vital to man's conceptualization. Titchener lost the totality (the one) in the constitutive total of basal elements (the many), and yet this self-organizing principle of mental life is most characteristic of the human experience. Rather than a full airing of the introspective-versus-extraspective *theoretical* slant implied, what developed was a temporary quibble over the rules of *methodological* procedure. (pp. 140–147)

Wundtian Influence and James Mark Baldwin

One very important endeavor in Wundt's scientific work was to study the facts pertaining to the nature of the human organism, to isolate these facts by observation, and to measure them in terms of intensity and duration, that is to say, to study the psychic compounds formed by and

Figure 2. James Mark Baldwin.

revealed to us by our "introspective experience." It was through the form of *representation* and *emotions* that Wundt attempted to fix the empirical laws of the mind and their relationship to the body. This interest in representations was more than likely one of the things that attracted James Mark Baldwin to Wundtian psychology early in his career. Baldwin's frequent citations of Wundt in his *Handbook of Psychology* (1889) demonstrated Wundt's importance to Baldwin at that point in time.[4]

But, alas, Wundt's importance to Baldwin did not last very long, for in his *History of Psychology* (1913), Baldwin has only a few references to Wundt and in his only discussion of Wundt, in a footnote, adds insult to injury by pointing out that "this work [the *Völkerpsychologie*] is less effective because of the writer's tendency to abstract classification and schematicism" (p. 16). This extraordinary, deliberate abatement of Wundt clearly demonstrates Baldwin's desire to forget him and to help others do

[4]There were many textbooks in psychology at the turn of the century. One very interesting and important text—J. Clark Murray's entitled a *Handbook of Psychology* (1888), which was successful both in Canada and in the United States—demonstrates the influence of Wundt on Canadian psychology and contains many references to Wundtian and other related ideas.

the same, especially since Baldwin devoted whole sections to such important scholars as Herbart, Lotze, Helmholtz, Spencer, James, Fechner, and Ribot.

Baldwin's importance in American psychology during his early period is represented in a very important paper by Wozniak (in press), in which Wozniak argued a position that is basically compatible with the point of view of this chapter: namely, that Baldwin's most powerful influences stemmed not from Wundt and the Europeans but from more indigenous influences in America, represented by the American mental and moral philosophy movement during the middle of the nineteenth century. Nevertheless, Baldwin's references to Wundt in his *Handbook* (1889) constitute the largest number of references to any one author in that work.

Baldwin quoted Brentano's criticism of psychological theories that do not include an appreciation of the unity between body and mind. Brentano (cited in Baldwin, 1890) pointed out that "Wundt, for example, forfeits unity in the mental life and finds three problems on his hands instead of one. First to account for the purely mental, second to account for the psychophysical, and third to account for this duality." Baldwin continued his critique of Wundtian psychology by pointing out the narrow and limited importance that Wundt gave to the concept of the unconscious. Furthermore, still in a critical vein, Baldwin then discussed the concept of association of ideas with a fascinating diagram (see Figure 3) putting Wundt in his proper place, as it were.

A similar criticism of Wundt's use of the association of ideas was given by Royce (1903) in his discussion of the general laws of docility. Here, Royce referred to Wundt's fictitious mental elements and criticized

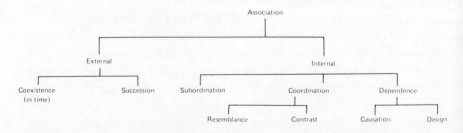

Figure 3. The prevailing German classification of the principles of association followed by Herbart, Wundt, Taine, and Trautscholdt. (From *Handbook of Psychology: Sense and Intellect*, New York, 1889.)

Wundt for his narrow volitional approach to the understanding of the mind. More specifically, Royce took issue with the Wundtian theory of emotion and had the following to say:

> In view of the facts which constitute Wundt's admittedly still incomplete evidence for his three "directions" of feelings, and in view of the really very large body of inexact but impressive evidence on the subject which the literature of the emotions seems to contain, I am disposed to regard it as *decidedly improbable that the dual theory of the feelings gives an adequate account of the phenomena.*

Wundt and Darwinism in America

In the latter half of the nineteenth century, an influential movement advocating the theories of Darwin and Spencer developed in America. This Americanization of evolutionary theory had a considerable impact on intellectual, scientific, and pedagogical thought during that period. The movement was mainly led by the American scientist and editor Edward Livingston Youmans.[5]

Many works of English and European scientists were either reprinted or translated by American publishers during the period between 1860 and 1890. An important related fact is that in America, very little importance was given to Wundt during this period and, conversely, that Darwin and Spencer received only brief mention in passing in the writings of Wundt. As Blumenthal points out in Chapter 4 of this book, quoting Hofstadler, "Social Darwinism à la Spencer fell from American popularity very quickly." In some measure this may have been the case. Nevertheless, Darwin's and Spencer's influence on scientific thought in general and on scientific psychology in particular continued in the decades to come, and remnants of this development can still be seen even in today's psychology.

[5]E. L. Youmans was the catalytic agent for the connection between John Fiske and Herbert Spencer. He developed a close association with both of these men during the late 1860s and the 1870s. His close association with D. Appleton & Co., a prominent American publishing firm of the time, helped popularize evolutionary theory in America. With the creation of the journal that Youmans edited for many years entitled *The Popular Science Monthly* and a most influential group of books entitled the *International Scientific Series*, Youmans arranged for the publication and the simultaneous translation into English and other languages of important scientific works by authors from England and other European nations. Youmans corresponded and worked with many of the most distinguished European scientists, and Wilhelm Wundt was conspicuously absent from this list.

The difference between Darwin and Wundt alluded to earlier centered mostly on Wundt's criticism of Darwin's theory of emotional expression.[6] Emotions, according to Wundt (1907) are capable of being

[6]Solomon Diamond has been good enough to translate for us an interesting passage in which Wundt discusses Darwin's theory of expressive movements. He has also written the paragraph of comment at the end of this footnote. At several points, where Wundt is restating Darwin's theory, the German words have been left in the text and Darwin's own words are given in brackets.

Darwin subsumes all expressive movements of animals and humans under three general principles, which are however essentially different from those which have been stated above. He calls the first principle of zweckmässig associerter Gewohnheiten [serviceable associated habits]. Certain complicated behaviors, which unter Umständen [under certain states of the mind] were of direct or indirect use, are supposedly performed as a consequence of habit and association even when they are not useful. The second principle is that of Gegensatz [antithesis]. When certain mental states are connected with particular habitual behaviors, the opposite states are supposed to become connected with the opposite behaviors by the mere fact of contrast. Finally, according to the third principle, some acts are from the first caused by the constitution of the nervous system, independently of the will and [omitted: to a certain extent] of habit. I cannot conceal the fact that to me these three laws seem to be neither correct generalizations of the facts nor capable of embracing them adequately. Naturally, real or apparent usefulness can be observed in expressive movements, to a certain extent, because they are originally reflexes and as such they are subject to the law of purpose and adaptation. They are this, however, at least for individuals, because of the constitution of the nervous system. Darwin's first and third principles therefore coincide at this point. As to why such purposive reflexes are also transferred to other stimuli, when there is no longer any question of their being useful, Darwin's rules provide no explanation. The factors that come into play here are in part the law of association of analogous sensations, and in part the law of the relation of movements to sensory ideas, and neither of these is included in Darwin's statement. The law of contrast is an obvious makeshift to meet this situation. If one expressive movement is to arise by contrast with another, some psychological basis for this must be discovered. Such a basis will, however, always bring us back again to the principles of expression which we formulated above, and thus to a *positive* reason for the movement in question. For example, if a dog that is expressing affection for its master displays a posture that is just the opposite of the one it takes when it approaches another dog with the intention of fighting (cf. Darwin, 1872, p. 51ff.), the reason lies partly in the qualities of the tactile and muscular sensations which accompany the wagging of its tail and the Windungen [continuous flexuous movements] of its body, and partly in the fear of its master which shows itself in the crouching attitude; that is, in movements which have their basis either in sensory analogies or in the connection of these movements with ideas. Aside from this inadequate psychological development of his theory, Darwin does have the merit of having collected an extraordinarily rich set of observations and of having given numerous examples which prove the importance of heredity in this area. (Wundt, 1874, pp. 856–857)

Wundt's *Grundzüge* was to substitute "principle" for "law" where the latter word occurs in sentences 7 and 12 as translated (but not in sentences 8 and 13!). This substitution was introduced in the third edition, when Wundt (1887, vol. 2, pp. 514–515) also added a paragraph stating that even his own "principles" of expressive movement (previously divided into three classes: (1) purely intensive symptoms; (2) qualitative expressions of feelings: these are mimetic movements; and (3) expression of ideas: these are generally pantomimetic movements. Wundt's critique of Darwin centers mainly on Wundt's claim that Darwin had subsumed all expressive movements of humans and animals under three general principles that were different from the principles that Wundt postulated. This is a rather good illustration of how Wundt rejected Darwin's theory, giving him credit for being a good observer and nothing more and thus rejecting all that was really essential to the Darwinian position.

Edward Wheeler Scripture: The Yale Laboratory and the New Psychology

The last of the important figures in our discussion who studied under Wundt, and who was strongly influenced by him, was E(dward) W(heeler) Scripture. After studying with Wundt, Scripture held his first job at the Yale Psychology Laboratory under the supervision of George T. Ladd. The general conclusion that Scripture took from his studies at Leipzig to his position at Yale was that statements were dependent on reliable measurements and, correspondingly, that statements without measurements were of little value; he adhered to the principle: "If it can't be measured, then it can't be any good." His time at Yale was a chaotic period for Scripture. For almost a decade, Scripture was in conflict with Ladd. This conflict dealt with intradepartmental and philosophical struggles, essentially focusing on philosophical–theoretical versus laboratory psychology, and it led to the termination of the services of both men. Carl E. Seashore (1930), a student of Scripture's while at Yale, commented on this conflict, saying, "the President should have recognized in Scripture the new approach to mental science of which Scripture was champion. Instead, he threw the baby out with the bath."

In some measure, the Yale conflict stemmed from a dispute over

---

called laws) were purely descriptive, because any causal explanation of movements must be in physiological rather than psychological terms. In the fifth edition, in a broader context, Wundt (1902–1905, vol. 3, p. 689) stated further that the principle of natural selection is a teleological rather than a causal concept, and that by describing as "accidental" the variations on which natural selection operates, Darwin had expressly foregone any attempt at causal explanation. All in all, this is a good example of how Wundt often acknowledged Darwin's acuity as an observer, but consistently rejected Darwinian theory.

Wundt,[7] although personality conflicts played a major part as well. Although Scripture was basically a "Wundtian," nevertheless, he was gradually contributing to the Americanization process as previously described. An important aspect of this development was particularly evident in James Rowland Angell's review (1895) of Scripture's *Thinking, Feeling, and Doing*, particularly as it is a partial reflection of the functionalist–structuralist controversy that has been previously described. Angell attacked Scripture for gross carelessness in his use of quotation marks by saying:

> In Chapter XXI, Dr. Scripture has the occasion to quote Wundt's human and animal psychology in these passages. The English varies widely from that of Creighton's and Titchener's translation of this work. But throughout nearly the whole of Chapter XVII where the author vaguely states that he follows Wundt the English is not only a translation of the German but is furthermore identical with that of the published translation just mentioned. (pp. 606–607)

Scripture's involvement in the Americanization process lead to the applications of quasi-Wundtian methods in industrial psychology (e.g., time–motion studies; see Gilbreth, 1916) and clinical applications in the area of communication disorders (Scripture, 1912).

Carl E. Seashore, a student of Scripture's as previously indicated, was strongly influenced by Scripture, as is evident from two of his works. Seashore's book, the *Psychology of Music* (1933), more than likely had its origins through Scripture because of his dispute with Carl Stumpf (one of

---

[7]Ladd, who is best known for his *Elements of Physiological Psychology* (1887), acknowledged the importance of Wundt's work as a tool in helping him produce his textbook. Nevertheless, Ladd's early training at Andover Theological Seminary instilled in him a powerful and lasting appreciation of early-nineteenth-century mental and moral philosophy. Boring (1957) indicated that Ladd, like James and others, stressed the importance of the concept of self within psychology, thus making consciousness a matter of activity, namely, the activity of a self. Therefore, Boring considered Ladd basically a functional psychologist. Clearly, this difference must have been one of the sources of tension between Scripture and Ladd when they were both at Yale. In the revised edition of the *Elements of Physiological Psychology*, prepared in collaboration with Woodworth, Ladd and Woodworth (1911), the authors, in their introduction, pay a token tribute to Wundt but are quick to point out, "In brief, it may be said that introspective psychology, important as its results have been and indispensible as its method is, has shown its incompetency to deal with the many and most interesting inquiries which it has itself raised." The authors go on to say, "We may affirm with Wundt without fear of successive contradiction: 'psychology is compelled to make use of objective changes in order by means of the influences which they exert on our consciousness to establish the subjective properties and laws of that consciousness.' (Quote taken from "Über psychophysischen Methoden," *Philosophische Studien* [1881], Heft 1, p. 4.)" Ladd and Woodworth (1911) (p. 10).

Brentano's students). Wundt's students taught that melodies were actually constituted of elemental sounds and that tunes were a combination of these sounds. Stumpf argued that Wundt's data contradicted what a trained musician's ear would discover to be important to the melody. As a result, Stumpf disagreed with Wundt's findings and criticized him for not supplying us with an explanation that was truly reflective of what musical experience actually was. Additionally, Seashore's book that was written before the *Psychology of Music* and was entitled *Elementary Experiments in Psychology* (1908), was considered a manual for the instructor and clearly was in the tradition of other works of the period that were written by Wundtian students, such as Titchener's *Experimental Psychology* (1901), Witmer's *Analytical Psychology* (1902).

By far the most loyal American student of Wundt was Charles Herbert Judd, who took over at Yale when both Ladd and Scripture were fired. At least, during the first ten years or so of the new century, Judd represented his master in Leipzig with the greatest of fidelity. The English translations of Wundt's *Outlines of Psychology* were all translated and prepared by Judd with the cooperation of the author, as the title specifically indicates. They were printed in Leipzig by Wundt's publisher, an unusual arrangement; but one that gave him complete assurance that the final copy would be exactly the way he wanted it. This example serves as an important contrast to all the translations of Wundt prepared by Titchener and his associates, none of which were translated with the cooperation of the author, as were the Judd translations.

Judd remained a loyal Wundtian until very near the end of Wundt's career, when it became apparent that application, particularly in the area of educational psychology, was both important and inevitable in American psychology, thus illustrating that even the most faithful of all the American Wundtians had eventually to succumb to the Americanization process.

As we can see from the information provided in this essay, the American psychologists' relation to Wundt may be exemplified best as an affair that ran its course from flirtation to abandonment. This short but intense relationship, especially through the political polemics and the tensions that came out of the functionalist–structuralist controversy, opened the door to two potentially powerful but nevertheless sleeping tigers, that is, positivism and behaviorism. A flicker of light in the form of a more dynamic, humanistic psychology was quickly blown out along with the remnants of the Wundtian structuralism as the second decade of the twentieth century proceeded to build a new psychology that would hope to be as truly scientific as chemistry and physics.

References

Angell, J. A review of Thinking, feeling, and doing by E. W. Scripture. Psychological Review, 1895, 1, 606–609.

Angell, James Rowland. Psychology. New York: Henry Holt, 1906.

Baldwin, J. M. Handbook of psychology: Sense and intellect. New York: Henry Holt, 1889.

Baldwin, J. M. History of psychology. London: Watts & Co., 1913.

Boring, E. G. A history of experimental psychology (2nd ed.). New York: Appleton-Century-Crofts, 1957.

Boring, E. G. Titchener, meaning, and behaviorism. In D. Krantz (Ed.), Schools of psychology: A symposium. New York: Appleton-Century-Crofts, 1969.

Calkins, M. W. A reconciliation between structural and functional psychology. Psychological Review, 1906, 13, 61–81.

Diamond, S. Francis Galton and American psychology. In R. W. Rieber and K. Salzinger (Eds.), Psychology: Theoretical and historical perspectives. New York: Academic Press, 1980.

Gilbreth, F. W. Fatigue study. New York: Sturgis & Walton, 1916.

Green, M., and Rieber, R. W. Assimilation of psychoanalysis in America. In R. W. Rieber and K. Salzinger (Eds.), Psychology: Theoretical and historical perspectives. New York: Academic Press, 1980.

Hall, G. S. Preface to the American edition. In Sigmund Freud, A general introduction to psychoanalysis. New York: Edward L. Bernay, 1920.

Hall, G. S. Life and confessions of a psychologist. New York: D. Appleton, 1923.

Heidbreder, E. Functionalism. In D. Krantz (Ed.), Schools of psychology: A symposium. New York: Appleton-Century-Crofts, 1969.

Judd, C. H. Psychology: General introduction. New York: Scribner's, 1907.

Krantz, D. L. (Ed.). Schools of psychology: A symposium. New York: Appleton-Century-Crofts, 1969.

Ladd, G. T. Elements of physiological psychology. New York: Scribner's, 1887.

Ladd, G. T., and Woodward, R. Elements of physiological psychology (rev. ed.). New York, 1911.

Münsterberg, H. On the witness stand: Essays on psychology and crime. New York: McClure, 1908.

Münsterberg, H. Psychology: General and applied. New York: D. Appleton, 1914.

Münsterberg, M. Hugo Münsterberg: His life and work. New York: D. Appleton, 1922.

Murray, J. C. Handbook of psychology. Boston: Cupples & Hurd, 1888.

Radstock, P. Habits and its importance in education: Essay in pedagogical psychology (trans. F. A. Caspari). Boston: D. C. Heath, 1886.

Rieber, R. W. Psychology in America before William James. In R. W. Rieber and K. Salzinger (Eds.), Psychology: Theoretical and historical perspectives. New York: Academic Press, 1980.

Royce, J. Outlines of psychology. New York: Macmillan, 1903, p. 177.

Rychlak, J. F. The psychology of rigorous humanism. New York: Wiley, 1977.

Scripture, E. W. Thinking, feeling, and doing (1st ed.). New York: Meadville, Flood & Vincent, 1895.

Scripture, E. W. Thinking, feeling and doing (2nd ed.). New York: G. P. Putnam & Sons, 1907.

Scripture, E. W. *Stuttering and lisping*. New York: Macmillan, 1912.

Seashore, C. E. *Elementary experiments in psychology*. New York: Henry Holt, 1908.

Seashore, C. E. In C. Murchison (Ed.), *History of psychology: An autobiography*. Worcester, Mass.: Clark University Press, 1930, pp. 225–297.

Seashore, C. E. *Psychology of music*. New York: McGraw-Hill, 1933.

Titchener, *Experimental psychology: A manual of laboratory practice*. New York: Macmillan, 1901.

Witmer, L. *Analytical psychology*. New York: Gin & Co., 1902.

Wozniak, R. Metaphysics and science, reason and reality: The intellectual origins of epistemology. In J. Broughton & J. Freeman-Moir (Eds.), *The cognitive developmental psychology of James Mark Baldwin: Current theory and research in genetic epistemology*. Norwood, N.J.: Ablex Publishing, in press.

Wundt, W. *Outlines of psychology* (trans. C. H. Judd). Leipzig: William Engelmann, 1907.

III

WUNDT IN ENGLISH TRANSLATION

6

SELECTED TEXTS FROM WRITINGS OF WILHELM WUNDT*

This chapter consists of three parts: (1) Wundt's introductory statement on "The Task of Physiological Psychology," as published in 1873; (2) a listing of variant texts that traces how this statement of objectives was subsequently revised in later editions; (3) the "Closing Remarks," in which Wundt stated his position on the mind–body problem. There is a separate introductory note for each part, as well as some further discussion in the second part.

The Task of Physiological Psychology

The opening pages of Wundt's *Principles of Physiological Psychology*, in the original edition, are given here for the first time in English translation. Less than two lines of this version survived in the fifth edition, which was the basis of Titchener's translation, parts of which are often quoted as if to illustrate Wundt's objectives in writing that work. Indeed, the key words in that fragment ("zwei Wissenschaften in Verbindung zu bringen") were mistranslated by Titchener ("to show the connexion between two sciences"), apparently in an attempt to make them consistent with what follows in that edition.

The heading for this selection is that given by Wundt to the first section of his introduction, but the selection does not include everything under that heading. It omits several pages in a smaller type face that carry

*The selections in the three parts have been translated by Solomon Diamond, who has also written the editorial notes in this chapter. He gratefully acknowledges helpful criticism in respect to both tasks from Arthur L. Blumenthal and Kurt Danziger, but he is alone responsible for the views expressed.

Figure 1. A gathering of friends celebrating Wundt's 80th birthday. Wundt is in the second row, second from the left.

a separate running head, "The Application of Mathematics to Psychology." That portion is concerned primarily with Herbartian psychology, and its content does not bear directly on the issues here discussed, nor does it anticipate changes that were to be made in the opening portion in later editions.

Readers must try not to be distracted by the [brackets], {braces}, //slashes//, and superior indexes used to identify passages that were omitted or altered in later editions, or to show the position of additions. Their use is explained in the note to the second part of this chapter.

———— • ————

The present work shows by its very title that it seeks to establish an alliance between two sciences that, [[3a]although they both deal with almost the same subject, that is, preeminently with human life, nevertheless have long followed different paths. *Physiology* informs us about those life phenomena that we perceive by our external senses. In *psychology*, the person looks upon himself as from *within* and tries to explain the interrelations of those processes that this internal observation discloses. Yet, however differently structured the content of our internal and external life, taken as a whole, may seem, there are nevertheless numerous points of contact between them.]{[5b]Inner experience is continuously being influenced by external stimulation, and our internal states help to determine the course of external events in many ways. Thus, there exists a wide range of life processes that are simultaneously accessible to external and internal observation, a border region that, at least so long as physiology and psychology remain separate from each other, may usefully be assigned to a special [[3b]science] standing between them. However, such a border region offers its own prospects toward both sides. A science that has as its subject matter the points of contact between internal and external life will be disposed to compare so far as possible, on the basis of the points of view thus gained, the full scope of the two disciplines between which it stands as intermediary, and all its investigations will finally reach their climax in the question how, [[2x]indeed,] in the last analysis, internal and external existence are connected with each other. Physiology and psychology each by itself can easily evade this question, but physiological psychology cannot sidestep it.}

[[5c]Thus, the task we assign to our science is this: *first*, to investigate those life processes that, standing midway between external and internal experience, require the simultaneous application of both methods of observation, the external and the internal; and *second*, to throw light upon the totality of life processes from the points of view gained by investigations of this area and in this way perhaps to mediate a total comprehension of human existence.]

{[5dHowever, there is *one* connection in which this task still requires sharper definition. When physiological psychology traverses the paths between internal and external life, it strikes out first along that which leads from outside in. It begins with physiological processes and seeks to demonstrate how these influence the domain of internal observation; only secondarily does it deal with the reciprocal influence that external existence receives from the internal. Thus, it casts its attention primarily toward only one of the two basic sciences between which it has been set up, toward the psychological side. The name *physiological psychology* implies this, for it points to psychology as the real subject of our science and only adds the physiological standpoint as a further stipulation. The basis for this relationship lies [4aessentially] in the fact that all those problems that relate to the mutual connections of internal and external life have hitherto formed [4bessentially] a portion of psychology, while physiology has willingly excluded from the area of its investigations those topics in the investigation of which speculation must be given an essential role. However, in the recent period, psychologists have begun to acquire greater familiarity with physiology, while simultaneously, physiologists have felt the need to call upon psychologists for counsel with regard to certain border problems that they have come up against. The contact brought about by these similar needs gave rise to physiological psychology. As important as the problems of this science are to physiology— often indeed overlapping its own proper field—they have belonged hitherto mostly to the domain of psychology, but the methods that are brought into play to conquer them are taken equally from both mother sciences. Psychological introspection goes hand in hand with the methods of experimental physiology, and the application of the latter to the former has given rise to the [4cpsychophysical methods as a separate branch of experimental research]. If one wishes to place major emphasis on methodological characteristics, our sciences might be called *experimental psychology* in distinction from the [4dusual] science of mind based purely on introspection.}

[4xThere are two principal phenomena that clearly indicate that frontier where external observation no longer suffices without internal observation, and where the latter finds itself in need of help from the former. *Sensation* is a psychological fact that is immediately dependent on certain fundamental external conditions. *Movement resulting from inner impulse* is a physiological process, the causes of which can in general be recognized only introspectively. In the case of sensation, we look upon the dividing wall between the two areas as if from within, from the psychological side; in the case of movement, from without, from the physiological side.]

{[4x]With respect to its intensity and its quality, sensation is determined first of all by external causes, the physiological sense stimuli. But it undergoes further transformations under the influence of prior conditions given in introspection. It is through these that sensations give rise to ideas of external objects, [2x]that simple ideas give rise to complex ones,] that the ideas [2a]combine into] groups and series and, in such combinations, remain accessible to consciousness for a longer or a shorter time [2b]. Still, even here, external influences constantly make themselves felt: the combinations and the flow of ideas are conditioned in part by the combinations and the flow of impressions, the building up of complex ideas from simple ones is tied to [2c]certain physiological relationships between] our sensory and motor apparatus, and finally, even the [2x]apparently] altogether internal course of our thoughts is accompanied by certain states and processes in the [2d] central nervous system. Thus, ramifications extend from the psychophysical periphery deep into the midst of mental life.}

{[4x]On the other side, inner processes are reflected in external movements. These complete the circle of process that moves this way and that between external and internal existence, bringing it back to its starting point. The simplest movements lack the intermediate psychological member, or at least it escapes our introspection; here the movement seems to be an immediate reflex of the stimulus, [2x]and therefore the name *reflex movement* has been chosen for this case]. But in the measure that psychological processes enter between the impression and the movement released by it, the latter becomes less dependent on the former with respect to its spatial extent and its temporal occurrence; and it requires for its explanation more and more of those factors revealed by internal observation, until at last it is only they that provide an immediate accounting of the appearance of such movements. Here we reach the final member of the series: just as the psychological mid-member is missing in the reflex movement, so now the physiological initiatory process escapes us [²ˣor at least cannot be demonstrated], and only the inner process and the external reaction to it remain accessible to observation.}

{⁵ˣ[²ᵉ] Psychology occupies an intermediate position between the natural and the mental sciences. It is related to the former because similar principles of investigation and explanation are applicable to both internal and external events, insofar as those principles depend on the very concept of sequential events. For the mental sciences, it is the fundamental discipline. Every manifestation of the human mind has its ultimate source in the elementary phenomena of our inner experience. History, jurisprudence, political science, the philosophies of art and religion, all lead back to psychological principles of explanation. But physiological psychology remains half a natural science, because it must especially investigate the relations between external and internal events, and from this position, it must serve as the closest intermediary to the mental sciences.}

//⁵ˣAmong the natural sciences, a distinction is made between those that are *descriptive* and those that are *explanatory*, or between natural history and the natural sciences. [³ᶜEach is dependent on the other.] Description has scientific value only when it is based on explanatory principles, [⁴ᵉwhile] [³ˣconversely,] description, and the classification of phenomena based on it, prepare the way for explanation. [³ᵈThe less developed a science is, the more do description and explanation merge together in it. As a rule, attempts at classification are regarded as explanations. Most treatments of empirical psychology belong primarily in the domain of a natural history of mind, {³ᵉalthough they are not always aware of this fact. The psychological study of history and ethnology, which in the recent period has become a separate branch of science, also belongs to a natural history of mind in the broad sense. For ethnic psychology deals throughout with complex phenomena that must be clarified through individual consciousness. They must be organized according to psychological laws derived from its study, [²ˣand this is essentially a task of classification]. On the other hand, the investigations of physiological psychology belong essentially to the realm of a natural science of the mind. It is wholly directed toward demonstrating the elementary mental phenomena.} It seeks to discover them by starting out from the physiological processes to which they are related. Therefore, our science does not at once take its position on the stage of introspection but seeks rather to penetrate it from without. That is why it is able to utilize the most effective technique of explanatory natural science, the experimental method.//[5e] For the essence of experimentation consists in varying the conditions of events in a manner that is both *arbitrary* and—if we wish to establish lawful relationships between causes and effects—*quantitatively determinable*. Now, it is only the external, physical conditions of the internal processes that we are able to alter at will, at least with any certainty, [[3x]and above all, it is only they that are accessible to direct measurement. It is therefore clear that the application of experimental method can take place only in the psychophysical border region.] Nevertheless, it would be incorrect to deny the possibility of an experimental psychology for this reason. It is true that there are only psychophysical and not purely psychological experiments, if by the latter one understands those that completely disregard the external conditions of internal events. But the change that takes place as a result of varying a condition depends not only on the nature of that condition but also on the nature of what is conditioned. Therefore, changes in an internal process that are brought about by variations in external influences on which it depends also throw light on the internal process itself. In this sense, every *psychophysical* experiment may also be called a psychological experiment.} [[3f]]

Wundt's Restated Objectives for Physiological Psychology

It is assumed that the reader has already read the original version of the opening pages of the *Principles of Physiological Psychology* in the first part of this chapter. No other passage in all of Wundt's writings was more frequently or more drastically revised. In successive editions, these revisions became increasingly extensive, until their cumulative effect produced a totally new document. Did this process do no more than make explicit views that Wundt already held when he wrote the first edition, or did it express significant shifts in his own values and objectives? If (as the translator believes) the latter is the case, it follows that we must not regard the psychological system set forth in Wundt's later books as necessarily consistent with the initial program that fired the imagination of young psychologists worldwide and played such an important part in promoting the development of experimental psychology. This listing of variant texts, which makes it possible to read Wundt's introductory statement on "the task of physiological psychology" in each of its six versions, is offered as a tool to be used in studying this important problem.

The variants listed below have been culled by comparing the opening pages of each later edition (1880, 1887, 1893, 1902–1903, and 1908–1911) with the one preceding. Each variant is identified by an index that includes a number that represents the edition in which it first appeared and a letter to define its sequential position. Its place in the original text (or within an earlier variant) is marked by a similar index, which is placed immediately after the first of a pair of brackets, braces, or, in one instance, a pair of double slash marks. When the letter in such an index is an x, it signifies that the enclosed text was deleted in that and subsequent editions without the substitution of any variant. Any other letter identifies a variant that replaces the enclosed portion of text, and is listed below. If the index is inside a pair of brackets that is otherwise empty, it designates a variant that was added at that point without any deletion. Minor stylistic changes, which do not change the meaning enough to alter a translation, are not noted.

Many readers will wish only to compare the first and fifth editions. The version in the fifth edition consists of the first 19 words of the translation as given previously (p. 157), followed by several lines from variant 3a, then by variants 5a–5e, and finally by a substantial part of variant 4f as modified by variants 5f–5h.

The list of variants is followed by a discussion.

The Variants

2a. are arranged in
2b. and by which affective processes of many kinds are tied in with the ideas and their processes.
2c. physiological characteristics of
2d. organs of the
2e. From the nature of its task,
3a. although their subject matters are intimately related, nevertheless have traveled altogether divergent paths. Physiology and psychology share between them the observation of life phenomena generally and those of human life in particular. Among these phenomena, physiology investigates [5aprimarily those that can be perceived by our external senses. Psychology seeks to render an account of the relationships among

those processes that are presented to us by inner perception. There are, however, numerous points of contact between these areas of internal and external life.]

3b. discipline

3c. The two fields permit no lasting separation.

3d. However, the less developed a science is, so much the more will attempts to classification, which arise out of the description of facts, be regarded as in themselves causal explanations.

3e. which sees its task as classifying the individual complex facts under such general concepts as feeling, will, and ideas, which are for the most part already established in language, or under such comprehensive goal-related concepts as memory, reason, understanding, etc. In contrast, the efforts of physiological psychology are wholly directed toward establishing the elementary mental phenomena, their causal relationships and interconnections.

3f. [As a new paragraph.]

[[4f]By its use of objective techniques, experimental psychology enters into close relationship with another important branch of psychological research, ethnic psychology. While the task of the former is the exact investigation of individual consciousness, the latter seeks to learn the psychological laws that govern the products of collective mental life—in particular, language, myth, and custom. However, not only do these two areas of objective psychology supplement each other, but in many ways, they are also dependent on each other. For the collective mental life of a people points everywhere to the individual energies that have entered into it, and individual consciousness, especially in its higher forms of development, is supported by the mental life of the collectivity to which it belongs.

Psychological research may therefore be divided into the following branches, according to the resources that it employs:

1. subjective psychology, which limits itself to immediate inner perception; and

2. objective psychology, which seeks partly to supplement and partly to improve on inner perception by objective means. This is further subdivided into:

a. experimental or physiological psychology, which places inner perception under the control of experimental influences by means of external operations that are arbitrarily introduced and regulated; and

b. ethnic psychology, which seeks to derive general psychological laws of development from the objective products of the collective: language, myth, and custom.

Considered with respect to the subject matter that they investigate, subjective and experimental psychology, as different orientations within individual psychology, may be contrasted with social or ethnic psychology.]

4a. chiefly

4b. for the most part

4c. experimental methods of psychological research

4d. older

4e. whereas

4f. [replaces variant 3f] {[6x]The decisive merit of this technique lies in the fact that by its help, introspection, in the scientific sense of the word, first becomes at all possible. [[5f]Such] observation presupposes that its object (which in this case is the mental process that is being investigated) can be fixed in attention and followed through whatever changes it undergoes. However, to be so fixed in attention requires further that what is being observed shall be independent of the observer. It is obvious that this is not the case in any attempt at immediate introspection without experimental assistance. The effort to observe oneself inevitably produces changes in the internal events, and consequently, as a rule, what we wish to observe disappears from consciousness.} The psychological experiment establishes external conditions that are intended to induce a certain mental event at a given moment, and in addition, it enables us so to control the attendant circumstances that the state of consciousness accompanying the event remains approximately the same. Therefore, the principal significance of the experimental method is not simply that, as in the physical realm, it makes the conditions of observation subject to arbitrary variation, but also, and essentially, that by this means exact observation comes about. Its results can also be fruitful with respect to such mental phenomena as are by their nature not subject to direct experimental influence.

Fortunately, it happens that just where the experimental method fails us, other objectively valuable resources become available to psychology. These consist of those products of collective mental life that [[5g]embody certain psychological laws]. Chief among these products are language, myth, and custom. Because they are shaped not only by historical conditions but also by general psychological laws, these phenomena have become the materials of a special psychological discipline, ethnic psychology, and its findings constitute the principal resource for the general laws of complex mental processes. *Experimental* psychology and *ethnic* psychology thus constitute the two principal branches of *scientific* psychology. *Animal* psychology and *child* psychology are joined to these as amplifying fields that seek, along with ethnic psychology, to solve the problems of psychogenesis. [6xInsofar as possible, these latter fields will make use of experimental methods to test their results and expand on them, but for them, experiment lacks that special significance that it has in experimental psychology as an auxiliary technique of introspection, because in them, its effects are accessible only to objective observation.]

[5xNevertheless, animal psychology and child psychology can be included within experimental psychology in the wider sense of that word, because of the role that experimental method has in them.] Together, child psychology and experimental psychology in the narrow sense constitute *individual* psychology, while ethnic psychology and animal psychology form the two parts of a *general* or *comparative* psychology. However, these distinctions have less significance here than the analogous ones in physiology, because [5xethnic psychology must serve individual psychology as a major auxiliary resource wherever the question of investigating complex mental processes arises, while] animal and child psychology have much less importance than the corresponding physiological disciplines of human and comparative development, ontogenetic and phylogenetic, [5xbecause the former throw very little light on mental life in general]. [5h]

[5xPsychophysics forms a special part of experimental psychology. As an exact science of the relations between body and mind, it seeks in part to determine the laws governing sensations in relation to the corresponding external stimuli, and in part to investigate other interrelationships between physical and mental life by experimental means.]

[5xAlongside those fields of scientific psychology that have been mentioned, what is called *empirical* psychology still plays a certain part. It offers a doctrine of mind that is indeed based solely on internal perception or supposed introspection. Now, it is naturally true that in this day, any treatment of psychology that still wishes to assert a claim to attention must be empirical, because it is simply impossible to see how conclusions about mental life can be taken from any other source than from experience. But in the empirical treatment of a science, one is obligated to draw on all those types of experience that the existing state of scientific methodology makes available. An empirical physics that would still restrict itself today to the immediate observation of natural phenomena, as they present themselves to the unaided senses, would no longer deserve to be called a science. Psychology, however far it may lag behind the natural sciences in the solution of its problems, is now in the same position. Therefore, there exists today only *one* empirical psychology of scientific character; that one is subdivided, according to the objective techniques that it employs, into experimental psychology and ethnic psychology. The psychology of mere introspection is only a survival of the past.]

5a. those that appear to us in sensory perception as bodily processes, and as such form a part of the whole outer world that surrounds us. Psychology, on the contrary, seeks to render an account of all those processes that appear to us in our own consciousness, or that we infer from those [⁶ᵃbodily processes of] other living creatures that indicate the presence of a consciousness similar to our own.

5b. [As new paragraph] This division of life processes into the physical and the mental is useful and even necessary for the solution of scientific problems. However, the life of an organism is in itself a unitary concatenation of processes. We can therefore no more separate the events of bodily life from conscious events than we can mark off an outer experience, mediated by sense perception, and oppose it, as an entirely separate state of affairs, to what we call "inner" experience, the events of our own consciousness. Rather, just as one and the same thing—for example, a tree perceived by me—lies as an external object within the scope of natural science, and as conscious content within that of psychology, so there are many phenomena of physical life that are persistently associated with conscious processes, and the other way around. Thus, it is a matter of everyday experience that we refer certain bodily movements directly to volitions, which we can observe as such only in our consciousness. Conversely, we refer the ideas of external objects that arise in consciousness either to direct affection of the organs of sense or, in the case of memory images, to physiological excitation of the sensory centers that we interpret as aftereffects of previous impressions.

5c. From this it is clear that, despite the generally unambiguous separation of their scientific tasks, physiology and psychology are dependent on each other in many ways. Psychology must pursue the relations that exist between conscious processes and certain physical life phenomena, just as physiology must take account of the conscious contents through which we become aware of various physical expressions of life. Indeed, this mutual interrelation finds clear expression in the fact that most of what physiology has been able to discover or infer about processes in the sense organs and the brain has been based on various mental symptoms. But although psychology has long been recognized, explicitly or implicitly, as an indispensable auxiliary to physiology, psychologists, for the most part, have believed that they have no need to take any notice of physiology and that psychology can get along by itself, with the immediate apprehension of conscious processes. The present exposition is called a "physiological psychology" in order to signify that it deviates from all such attempts to base psychology either on pure introspection or on philosophical presuppositions. It will make use of physiology as an auxiliary discipline whenever that seems necessary, just as physiology has never been able to dispense with facts that, in themselves, belong to psychology—although often it has been hampered in this by the fact that the traditional empirical or metaphysical psychology could provide only inadequate assistance. 5d. Physiological psychology is, accordingly, first of all, *psychology*, and like any other treatment of this science, the task it sets itself above all is to investigate *conscious processes in their own interrelationships*. It is not a province of physiology, nor does it attempt, as has been mistakenly asserted, to derive or explain the phenomena of the mental from those of the physical life. The name no more implies such a purpose than, for example, the title of a "microscopic anatomy" would express the intention to use anatomy to elucidate the accomplishments of the microscope. Accordingly, the present work will apply the concept of a physiological psychology only in the sense that it makes use, in two ways, of the means that contemporary physiology makes available for the analysis of conscious processes.

First: because of the nature of its problems, physiology reached the stage of employing exact experimental methods earlier than psychology, which remained in the service of philosophy until very recently. The experimental modification of life processes, as practiced by physiology, often produces direct or indirect changes in the conscious events that form a part of those processes. Thus, in the nature of the case, physiology was destined to serve psychology as an auxiliary discipline, just as physics had served physiology. To the extent that physiological psychology leans on physiology in developing its experimental methods, it is *experimental* psychology. This expression implies at the same time that the application of experimental physiological methods by no means consists in taking them over unchanged; rather, those methods are independently transformed and even restructured to serve specific psychological purposes, just as was the case when physiology took over the methods of physics.

Second: as we have already remarked, our total concept of life includes both physical and conscious processes. Consequently, wherever specific life phenomena present both physical and mental aspects, a question necessarily arises concerning their relations to each other. This gives rise to a series of problems that are indeed sometimes touched upon by physiology as well as by psychology but that cannot be thoroughly dealt with by either science, because of the division of labor to which they are both committed in principle. Experimental psychology conducts itself no differently in this regard, because it differs from other approaches to psychology only in method, not in respect to its problems. On the other hand, insofar as physiological psychology investigates relationships between physical and mental events, the term *psychophysics*, coined by Fechner,[1] can be applied to it. If we understand this term to mean only the investigation of empirically demonstrable relations between physical and mental aspects of life processes, quite without metaphysical assumptions about the relation between body and mind, it follows directly that such a psychophysics is not, as is sometimes assumed, a field that lies between physiology and psychology, but rather one that is *auxiliary* to both, but especially to psychology. This is because the connections that exist between conscious events and certain relationships within the physical organism are primarily of interest to psychology. As to its final objectives, therefore, the psychophysical problem is a psychological one, but in its execution, it is predominantly physiological; what it comes down to is a closer examination of the findings of anatomy and physiology concerning the physical substrates of conscious events, with the object of relating those findings to mental life.

---

[1] *Elemente der Psychophysik*, 1860, I, p. 8. Fechner here defines psychophysics as an "exact study of the functional relationships or dependencies between body and mind, more generally, between the corporeal and spiritual, physical and mental worlds." Accordingly, his work is directed chiefly at establishing *laws* governing the interaction of the mental and the physical. The metaphysical assumption of a difference in substance is thereby implied, for without this we cannot conceive of such an intermediate zone with its own laws. However, Fechner denies this substantial difference in principle, and therefore, strictly speaking, he could hardly object to a purely empirical formulation of the psychophysical problem, as stated above. Cf. our concluding chapter. [Wundt's note.]

5e. Of the two tasks that are thus implied by the name *physiological psychology*—one *methodological,* relating to the use of experiment, the other *amplificatory,* relating to the corporeal basis of mental life—it is the former that is more essential to psychology itself, while the latter has value chiefly with respect to the *philosophic* question about the overall unity of life processes. As an *experimental* science, physiological psychology strives to effect a reform in psychological research no less significant than the revolution of thinking in the natural sciences that resulted from the introduction of experimentation into them. Indeed, in *one* respect, this reform is perhaps more significant; for, under favorable conditions, it is possible to make exact observations in the natural sciences without experimentation, but there is no such possibility in psychology. It is only with important qualifications that so-called "pure introspection" can be regarded as a form of observation, and it can make no claim whatever to exactness. On the other hand, it is of the essence of experiment that we can vary the conditions of an event at will and, if it is desired to establish exact relationships, in a *quantitatively determinable* manner. That is why the experimental method has become an indispensable auxiliary of the natural sciences wherever they deal with the analysis of swiftly occurring, transient phenomena, rather than with the observation of relatively constant objects. However, it is precisely conscious events that never present such constancy; they are processes, fleeting events that continuously dissolve into one another.
5f. All scientific
5g. permit inferences about specific mental factors
5h. On the other hand, the investigations of ethnic psychology are essential supplements to individual psychology, whenever the developmental forms of complex mental processes are being studied.
6a. manifestations of life in

Discussion

This discussion is limited to outlining the most important revisions that Wundt introduced into his definition of the task of physiological psychology and a brief comment on their significance.

Changes in the second edition were minimal.

The third edition, which was published after Wundt had written his *Ethics,* at a time when he was actively pursuing his interest in ethnic psychology, was revised as follows:

1. The statement that experimental method can be applied to psychology "only in the psychophysical border region" was deleted.

2. Also deleted was the description of ethnic psychology as having the character of natural history rather than science and as dependent on psychological laws derived from the study of individual consciousness.

3. About thirty lines were added, defining several disciplines within psychology and crediting ethnic psychology with the ability to derive "general psychological laws" from its own data.

The fourth edition, prepared in a period when the Leipzig laboratory reached a peak of activity, shows throughout an increased concern with experimental methodology. In keeping with this, the introduction states that psychology's debt to physiology is not for "psychophysical methods" (as stated previously) but for help in establishing "experimental methods of psychological research" (see variant 4c). Emphasis was thus given to the distinctiveness of psychology's methods. Paragraphs 4–6 of the original statement, which had specified the close dependence of conscious events on physiological influences (as well as conversely) and had implied the need for coordinated psychological and physiological research, were deleted *in toto*. Finally, the thirty lines that had been added in the third edition were replaced by a much longer passage (4f) that did the following:

1. It stated that the chief purpose of experimental method in psychology is to control the conditions under which introspection takes place.

2. It placed ethnic psychology on a par with physiology as an auxiliary to experimental (individual) psychology.

3. It acknowledged that both animal and child psychology might be regarded as parts of experimental psychology "in the broad sense" and as assisting the effort of ethnic psychology to trace mental evolution.

4. It dismissed the empirical psychology of "mere introspection" as "only a survival of the past."

Despite these extensive changes, the introduction still stated that there exists "a border region that, at least so long as physiology and psychology remain separate from each other [a proviso that seemed to hint at the desirability of abandoning such separateness], may usefully be assigned to a special discipline between them," and that the character of this new science is such that it "cannot sidestep" the responsibility to seek a solution to "the question how internal and external existence are . . . related to each other." On its second page, it still declared that physiological psychology "begins with physiological processes and seeks to demonstrate how these *influence* [emphasis added] the domain of internal observation." It is an anachronism that such statements remained in the fourth edition, since they were no longer in harmony with what Wundt was writing elsewhere, but this anachronism shows how difficult it was for Wundt to break completely with his original concept of an active "alliance" (*Verbindung*) between physiology and psychology.

In the preface to the fifth edition, Wundt declared his determination to eliminate those earlier "passages which [he] could not allow to pass as an adequate expression of [his] present convictions." To accomplish this, he had to remove every vestige of the original introduction. Where once he had written that physiological psychology "seeks to demonstrate how [physiological processes] influence the domain of internal observations," he now wrote that it does not attempt, "as has been mistakenly asserted, to derive or explain phenomena of the mental from those of the physical life." He deleted the last remaining reference to a "border zone" of problems common to the two sciences and wrote instead that psychophysical research "is not, as is sometimes assumed, a field that lies between physiology and psychology, but rather one that is auxiliary to both." However, he apparently could not bring himself to erase the memorable lines with which the introduction opened, even though the book no longer constituted an effort "to establish an alliance" between physiology and psychology. It was no doubt an awareness of this inconsistency that led Titchener to the softened translation, "to show the connexion" between those sciences.

In summary, it seems quite clear that Wundt left us two sharply different definitions of physiological psychology, as well as some intermediary, transitional forms. Both documents are historically important. But when the 1902 version is quoted, as repeatedly happens, in discussions of Wundt's services as a pioneer of experimental psychology, this can only result in a distorted picture of what took place almost three decades earlier.

Wundt's "Closing Remarks"

The opening paragraph of the *Principles of Physiological Psychology* committed the new science to face without evasion "the question how, in the last analysis, internal and external existence are connected with each other." To fulfill this pledge, the book ended with a short chapter of "Closing Remarks" (pp. 858–863) on the implications that the empirical findings had for the problem of the mind–body relationship. After affirming the importance of "specific physiological processes" as the "foundation" of psychological events, and rejecting all prior solutions of the problem as misdirected, Wundt saw the key to its solution in a recognition that mind is not a "simple" substance and that its unity is of the same order as the functional unity of the physical organism. He described mind as "an ordered unity of many elements" that had arisen as an "evolutionary product of nature's course" (p. 863) and as "the inner being of the same unity as the body which belongs to it" (p. 862).

Some readers (e.g., the reviewer in the *Literarisches Centralblatt*; cf. page 60) were taken aback by this metaphysical climax to an ostensibly antimetaphysical book. As we looked at Wundt's revisions to his introduction (pp. 162–169), so in chapter 7 we will see something of the later development of Wundt's thinking on this problem.

Wundt's 1874 "Schlussbemerkungen"[2]

On every side, psychological investigations lead us into metaphysical problems. However, the empirical facts and laws that are brought together as the outcome of such investigations form only a part of what is needed for solution of those problems. The philosophy of nature and the critique of knowledge must provide the rest. The concepts of inner experience are codetermined with those of outer experience, and the testing of their origin and their validity must be done jointly. Having come to the end of our task, we therefore wish only to indicate some points of view that the results of physiological psychology bring to this more general undertaking.

We may with sufficient assurance regard it as an established fact that nothing happens in our consciousness that does not have its bodily foundation in specific physiological processes. Simple sensation, the synthesis of sensations into ideas, the association of ideas and their recall, and finally the processes [859] of apperception and volitional arousal are accompanied by physiological nerve processes. Other bodily processes such as, in particular, the simple and complex reflexes do not themselves

[2]Translated from *Grundzüge der physiologische Psychologie*, 1874, pp. 858–863. Bracketed numbers indicate page in original.

enter into consciousness, but they constitute essential preconditions of conscious facts or of psychological facts in the more narrow sense.

This *principle of thoroughgoing interaction [Wechselwirkung] between mind and body*—which, as often as attempts have been made to limit it, asserts itself with irresistible force over the whole range of inner experience—has since ancient times been given various metaphysical interpretations. The dualism that looks on body and mind as two different forms of being was transplanted from vulgar intuition into philosophy, where it gave rise to no fewer than three points of view regarding this interaction. According to the most immediate, the mind receives impressions from bodily organs just as if it were a corporeal thing to be pushed about, and in the phenomena of movement, it is seen as acting on them in the same manner. But this system of "physical influence" can no longer be maintained as soon as we become aware of the thoroughgoing differences between bodily and mental events. For the mind to receive impulses from the body and return impulses to it, it would itself have to possess a bodily character. Weighing these difficulties, DESCARTES—who, indeed, saw them as present even in the interaction of bodily substances—came to the idea that the influence of soul and body on each other is brought about in each instance by a special divine act of "supernatural assistance." LEIBNIZ, although he recognized that the first principle of the connection between body and mind escaped explanation, was not satisfied with a system that thus reduced each psychological fact to an immediate miracle. According to him, therefore, this connection is divinely foreordained. Bodily processes and ideas are linked together by a "preestablished harmony." The repeated miracle of supernatural assistance was thus reduced to a one-time joining, but the miracle still remained. Dualism had exhausted all possible means of explanation open to it without being able to find one that was satisfactory, and thus it gave the proof of its own untenability. This led necessarily to the development of *monistic* views.

Among these, *materialism* seeks to comprehend the mental as a form or a product of bodily processes. It is older in origin than the dualistic systems and has the advantage as long as it [860] campaigns against the usual dualism by pointing to the dependence of ideation and thinking on physiological conditions. But it has never itself provided an explanation of psychological experience, and the hope that it might some day succeed in this runs aground on the resistance that it meets in the most securely founded principles of epistemology. The facts of consciousness are the foundation of all our knowledge, and therefore, outer experience is only a special domain of inner experience. Even though this leads to a necessary assumption of objective existence, still the form in which we apprehend that existence is in essence codetermined by the characteristics of consciousness. Sensation is the subjective form of our responses to external impressions; space and time rest on subjective laws of the synthesis of ideas; finally, the concepts of cause and substance, which are everywhere necessary to explain nature, are of psychological origin.

Idealism seizes hold of these results of the critique of knowledge. Since outer experience is a part of inner experience, it views the world as a reflection of consciousness. As long as it combats the claim of the materialists, it keeps the upper hand, but when it passes on to attempts at explanation of nature, it runs aground on unyielding reality. Despite the ubiquitous traces of subjective influences on the forms in which reality is apprehended by us, they point no less clearly to an objective existence that would persist even if we had no intuitions or concepts. We are therefore forced to admit that not only our knowledge of nature but also the forms by which we apprehend it depend on external factors. Space and time, cause and substance, would never arise within us if the objective world did not offer the stimulus to the formation of these intuitions and concepts. *Realism* seeks to give equal justice to these different sources of knowledge. However, if it wishes to be in full harmony with the results of the critique of knowledge, it must recognize the priority of inner experience. Thus, psychology in particular necessarily leads beyond pure realism to *ideal-realism.*

Realism tried to develop a concept of substance that would be equally applicable to inner and outer experience. Thus, it came to assert the existence of simple entities whose external interactions represent the juxtaposition of atomistically conceived matter, while their inner essence forms the basis of a unitary consciousness. This gave rise to those monadological systems in which the human mind appears as one entity among the many which constitute the body and the environment, [861] being distinguished from them only by its greater worth or by the favorable situation that it occupies because of its special connections. Yet even in LEIBNIZ, the inventor of monads, we see how easily such views fall prey to vulgar dualism, with all its contradictions, as soon as an attempt is made to find an explanation for the problem of interaction. He so exalted the mind, as the ruling monad, over the corporeal monads that serve it that it needed only a small step for WOLFF to return completely to dualism, especially since he found ready at hand the truly dualistic hypothesis of preestablished harmony. HERBART dealt more seriously with the problem of interaction. For him, psychology and the philosophy of nature were both alike to be deduced from the mutual interferences and the acts of self-preservation of simple entities. But he, too, retained the view that the mind is a single simple entity among many that are subordinate to it. Its ideas are its acts of self-preservation against the interferences it undergoes from other monads, and the whole content of inner experience flows out of the relationships among ideas. This point of view is most easily related to some hypothesis like that which DESCARTES had already advanced about connections with the nervous system. The mind must have its seat at some point in the brain—for example, in the pineal gland—and from everywhere in the brain, fibers must run to that same point, so that by their excitation it will be informed about the state of all other parts of the brain. However, this notion is so much in contradiction with physiological findings that no one in recent times has given any thought to making use of it. Instead, they let the soul move about the brain, wandering here and there, so that the changes taking place in various regions of the brain can influence it. However, the findings of physiological psychology would not only require that the soul wander about far more extensively than the proponents of this theory can well have supposed to be the case, but we can also scarcely escape the inference that one and the same soul is simultaneously at different points, since countless elementary sensations, which cannot possibly be localized at one and the same point in the brain, cooperate in every single idea. However, if we ask why the mind monad moves at each moment to just the place where it must be in order to receive the bodily influences, we have no answer. Here, again, the miracle of supernatural assistance or preestablished harmony has been assumed.

In the face of such difficulties, the question arises whether [862] the foundation of all these ideas is itself sufficiently secure. Whence arises the conviction that the mind is a single *simple* entity? Obviously, from the unitary relationship of all conscious states and processes. The concept of unity is then replaced by the concept of simplicity. But a unitary entity is not necessarily a simple one. The bodily organism also is a unit, but it consists nevertheless of a multiplicity of organs. In this case, it is the connection of the parts that determines their unity. Indeed, we meet in consciousness a complexity that is both successive and simultaneous and that points to the multiplicity of its foundations.

The mind is therefore a unity. But this unity rests not on the simplicity of its substance but presumably on the relationship among many simple entities. Its inner being possesses a unity like that which must be assumed for the external apprehension of the bodily organization, and the thoroughgoing interaction between body and mind necessarily leads *to the idea that the mind is the inner being of the same unity as the body that belongs to it.* The manifestations of the mind are also tied to the ruling organs of the body, the central organs of the nervous system. The mental functions, like the bodily functions, are distributed over different central regions, and to each external change there corresponds a change of inner state. Self-awareness, or consciousness of these inner states, becomes possible only when the connections that constitute the foundations of the internal and the external organism include the conditions for independent renewal of these processes and for connecting present and former states. Therefore, there are creatures that never develop a consciousness, and not all organs that belong to those that are endowed with consciousness participate in it.

This conception of the problem of interaction leads unavoidably to the metaphysical assumption that the world consists of simple entities, among which there are multiple connections, and that their external changes are always accompanied by changes in their inner states. However, these become sensations and ideas only where the connections between the simple entities are sufficiently perfect to ensure the duration and the continuity of the inner states. So far as we know, this stage reaches a preparatory development in animals, but it is perfected only in the consciousness of human beings. Thus, human consciousness constitutes a decisive point in nature's course, a point at which the world becomes aware of itself.

[863] This genetic conception of the psychological facts leads unavoidably to regarding human consciousness as a developmental product of nature's course. However, psychological research just as certainly gives rise, on the other hand, to a conviction that human self-perception is the foundation on which all knowledge rests. This self-perception is more firmly established than our perception of the outer world, which we know only intuitively through the medium of our consciousness. Its immediate result is that we experience ourselves as unitary entities. Our consciousness encompasses only an infinitesimal point of the world in its inner being. We cannot assume that the world outside ourselves lacks this inner being. But if we wish to imagine what it is like, we cannot possibly

do so otherwise than in the form of our own self-perception and of our apprehension of mankind as a whole, which is erected on that—that is, as a unified complex that is articulated into independent units of different orders, each developing in accordance with inner ends. Thus, psychological experience is compatible only with a monistic world view that acknowledges the worth of the individual without dissolving it into the contentless form of a simple monad that can attain complexity only through the miracle of supernatural aids. It is not as a simple entity but as an ordered unity of many elements that the human mind is what LEIBNIZ called it: *a mirror of the world.*

7

Wilhelm Wundt

OUTLINES OF PSYCHOLOGY*
V. THE PRINCIPLES AND LAWS OF PSYCHICAL CAUSALITY

INTRODUCTION

After Wundt's change of status from being a physiologist of no particular note to professor of philosophy at Germany's largest university, it was natural that he should make a more careful statement of his metaphysical position than the "Closing Remarks" with which he ended the *Principles of Physiological Psychology* (pp. 171–177). In the second edition, accordingly, that short chapter was expanded into two chapters, each twice as long as the original. Section 23 ("Metaphysical Hypotheses about the Nature of Mind") is an expanded treatment of the topics included in paragraphs 3–7 of the earlier statement. Errors that had been committed in stating the views of Descartes and Leibniz were corrected by substituting for their names, at the appropriate places, "the Cartesians" and "followers of Leibniz." Unguarded references to interaction (*Wechselwirkung*) of body and mind were not eliminated from this chapter.

Section 24 ("General Points of View Concerning the Theory of Inner Experience") includes a statement of Wundt's own "psychological" standpoint and how it differed from a "psychophysical" position. Its final paragraph presents an interesting interweave of threads from the last three paragraphs of the original section:

*Translated with the cooperation of the author by Charles Hubbard Judd. Leipzig: Wilhelm Engelmann, 1907. The numbering system used in this chapter has been retained from the original volume. At some points, punctuation has been modernized. The Introduction was written by Solomon Diamond.

In its physical as well as in its mental aspect, the living body is a unity. However, this unity rests not on its simplicity but, contrariwise, on the very composite character of its substance. Consciousness has manifold states that are thoroughly interconnected, yet we apprehend it inwardly as a unity of the same sort as the bodily organism is to our external apprehension. Hence, the thoroughgoing interrelation between the physical and the mental leads to the supposition *that what we call mind is the inner being of the same unity that we apprehend externally as the body that belongs to it.* However, this conception of the problem of interrelation also leads unavoidably to the hypothesis that mental being is the reality of things and that their most essential characteristic is development. For us, human consciousness is the peak of that development: it forms the nodal point in nature's course, at which the universe becomes aware of itself. It is not as simple being but as the evolved product of countless elements that the human mind is what Leibniz called it, *a mirror of the universe.* (Wundt, 1880, Vol. 2, pp. 463–464)

In this finale, "interaction" (*Wechselwirkung*) has been changed to "interrelation" (*Wechselbeziehung*); "the mind" appears as "what we call mind"; and the "human mind," as an "ordered unity of many elements," gives way to "human consciousness" as "the evolved product of countless elements."

The two chapters were set off as Part VI, "On the Origin of Mental Evolution." They remained virtually unchanged through the fourth edition, but in the fifth, their content was totally revised and greatly expanded. Those new "Closing Remarks"—for Wundt then returned to this unpretentious title, which had not been used since the first edition—were also published separately under the title *Science and Psychology* (*Naturwissenschaft und Psychologie*).

Meanwhile, in his *Outlines of Psychology* (*Grundriss der Psychologie*, 1896, 15th ed., 1922), Wundt had summarized his psychological system for a broader audience than that to which the *Physiological Psychology* was addressed. Its final section, on "The Principles and Laws of Psychical Causality," as it appeared in the later editions of that work, covers the same ground and is a more concise as well as less technical statement of what Wundt regarded as the major fruits of all his labors in psychology. It is reprinted here as translated by Charles Hubbard Judd.

———— • ————

OUTLINES

OF

PSYCHOLOGY

BY

WILHELM WUNDT

TRANSLATED WITH THE COOPERATION OF THE AUTHOR

BY

CHARLES HUBBARD JUDD, Ph. D. (LEIPZIG)

PROFESSOR OF PSYCHOLOGY AND DIRECTOR OF THE PSYCHOLOGICAL LABORATORY
YALE UNIVERSITY

THIRD REVISED ENGLISH EDITION
FROM THE SEVENTH REVISED GERMAN EDITION

LEIPZIG

PUBLISHED BY WILHELM ENGELMANN

LONDON	NEW YORK
WILLIAMS & NORGATE	GUSTAV E. STECHERT

1907

Figure 1. Title page from *Outlines of Psychology*, 1907.

§ 22. *Concept of Mind*

1. Every empirical science has, as its primary subject of treatment, certain particular facts of experience the nature and reciprocal relations of which it seeks to investigate. In dealing with such facts it is found to be necessary, if science is not to give up entirely the grouping of the facts under leading heads, to have *general supplementary concepts* which are not contained in experience itself, but are gained by a process of logical treatment of experience. The most general supplementary concept of this kind which has found its place in all the empirical sciences, is the concept of *causality*. It comes from the necessity of thought which prescribes that all our experiences shall be arranged according to reason and consequent, and that we shall remove, by means of *secondary* supplementary concepts and if need be by means of concepts of hypothetical character, all contradictions standing in the way of the establishment of a consistent interconnection of experience in accordance with the principle of reason and consequent. In this sense we may regard all the supplementary concepts which serve for the interpretation of any sphere of experience, as applications of the general principle of causation. These concepts are legitimate insofar as they are required, or at least rendered probable, by the causal principle; they are unwarranted as soon as they prove to be arbitrary fictions resulting from foreign motives, and contributing nothing to the interpretation of experience.

2. The concept *matter* is a fundamental supplementary concept of natural science formulated under the principle stated. In its most general significance matter is the permanent substratum assumed as existing in universal space, that is, the substratum of the activities to which we must attribute all natural phenomena. In this sense the concept *matter* is indispensable to every explanation of natural science. The attempt, therefore, which has been made in recent times to raise *energy* to the position of a governing principle does not succeed in doing away with the concept matter, but merely gives it a different content. This content, however, is given to the concept by means of a second supplementary concept, which relates to the *causal activity* of matter. The concept of matter which has been accepted in natural science up to the present time is based upon the mechanical physics of Galileo, and uses as its secondary supplementary concept the concept of *force*, which is defined as the product of the mass and the momentary acceleration. A physics of energy seeks to introduce

everywhere instead of this concept *force,* the concept *energy,* which in the special form of mechanical energy is defined as half the product of the mass multiplied by the square of the velocity. Energy, however, must, just as well as force, have a position in objective space, and under certain particular conditions the points from which energy proceeds may, just as well as the point from which force proceeds, change their places in space, so that the concept of matter as a substratum contained in space, is retained in both cases. The only difference, and it is indeed an important one, is that when we use the concept force, we presuppose the reducibility of all natural phenomena to forms of mechanical motion, while when we use the concept *energy,* we attribute to matter not only the property of motion without a change in the form of energy, but also the property of the transformability of qualitatively different forms of energy into one another without a change in the quantity of the energy.

3. The concept of *mind* is a supplementary concept of psychology, in the same way that the concept *matter* is a supplementary concept of natural science. It too is indispensable insofar as we need a concept which shall express in a comprehensive way the totality of psychical experiences in an individual consciousness. The content of the concept, however, is in this case also entirely dependent on the secondary concepts which give a more detailed definition of psychical causality. In the definition of this content, psychology shared at first the fortune of the natural sciences. Both the concept of mind and that of matter arose primarily, not so much from the need of explaining experience as from the effort to reach a fanciful doctrine of the general interconnection of all things. But while the natural sciences have long since outgrown this mythological stage of speculative definition, and make use of some of the single ideas which originated at that time only for the purpose of gaining definite starting points for a strict definition of their concepts, psychology has continued under the control of the mythological metaphysical concept of mind down to most modern times, and still remains, in part at least, under its control. The concept *mind* is not used as a general supplementary concept which serves primarily to gather together the psychical facts and only secondarily to give a causal interpretation of them, but it is employed as a means of satisfying so far as possible the need of a general universal system, which system includes both nature and individual existence.

4. The *concept of a mind substance* in its various forms, is rooted in this mythological and metaphysical need. In the development of this concept there have not been wanting efforts to meet as far as possible, from the

metaphysical position, the demand for a psychological causal explanation, but such efforts have in all cases been afterthoughts, and it is perfectly obvious that psychological experience alone, independent of all foreign metaphysical motives, would never have led to a concept of mind substance. This concept has beyond a doubt exercised a harmful influence on the scientific treatment of experience. The view, for example, that all the contents of psychical experience are ideas, and that these ideas are more-or-less permanent objects, would hardly be comprehensible without such presuppositions. That this concept is really foreign to psychology is further attested by the close relation in which it stands to the concept of material substance. Mind substance is regarded either as identical with material substance, or else as distinct in nature but yet reducible in its most general formal characteristics to one of the particular concepts of material elements, namely, to the concept of the *atom*.

5. *Two* forms of the concept *mind substance* may be distinguished, corresponding to the two types of metaphysical psychology pointed out above (§ 2, p. 6). The one is *materialistic* and regards psychical processes as the activities of matter or of certain material complexes such as the brain elements. The other is *spiritualistic* and looks upon psychical processes as states and changes in an unextended and therefore indivisible and permanent being of a specifically spiritual nature. In this case matter is thought of as made up of similar atoms of a lower order (monistic, or monadological spiritualism), or the mind atom is regarded as specifically different from matter proper (dualistic spiritualism).

In both its materialistic and spiritualistic forms, the concept *mind substance* does nothing for the interpretation of psychological experience. Materialism does away with psychology entirely and puts in its place an imaginary brain physiology of the future, or when it tries to give positive theories, falls into doubtful and unreliable hypotheses of cerebral physiology. In thus giving up psychology in any proper sense, this doctrine gives up entirely the attempt to furnish any practical basis for the *mental sciences*. Spiritualism allows psychology as much to continue, but in the type of psychology which it permits actual experience is entirely subordinated to arbitrary metaphysical hypotheses, through which the unprejudiced observation of psychical processes is obstructed. This appears as a rule in the incorrect statement of the problem of psychology, with which the metaphysical theories start. Such theories regard inner and outer experience as totally heterogeneous, though in some external way interacting, spheres.

6. It has been shown (§ 1, p. 3) that the phases of experience dealt with in the natural sciences and in psychology are nothing but phases of *one* experience regarded from different points of view; in the natural sciences experience is treated as an interconnection of objective phenomena and, in consequence of the abstraction from the knowing subject, as *mediate experience*; in psychology experience is treated as *immediate and underived*.

When this relation is once understood, the *concept of a mind substance* immediately gives place to the *concept of the actuality of mind* as a basis for the comprehension of psychical processes. Since the psychological treatment of experience is supplementary to that of the natural sciences, in that the psychological treatment deals with the immediate reality of experience, it follows that there is no place in psychology for hypothetical supplementary concepts such as are necessary in the natural sciences because of the presupposition in the natural sciences of an object independent of the subject. The concept of the actuality of mind, accordingly, does not require any hypothetical determinants to define its particular contents, as does the concept of matter, but quite to the contrary, the concept of actuality excludes such hypothetical elements from the first, by defining the nature of mind as the immediate reality of the processes themselves. However, since one important component of these processes—namely, the totality of ideational objects—is, at the same time, the subject of consideration in the natural sciences, it necessarily follows that substance and actuality are concepts which refer to one and the same general experience, with the difference that in each case experience is looked at from a different point of view. If we abstract from the knowing subject in our treatment of the world of experience, that world appears as a manifold of interacting substances; if, on the contrary, we regard the world of experience as the total content of the experience of the subject including the subject itself, then the world appears as a manifold of interrelated occurrences. In the first case, phenomena are looked upon as *outer phenomena,* in the sense that they would take place just the same, even if the knowing subject were not there at all, so that we may call the form of experience dealt with in the natural sciences *outer* experience. In the second case, on the contrary, all the contents of experience are regarded as belonging directly to the knowing subject, so that we may call the psychological attitude the attitude of *inner* experience. In this sense outer and inner experience are identical with mediate and immediate, or with objective and subjective forms of experience. All these terms serve to designate, not different spheres of experience, but different supplementary points of view in the analysis of an experience which is presented to us as an absolute unity.

7. That the method of treating experience employed in natural science should have reached its maturity before that employed in psychology is easily comprehensible in view of the practical interests connected with the discovery of regular natural phenomena thought of as independent of the subject. It was, furthermore, almost unavoidable that this priority of the natural sciences should, for a long time, lead to a confusion of the two points of view. This did really occur as we see by the different psychological substance concepts. When the reform came in the fundamental position of psychology, and the characteristics and problems of this science were sought, not in the specifically distinct nature of its sphere, but in its method of considering all the contents presented to us in experience in their immediate reality, unmodified by any hypothetical supplementary concepts—when this reform came, it did not originate in psychology itself, but in the *single mental sciences*. The view of mental processes based upon the concept of actuality, was familiar in these mental sciences long before it was accepted in psychology. This inadmissible difference between the fundamental position of psychology and the mental sciences is what has kept psychology, until the present time, from fulfilling its mission as a foundation for all the mental sciences.

8. When the concept of actuality is adopted, one of the questions on which metaphysical systems of psychology have long been divided is immediately disposed of. This is the question of the *relation of body and mind*. So long as body and mind are both regarded as substances, this relation must remain an enigma in whatever way the two concepts of substance are defined. If they are like substances, then the different contents of experience as dealt with in the natural sciences and in psychology can no longer be understood, and there is no alternative but to deny the independence of one of these forms of knowledge. If they are unlike substances, their connection is a continual miracle. If we start with the theory of the actuality of mind, we recognize the immediate reality of the phenomena in psychological experience. Our physiological concept of the bodily organism, on the other hand, is nothing but a part of this experience, which we gain, just as we do all the other empirical contents of the natural sciences, by assuming the existence of an object independent of the knowing subject. Certain components of mediate experience may correspond to certain components of immediate experience, without

there being any necessity of reducing the one component to the other or of deriving one from the other. In fact, such a derivation is absolutely impossible because of the totally different points of view adopted in the two cases. Since we have here not different objects of experience but different points of view in looking at a unitary experience, there must be at every point a thoroughgoing relation between the two modes of treatment adopted in the natural sciences and in psychology. It is, furthermore, obvious that the natural sciences never exhaust the total content of reality; there are always a number of important facts which can be approached only directly, or in psychological experience. These are all the contents of our subjective consciousness which do not have the character of ideational objects, that is, are not directly referred to external objects. This includes our whole world of feeling so long as this world is considered entirely from the point of view of its subjective significance.

9. The principle that all those contents of experience which belong at the same time to the mediate or natural scientific sphere of treatment and to the immediate or psychological sphere are related to each other in such a way that every elementary process on the psychical side has a corresponding elementary process on the physical side is known as the *principle of psychophysical parallelism*. It has an empiricopsychological significance and is thus totally different from certain metaphysical principles which have sometimes been designated by the same name, but which have in reality an entirely different meaning. These metaphysical principles are all based on the hypothesis of a psychical substance. They all seek to solve the problem of the interrelation of body and mind, either by assuming *two* real substances with attributes which are different but parallel in their changes, or by assuming *one* substance with two distinct attributes which correspond in their modifications. In both these cases the metaphysical principle of parallelism is based on the assumption that every physical process has a corresponding psychical process and vice versa, or on the assumption that the mental world is a mirroring of the bodily world, or that the bodily world is an objective realization of the mental. This assumption is, however, entirely indemonstrable and leads in its psychological application to an intellectualism which is contradictory to all experience. The psychological principle of parallelism, on the other hand, as above formulated, starts with the assumption that there is only *one* experience, which, however, as soon as it becomes the subject of scientific analysis, is, in some of its components, open to *two* different kinds of scientific treatment: to a mediate form of treatment, which

investigates ideated objects in their objective relations to one another, and to an *immediate* form, which investigates the same objects in their directly known character and in their relations to all the other contents of the experience of the knowing subject. So far as there are objects to which both these forms of treatment are applicable, the psychological principle of parallelism requires relation at every point between the processes on the two sides. This requirement is justified by the fact that both forms of analysis are in these two cases really analyses of one and the same content of experience. On the other hand, from the very nature of the case, the psychological principle of parallelism can *not* apply to those contents of experience which are objects of natural-scientific analysis alone, or at least it can apply only in so far as these belong to the ideational contents of our subjective consciousness. Furthermore, the principle in question cannot apply to those contents of consciousness which go to make up the specific character of psychological experience. Among the latter we must include the characteristic *combinations* and *relations* of psychical elements and compounds. To be sure, there are combinations of physical processes running parallel with the psychical processes, in so far at least as a direct or indirect causal relation must exist between the physical processes the regular coexistence or succession of which is indicated by a psychical interconnection, but the characteristic content of the psychical combination can, of course, in no way be a part of the causal relation between the physical processes. Thus, for example, the elements which enter into a spatial or temporal idea stand in a regular relation of coexistence and succession in their physiological substrata; or the ideational elements which make up a process in which psychical contents are related or compared have corresponding combinations of physiological processes of some kind or other, which are repeated whenever these psychical processes take place. But the physiological processes cannot contain anything of that which goes to form the specific nature of spatial and temporal ideas, or anything of that which goes to form the relating and comparing processes, because natural science purposely abstracts from all these processes. Then, too, there are two concepts which result from the psychical combinations, which, together with their related affective elements, lie entirely outside the sphere of experience to which the principle of parallelism applies. These are the concepts of *value* and *end*. The forms of combination which we see in processes of fusion or in associative and apperceptive processes, as well as the values which they possess in the whole interconnection of psychical development, can only be understood through *psychological* analysis, in the same way that objective phenomena, such as those of weight, sound, light, heat, etc., or the processes of the nervous system, can be approached only through physical or physiological analysis, that is, through a form of analysis which makes use of the supplementary substance-concepts of natural science.

10. Thus the principle of psychophysical parallelism, in the incontrovertible *empiricopsychological* significance above attributed to it, leads necessarily to the recognition of an *independent psychical causality*, which is related at all points to physical causality and can never come into contradiction with it, but is just as different from this physical causality as the point of view adopted in psychology, or that of immediate subjective experience, is different from the point of view taken in the natural sciences, which as has been pointed out is the point of view of mediate, objective experience due to abstraction. And just as the nature of physical causality can be revealed to us only in certain principles which are valid for all natural phenomena, as for example the principle of inertia, the principle of composition of forces, and the principle of conservation of energy, so also an account of the characteristics of psychical causality can be given only by extracting from the sum total of psychical processes by a process of abstraction *the principles of psychical phenomena*. Furthermore, as certain general laws of nature, such as the law of gravity, the laws of falling bodies, the laws of oscillation of elastic media, etc., can be derived from certain complex physical phenomena, through the application of the principle of natural causation, so also can the empirical laws of psychic phenomena be referred back to general psychical principles. Among these general laws, those are of special importance for the definition of the total character of mental life which underlie the development of mental products in their historical evolution. These laws may, accordingly, be designated as the *general laws of psychical evolution*.

References. VOLKMANN, Lehrbuch der Psychologie, vol. I, Sect. 1. (This presents the substance concept of the Herbartian School, together with an historical review of the development of this concept.) LOTZE, Medicin. Psychol., chap. 1. (This presents a substance concept which shows some tendencies toward the theory of actuality.) BAIN, The Relation of Mind and Body, 1873. (Physiological Theory). L. BUSSE, Geist und Körper, Seele und Leib (Assumes a psycho-physical interaction). Theory of Actuality: WUNDT, Ueber psychische Kausalität und das Prinzip des psycho-physischen Parallelismus, Phil. Stud., vol. 10; Ueber die Definition der Psychologie, Phil. Stud., vol. 12; Logik, 2nd ed. vol. II, pt. 2, chap. 2. Grundz., 5th ed., vol. III, chaps. 21 and 22; Lectures, lecture 30. PAULSEN, (English trans. by Thilley) Introduction to Philosophy. EDM. KÖNIG, Zeitschr. f. Philos., vol. 119 (Principle of Parallelism).

§ 23. *The Principles of Psychical Phenomena*

1. *Three* general principles of psychical phenomena may be regarded as fundamental. We designate them the principles *of psychical resultants, of psychical relations,* and *of psychical contrasts.*

2. The *principle of psychical resultants* finds its expression in the fact that every psychical compound shows attributes which may indeed be understood from the attributes of its elements after these elements have once been presented, but which are by no means to be looked upon as the mere sum of the attributes of these elements. A compound clang is more in its ideational and affective attributes than merely a sum of single tones. In spatial and temporal ideas the spatial and temporal arrangement is conditioned, to be sure, in a perfectly regular way by the combination of elements which make up the idea, but the arrangement itself can by no means be regarded as a property of the sensation elements themselves. The nativistic theories which assume this implicate themselves in contradictions which cannot be solved; and besides, insofar as they admit subsequent changes in the original space perceptions and time perceptions, they are ultimately driven to the assumption of the rise, to some extent at least, of new attributes. Finally, in the apperceptive functions and in the activities of imagination and understanding, this principle finds expression in a clearly recognized form. Not only do the elements united by apperceptive synthesis gain, in the aggregate idea which results from their combination, a new significance which they did not have in their isolated state, but what is of still greater importance, the aggregate idea itself is a new psychical content made possible, to be sure, by the elements, but by no means contained in these elements. This appears most strikingly in the more complex productions of apperceptive synthesis, as, for example, in a work of art or a train of logical thought.

3. In psychical resultants there is thus expressed a principle which we may designate, in view of its results, as the *principle of creative synthesis.* This principle has long been recognized in the case of higher mental creations, but it has not been generally applied to the other psychical processes. In fact, through an unjustifiable confusion with the principles of physical causality, it has even been completely reversed. A similar confusion is responsible for the notion that there is a contradiction between the principle of creative synthesis in the mental world and the general principles of natural causation, especially the principle of the

conservation of energy. Such a contradiction is impossible from the outset because the points of view of judgment, and therefore of measurements wherever such are made, are different in the two cases, and must be different, since natural science and psychology deal, not with different contents of experience, but with one and the same experience viewed from different sides. (§ 1, p. 3). Physical measurements have to do with *objective masses, forces, and energies.* These are supplementary concepts which we are obliged to use in judging objective experience; and their general laws, derived as they are from experience, must not be contradicted by any single case of experience. Psychical measurements, which are concerned with the comparison of psychical components and their resultants, have to do with *subjective values and ends.* The subjective value of the psychical combination may be greater than the value of its components, its purpose may be different and higher than theirs, without any change in the masses, forces, and energies concerned. The muscular movements of an external volitional act, the physical processes which accompany sense perception, association, and apperception, all follow invariably the principle of the conservation of energy. But the mental values and ends which these energies represent may be very different in quantity even while the quantity of these energies remains the same.

4. The differences pointed out show that *physical* measurement deals with *quantitative values,* that is, with quantities that admit of a variation in value only in the one relation of measurable magnitude. *Psychical* measurement, on the other hand, deals in the last instance in every case with *qualitative values,* that is, values that vary in degree only in respect to their qualitative character. The ability to produce purely *quantitative* effects, which we designate in *physical energy,* is, accordingly, to be clearly distinguished from the ability to produce *qualitative* effects, or the ability to produce values, which we designate as *psychical energy.*

On this basis we can not only reconcile the *increase of psychical energy* with the *constancy of physical energy* as accepted in the natural sciences, but we find also in the two facts reciprocally supplementary standards for the judgment of our total experience. The increase of psychical energy is not seen in its right light until it is recognized as the reverse* subjective side of

---

*[The original reads "reverse," an obvious typographical error. The two sentences that follow seem needlessly difficult to comprehend. An alternative and more literal translation would be: "Furthermore, while that increase is indefinite in its expression, because its standard may be very different under different conditions, it is valid *only on the presupposition* of the continuity of psychic processes. Therefore it has a psychological correlate, which

physical constancy. The increase of psychical energy, being, as it is, indefinite, since the standard may be very different under different conditions, holds only *under the condition that the psychical processes are continuous.* As the psychological correlate of this increase we have the fact which forces itself upon us in experience, that *psychical values disappear.*

5. The *principle of psychical relations* supplements the principle of resultants; it refers not to the relation of the components of a psychical interconnection to the value of the whole, but rather to the reciprocal relations of the psychical components within the compound. The principle of resultants thus holds for the synthetic processes of consciousness, the principle of relations for the analytic. Every resolution of a conscious content into its single members is an act of relating analysis. Such a resolution takes place in the successive apperception of the parts of a whole, which whole is ideated at first only in a general way. This process is to be seen in sense perceptions and associations, and in clearly recognized form in the division of aggregate ideas. In the same way, every apperception is an analytic process, the two phases of which are the emphasizing of a single content and the marking off of this one content from all others. The first of these two partial processes is what produces *clearness;* the second is what produces *distinctness* of apperception (p. 233, 4). The most complete expression of this principle is to be found in the processes of *apperceptive analysis* and in the simple *relating* and *comparing* functions upon which such analysis is based (p. 286 and 298). In comparison more especially, we see the essential import of the principle of relations in the fact that every single psychical content receives its significance from the relations in which it stands to other psychical contents. When these relations are *quantitative*, this principle takes the form of a law of *relative quantitative comparison* such as is expressed in *Weber's law* (p. 291).

6. The third principle, the *principle of psychical contrasts*, is, in turn, supplementary to the principle of relations. It refers, like the principle of relations, to the relations of psychical contents to one another. It is itself based on the fundamental division of the immediate contents of experience into objective and subjective components, a division which is due to the very conditions of psychical development. Under subjective components are included all the elements and combinations of elements which, like the feelings and emotions, are essential constituents of *volitional*

---

unquestionably forces itself upon us in experience, in the fact of the *disappearance of psychic values."* —S.D.]

processes. These subjective components are all arranged in groups made up of opposite qualities corresponding to the chief affective dimensions of pleasurable and unpleasurable feelings, exciting and depressing feelings, and straining and relaxing feelings (p. 91). These opposites obey in their succession the general *principle of intensification through contrast*. In its concrete application, this principle is always determined in part by special temporal conditions, for every subjective little process requires a certain period for its development; and if, when the process has once reached its maximum, it continues for a long time, it loses its ability to arouse the contrast effect. This fact is connected with another fact, namely, that there is a certain medium, though greatly varying, rate of psychical processes most favorable for the intensity of all feelings and emotions.

This principle of contrast has its origin in the attributes of the subjective contents of experience but is secondarily applied also to ideas and their elements, for ideas are always accompanied by more-or-less emphatic feelings due either to the ideational content or to the character of the spatial and temporal combinations involved. Thus, intensification through contrast appears most clearly in the case of certain sensations, such as those of sight, and in the case of spatial and temporal ideas.

7. The principle of contrast stands in close relation to the two preceding principles. On the one hand, it may be regarded as the application of the general principle of relations to the special case in which the related psychical contents range between opposites. On the other hand, the fact that under suitable circumstances antithetical psychical processes may intensify each other, while falling under the principle of contrast, is at the same time a special application of the principle of creative synthesis.

References. WUNDT, Ueber psychische Kausalität, Phil. Stud., vol. 10, and Logik, vol. II, Pt. 2, Sect. 4, chap. 2, § 4; System der Philosophie, 2nd. ed., Sect. 6; Grundz., 5th ed., vol. III, chap. 22.

§ 24. *General Laws of Psychical Development*

1. We have as many laws of psychical development as we had principles of psychical causality, and the former may be regarded as the application of the latter to more comprehensive psychical interconnections. We designate the laws of development as laws first of *mental growth*, second of *heterogony of ends*, and third of *development toward opposites*.

2. The *law of mental growth* is as little applicable to all contents of

psychical experience as is any other law of psychical development. It holds only under the limiting condition which applies to the principle of resultants, the application of which it is, namely the condition of the *continuity of the processes* (p. 369). But since the circumstances that tend to prevent the realization of this condition, are, of course, much more frequent when the mental developments concerned include a greater number of psychical syntheses than in the case of the single syntheses themselves, it follows that the law of mental growth can be demonstrated only for certain developments taking place under normal conditions, and even here only within certain limits. Within these limits, however, the more comprehensive developments, as for example the mental development of the normal individual and the development of mental communities, are obviously the best exemplifications of the fundamental principle of resultants, which principle lies at the basis of this development.

3. The *law of heterogony of ends* is most closely connected with the principle of relations, but it is also based on the principle of resultants, which latter is always to be taken into consideration when dealing with the larger interconnections of psychical development. In fact, we may regard this law of heterogony of ends as a principle of development which controls the changes arising as results of successive creative syntheses, in the relations between the single partial contents of psychical compounds. The resultants arising from united psychical processes include contents which were not present in the components, and these new contents may in turn enter into relation with the old components, thus changing again the relations between these old components and consequently changing the new resultants which arise. This principle of continually changing relations is most strikingly illustrated when an *idea of ends* is formed on the basis of the given relations. In such cases the relation of the single factors to one another is regarded as an interconnection of means, which interconnection has for its end the product arising from the interconnection. The relation in such a case between the actual *effects* and the ideated ends is such that secondary effects always arise which were not thought of in the first ideas of end. These new effects enter into new series of motives and thus modify the earlier ends or add new ends to those which existed at first.

The law of heterogony of ends in its broadest sense dominates all psychical processes. In the special teleological coloring which has given it its name, however, it is to be found primarily in the sphere of *volitional processes*, for here the ideas of end together with their affective motives are of the chief importance. Of the various spheres of applied psychology, it is especially *ethics* for which this law is of great importance.

4. The *law of development towards opposites* is an application of the principle of intensification through contrast to more comprehensive interconnections which form in themselves series of developments. In such series of developments there is a constant play of contrasting feelings in accordance with the fundamental principle of contrasts. First, certain feelings and impulses of small intensity begin to arise. Through contrast with the predominating feelings this rising group increases in intensity until finally it gains the complete ascendency. This ascendency is retained for a time, and then from this point on the same alternation may be, once, or even several times, repeated. But generally the laws of mental growth and heterogony of ends operate in the case of such an oscillation, so that succeeding phases, though they are like corresponding antecedent phases in their general affective direction, yet differ essentially in their special components.

The law of development toward opposites shows itself in the mental development of the individual, partly in a purely individual way within shorter periods of time, and partly in certain universal regularities in the relation of various periods of life. It has long been recognized that the predominating temperaments of different periods of life present certain contrasts. Thus, the light, sanguine excitability of childhood, which is seldom more than superficial, is followed by the slower but more retentive temperament of youth with its frequent touch of melancholy. Then comes manhood with its mature character, generally quick and active in decision and execution, and last of all, old age with its leaning toward contemplative quiet. Even more than in the individual does this principle of development toward opposites find expression in the alternation of mental tendencies which appear in social and historical life and in the reactions of these mental tendencies on civilization and customs and on social and political development. As the law of heterogony of ends applied chiefly to the domain of *moral* life, so this law of development toward opposites finds its chief significance in the more general sphere of *historical* life.

References. Compare § 23, page 373.

A CRITICAL APPRECIATION OF WUNDT AS REFLECTED IN THE LITERATURE OF THE PAST

William James

REVIEW OF *GRUNDZÜGE DER PHYSIOLOGISCHEN PSYCHOLOGIE**

On every hand, no less in Germany than in England, there are signs of a serious revival of philosophical inquiry; from a quarter, too, which leads one to indulge the hope that real progress will erelong be made. For it is the men engaged in the physical sciences who are now pressing hard in the direction of metaphysical problems; and although in a certain point of view their education may not specially qualify them for the task, it would be sheer folly not to expect from their trained cunning in experiment, their habits of patience and fairness, and their willingness to advance by small steps at a time, new results of the highest importance.

Nowhere is the new movement more conspicuous than in psychology, which is of course the antechamber to metaphysics. The physiologists of Germany, devoid for the most part of any systematic bias, have, by their studies on the senses and the brain, really inaugurated a new era in this science. Where quasi-scholastic distinction and nomenclature were the only instrument of advance, we now find measurements and objective reactions to help us on our way. And in the main, whilst in France thoroughly, and in England still faintly, the old jealousy between the objective and the subjective methods survives, the one as patronized by religious, the other by materialistic speculation, we find that in Germany the minds of the best investigators on either side are wholly un-

---

**Grundzüge der physiologischen Psychologie.* Von WILHELM WUNDT. Leipzig: Engelmann. 1874. 8vo. pp. 870. This *Review* was published originally in the *North American Review*, 1875, 121, 195–201.

preoccupied with any such militant consciousness. The spiritualist Lotze is as hearty a physiologist as the materialist Moleschott, while it is hard to guess from the psychologic contributions of Fechner, Helmholtz, Mach, and Horwicz, what their theologic or antitheologic bias may be, or if they have any at all. This detachment of mind is very healthy and is in striking contrast with what such writers as Mill, Maudsley, and Huxley show us in England, and McCosh and Porter in this country. But even here we find in Hodgson and Lewes the beginning of a new era of temper, destined surely to be more fruitful than the old regime of unfairness and recrimination.

The heaven-scaling Titans have had their day in Germany, and the confident systems lie in the dust; for the schoolboy performances of a Haeckel and the sensational paradoxes of a Hartmann cannot count as philosophy. A season of headache and apathy, with bald *Empirie*, the mere registration of facts, for a diversion, ensued, and was natural after such a metaphysical debauch. There is something almost dramatic in the way in which the thirsty spirit of man is seen to be regaining its normal appetite again and, with its new desires, indulging in new hopes. Only maturity has brought circumspection, and the old rash notion of scaling the opaque walls of existence by a quick *coup de main*, and ravishing the secret within in an instant, has been given up. The method of patience, starving out, and harassing to death is tried; Nature must submit to a regular *siege*, in which minute advantages gained night and day by the forces that hem her in must sum themselves up at last into her overthrow. There is little of the grand style about these new prism, pendulum, and galvanometer philosophers. They mean business, not chivalry. What generous divination, and that superiority in virtue which was thought by Cicero to give a man the best insight into nature, failed to do, their spying and scraping, their deadly tenacity and almost diabolic cunning, must some day accomplish.

Such as they are, Professor Wundt, the title of whose latest work heads our article, is perhaps their paragon, and his whole career is at the same time a superb illustration of that thoroughness in education for which Germany is so renowned. In that learned land Browning's fable of the Grammarian's Funeral is reenacted every day. Poor Waitz, for instance, who died a few years ago with his monumental *Anthropologie der Naturvölker* unfinished, began that work merely to educate himself for the study of psychology and the philosophy of religion. Wundt is more fortunate than Waitz, for he has at last reached, at Zurich, the goal he evidently strove for from the first, a university chair of philosophy. Still young, his apprenticeship is over and the fruit is to be reaped. But what an apprenticeship! To be Helmholtz's colleague as professor of physiology at Heidelberg; to spend years in a laboratory and to publish numerous elaborate experimental researches; to write a large treatise on physics, and an admirable handbook of physiology (both of which have had several editions and been translated into French), besides two volumes of lectures on psychology, an essay on the law of causation, and various fugitive articles; to study each new subject by giving a year's course of lectures upon it—these are *preparations* on a scale rather fitted to cool than to excite the ardor of an American neophyte in philosophy.

Nevertheless Wundt has now laid them behind him, and in this compactly printed volume he takes, so to speak, an account of stock before embarking on his new career. The work certainly fills a lacuna and circumscribes in a very convenient way all those phenomena of human life which can be studied both by introspection and by objective investigation. The anatomy and physiology of the nervous centers and organs of sense occupy about one third; the natural history of sensations, pleasures, and pains, and perceptions spatial and temporal, follow; and analyses of the aesthetic, volitional, and self-conscious life conclude. The style is extremely concise, dry, and clear, and as the author is as thoroughly at home in the library as in the laboratory, the work is really a cyclopedia of reference. If, through a large part of it, the reader finds that physiology and psychology lie side by side without combining, it is more the fault of the science than of the author. He has registered no detail without doing his best to reduce and weave it in with the mass. Indeed so uninterrupted is his critical elaboration, that we can think of no book (except perhaps the *Origin of Species*) in the course of which the author propounds so many separate opinions.

Their multiplicity forbids our even attempting to give an account of them. But we may single out one or two for notice. Everyone has heard of the measurements of the velocity of nervous action which Helmholtz inaugurated. Wundt, after having worked at the subject experimentally for fourteen years, with interruptions, may fairly claim to have brought it for the present to a conclusion. The principle is this: a signal is given to the subject, who immediately on its reception replies by closing an electric key. The instant of the signal and of the closure are chronographically registered and the time between them ascertained, and according to the circumstances of the experiment this time undergoes some very interesting variations, whose interpretation by Wundt seems to us particularly felicitous. In a previous chapter on attention and consciousness, he has adopted a convenient nomenclature which really is something more than a metaphor:

> If we say of all the representations present to the mind at any one time that they are in the *field of vision* of consciousness, we may call that part of them to which the attention is particularly directed the *inward point of sight*. The entrance of a representation into this inner field of vision may be called Perception; its entrance into the focus or point of sight, Apperception. (p. 717)

Now the latter act is often a volitional effort on the part of the subject, a focusing of the attention upon the impression, which adjustment occupies a distinct interval of time. This interval is a part of the time registered in the experiments just referred to. It, *plus* the time occupied in the volitional innervation of the motor nerves which provoke the movement by which the key is closed, are called by Wundt, together, the *time of reaction*. It is this interval of psychical activity which is variable according to the experimental conditions. The other subdivisions of the total time, that of transmission from the organ of sense to the brain, that of "perception," and that of transmission to the muscle, are probably invariable. Now the experimental circumstances which shorten the time of reaction are mainly those which define beforehand as to its quality, intensity, or time, the signal given to the observer, so that he may accurately expect it before it comes. The focusing of the attention takes place under these circumstances *in advance*. Where, for instance, we are warned preliminarily by a slight sound that the signal is going to occur, the registered time is reduced to a minimum. The attention, in other words, "is so exactly adjusted to the entrance of the signal into the inner field of vision, that at the very instant of perception, apperception likewise occurs, and with apperception, the volitional mandate." More remarkable still! the time registered may be reduced to zero, that is, the signal may be given and the key closed at objectively the same instant, so that not only the "reaction time" but also the physiological duration of nerve transmission to and from the brain are abolished. This paradox amounts to saying that the impression is apperceived before it actually occurs, or that expectant attention is equivalent to objective stimulation.[1] And the same phenome-

---

[1]The reason why, in these not very frequent cases, we do not notice the signal *twice* (once as apperceived in advance by our spontaneous attention, and once passively after it has occurred) is probably to be sought in another series of experiments which show that one act of apperception, if it be all intense, prevents the apperception of other nearly simulta-

non is made even more strikingly manifest by another set of Wundt's original investigations, which we have not space to describe.

We select these particular researches for notice because they demonstrate, as it were mathematically, what empiricists are too apt to ignore: the thoroughgoing participation of the spontaneous mental element in determining even the simplest experiences. The *a posteriori* school, with its anxiety to prove the mind a *product, coûte que coûte,* keeps pointing to mere "experience" as its source. But it never defines what experience is. *My* experience is only what I agree to attend to. Pure sensation is the vague, a semichaos, for the *whole* mass of impressions falling on any individual are chaotic and become orderly only by selective attention and recognition. These acts postulate *interests* on the part of the subject—interests which, as ends or purposes set by his emotional constitution, keep interfering with the pure flow of impressions and their association and causing the vast majority of mere sensations to be ignored. It is amusing to see how Spencer shrinks from explicit recognition of this law, even when he is forced to take it into his hand, so to speak. Mr. Bain, in principle, admits it, but does not work it out. The only English-writing empiricist who has come near to making any use of it is Mr. Chauncey Wright, in his article on the evolution of self-consciousness in this review for 1873.

Another section important to English readers is that devoted to touch, vision, and cognition of space. Wundt's account of vision is unapproached by anything in our language for thoroughness and subtlety. His conclusion as to the nature of our notion of space is in one word this: "It is the resultant of a distinct psychologic process . . . which may be called a *synthesis,* because the evolved product shows properties which are not present in the sensuous material used in its construction." That is to say, our *intuition* of space within the limits in which it exists—a very different thing from our *idea* of space, which has no limits—is that of an undivided

---

neous impressions. This is by virtue of what Wundt calls the "law of discrete flow" in representations: "Attention demands a certain time to pass from one impression to another. As long as the first impression lasts the entire attention is bent upon it, and cannot, therefore, focus itself in advance, in order to apperceive the second impression at the very instant of its occurrence." The second will then either be apperceived late, or abort, unless indeed it can coalesce in one conception with the first. Of all impressions "perceived," none are remembered for more than a minute, except those which are "apperceived," or brought to the inner focus. In the case related in the text, the *real* impression may either abort (pass unnoticed, unapperceived) or it may coalesce with the imaginary one.

plenum, a perfectly simple and specific *quale* or affection of consciousness. Whether this new quality of feeling once arisen is *fertile*, that is, whether it be analyzable into different elements from those by whose synthesis it arose, giving us new relations, new propositions concerning them, propositions not *merely* expressive of the *particular* tactile, retinal, and muscular experiences that generated the form of intuition—this is not decided by Wundt, nor do we here affirm it. To prove it would be essentially to reinstate the Kantian philosophy, that is, to vindicate for the mind not only a native wealth in forms of sensibility—every empiricist must admit that!—but the possession of forms with synthetic judgments involved in them.

Wundt's term *synthesis* reminds one of the term *mental chemistry* used by the Mills, or rather admitted into their works, but not used; for both they, Bain, and Spencer are so desperately bent on covering up all tracks of the mind's originality (especially in this field of space, preoccupied by Kant), that they utterly repudiate mental chemistry here and labor with an energy worthy of a better cause to procure out of mere "association" something never given in any one of the ideas associated, something which after all they have to *escamoter* out of their sleeve as it were, or, in the absurd Spencerian fashion, to call "nascent," and trust that, in that seemingly infantile and innocent guise, you will take no alarm at its intrusion.

We are not at all concerned with the ultimate philosophical bearings of this particular question. Settle the particulars, and philosophy will take its turn. But to be so bribed beforehand by philosophical antipathies as to ignore evidence and shirk conclusions is a poor business for either psychologist or physiologist.

The notion of mental synthesis or chemistry opens the way to interesting questions. Hitherto most thinkers have admitted that in a state of consciousness the *esse* and the *existere* were one and the same thing, namely, the *sentiri*. In the conscious sphere, reality and phenomenon, substance and accident, nature and property, cannot be distinguished as they are in the objective sphere. A thought has only one mode of being at all, namely, as that very thought. *It* cannot become a different thought, nor can it cease to be *thought* without ceasing to *be* altogether. But in the material world, that which we call one and the same thing, a *leaf*, for instance, has relations and differs according to the point of view. It was green and is now brown. It is a product of chemical forces, a reducing agent, a form of beauty, an effect of luminiferous ether, an affection of my sensorium each in turn, and yet preserves what we call its identity throughout.

Now when, in this matter of space, we see feelings of innervation and retinal impressions combining into a novel *quale* of consciousness, what are we to say? Do *they* really exist within the new *quale*, or, in other words, have they, in addition to their simple *sentiri*, another existence, a sort of objective substantiality which may betray itself by producing effects—we being conscious of the effect, but no longer of the original feeling? Or is the process a logical one, the simple feelings being really "perceived" by the mind, but only used as signs to suggest the higher product, that alone being "apperceived," whilst the signs are unnoticed and forgotten? Or, thirdly, have the simple feelings never existed at all as feelings, and has the resultant intuition of space a purely physiological antecedent, in the shape of the *combined* nervous action, whose components, when they were separately excited, corresponded to the retinal and other feelings? These problems lie over the whole field of psychology and are worthy of explicit discussion.

Wundt does not deal with them at all, except by implication, as above. Neither does he seem ever to have entertained the hypothesis advanced by several English writers recently, that conscious states have no dynamic relations either with each other or with the nervous system. He assumes throughout that feelings as such may combine with each other (as we have just seen in regard to space), and that they may also act as nervous stimuli. We think, for our part, that the Englishmen (only two of whom, Hodgson and Clifford, have deigned to give reasons for their belief) are prematurely dogmatic. Taking a purely naturalistic view of the matter, it seems reasonable to suppose that, unless consciousness served some useful purpose, it would not have been superadded to life. Assuming hypothetically that this is so, there results an important problem for psychophysicists to find out, namely, *how* consciousness helps an animal, how much complication of machinery may be saved in the nervous centers, for instance, if consciousness accompany their action. Might, for example, an animal which regulated its acts by notions and feelings get along with fewer preformed reflex connections and distinct channels for acquired habits in its nervous system than an animal whose varied behavior under varying circumstances was purely and simply the result of the change of course through the nervous reticulations which a minute alteration of stimulus had caused the nervous action to take? In a word, is consciousness an economical *substitute* for mechanism?

Wundt's book has many shortcomings, but they only prove how confused and rudimentary the science of psychophysics still is. More workers and critics are wanted in the field, propounders of questions as well as of answers. Whoever they may be, they will find this treatise indispensable for study and reference. All we have cared to do has been to call attention to its importance and to the merits of its singularly acute and learned author.

9

S. *Feldman*

WUNDT'S PSYCHOLOGY*

This year signalizes the hundredth anniversary of Wundt's birth. Yet it is probably still true that, as Titchener wrote soon after Wundt's death in 1920, "we stand too near to Wundt to see him in a just perspective."[1] Clear vision, however, requires more than a proper perspective; with increasing distance, outlines are likely to blur. While, then, the time for a just appraisal of Wundt is not yet, certain preliminary studies can and need to be carried out now.

Wundt's was a long life, and his works were many. In his formative period, moreover, which reached to his forty-second year when he published the first edition of the *Grundzüge der physiologischen Psychologie* (1874), he bore the marks of many influences: Leibniz, Kant, and Herbart; Helmholtz, Fechner, and Darwin. From 1874 to 1920, on the other hand, while he added greatly to the fields of experimental and social psychology, his psychological outlook persisted, through its many restatements, fairly unchanged. To see Wundt justly, therefore, we may best begin by going back more than half a century and examining the first of the six editions of the *Grundzüge*, the first rough draft of his permanent psychological system. Then we may go back still further to the earlier, discarded drafts, the *Beiträge zur Theorie der Sinneswahrnehmung* (1858–1862), and the *Vorlesungen über die Menschen- und Thierseele* (1863). Finally, we shall have to note how Wundt was influenced by contemporaries and predecessors.

*Accepted for publication September 29, 1931. From the Department of Psychology, Cornell University. This study was begun under the direction of Professor E. B. Titchener. Published originally in the *American Journal of Psychology*, 1932, XLIV (4), 615–629.
[1] E. B. Titchener, Wilhelm Wundt, *American Journal of Psychology*, 32, 1921, 176.

The writings of the *Grundzüge* in 1874[2] was one of Wundt's two achievements which marked the launching of psychology as an au-

[2]The first ten chapters were issued in 1873. On the changes in the plan of the *Grundzüge*, first outlined in a letter written by Wundt to his publisher (cf. E. B. Titchener), "On the plan of the *Physiologische Psychologie*," *American Journal of Psychology*, 32, 1921, 596f. The letter, a facsimile of which is inserted after p. 90 in Wilhelm Engelmann, *Jubiläumskatalog* (1911), reads, in translation, as follows:

Heidelberg, December 8, 1872

My dear Sir,

For some time past I have been busy with putting into shape a book whose preparation has occupied me for several years and which I now design to publish under the title "Grundzüge der physiologischen Psychologies."

The field which in this book is to receive its first complete survey owes its demarcation and present importance almost wholly to investigations of the last two decades. It grew originally out of the physiology of sense perception; and partly by way of the physiological investigations that bear upon that topic, partly by way of a series of independent psychophysical studies, it has gradually attained dimensions that make a summary survey of its whole extent and a development of the general scientific results to which these paths have led possible and, I believe, desirable. Although the new discipline has grown out of experimental physiology, the questions that interest it cannot in the nature of the case receive in the physiological texts the consideration that their importance demands—just as they lie also beyond the purview of current psychology. It therefore seems to me that physiological psychology is destined to form a middle term between physiology and psychology, in much the same way as at a somewhat earlier period physiological chemistry intervened between physiology and chemistry.

I have laid out the plan of my book as follows. I felt bound, first of all, to include in a physiological psychology the whole range of the interrelations between our outer life and our inner, psychological experience. But I have also felt that I could not avoid the question of the relation obtaining in the last resort between the worlds of inner and of outer occurrence, and of the explanation of the whole interconnection of psychological phenomena suggested by the survey of their borderland. I accordingly treat my subject in five sections. The first, introductory part deals with the physiological characters of the nervous system. The second contains the doctrine of sensation and apprehension; the third, the doctrine of organic movements. These two sections comprise the empirical material of physiological psychology proper; the one, in discussing sensation and apprehension, investigates the inner or psychological—the other, in discussing movement, investigates the outer or physiological consequence of the manifold interactions between our outer and inner experience. A fourth section then presents a criticism of psychological doctrines, directed and supported by the results obtained in these two; and a fifth and final section adds, as outcome of the whole enquiry, a general theory of psychophysical occurrence.

The complete book will fill some forty or fifty forms. Woodcuts are provided, especially in the first two sections, to illustrate the text. The work of preparation is so far advanced that the first steps toward publication can be taken in February of next year and the printing can proceed thereafter without interruption.

I now wish to ask, my dear sir, whether, and if so upon what terms, you are disposed to undertake the publication of the book. Hoping to receive an early reply to this question, I am,

Yours faithfully,

W. Wundt

tonomous experimental discipline.[3] Affording us, as it does, the most comprehensive survey of the state of psychology in that momentous period, the book has a permanent value. We therefore begin our serial study of Wundt's psychology with a brief summary, chapter by chapter, of these first *Principles of Physiological Psychology*.[4]

Introduction

While human life is the primary concern both of physiology and of psychology, the two sciences have so far, in dealing with their common subject matter, been following different paths. Physiology has informed us of the phenomena of life as they may be perceived through our external senses; in psychology, man looked at himself, as it were, from within, and dwelled upon the results of this internal observation. Yet there is a wide range of vital processes that calls for cooperative exploring; sensation and centrally initiated movement are outstanding examples. A psychological fact, sensation is nevertheless referable in the main to conditions outside of the organism, and while the various stages of sensory complication may be followed through psychological observation, such factors as order and grouping of impressions, interrelations of sensory and motor apparatus, and central processes of the nervous system need also to be considered. In the case of action, again, one must rely in large measure upon psychological observation in order to fill the gap between impression and movement.

So long, however, as physiology and psychology stand apart, the investigation of this common territory may be properly assigned to an intermediate discipline.[5] Such a border science would take over the

[3]The other was the founding of his laboratory in 1879.

[4]Only a part (the physiological section) of the fifth edition of the book has been translated into English: *Principles of Physiological Psychology*, translated by E. B. Titchener, 1904. Cf. E. G. Boring, Edward Bradford Titchener, *American Journal of Psychology*, 38, 1927, 494.

[5]In his preface, Wundt writes: "The work which I here present to the public is an attempt to mark out a new domain of science. I am well aware that the question may be raised, whether the time is yet ripe for such an undertaking. . . . At the same time the best means of discovering the gaps in the subject matter of a developing science is, as we all know, to take a general survey of its present status." The last sentence echoes a statement made ten years earlier by the Herbartian, M. W. Drobisch. Referring to Wundt's *Vorlesungen*, in a review entitled "Über den neuesten Versuch die Psychologie naturwissenschaftlich zu bebegründen" (*Zeitschrift für exacte Philosophie*, 1864, 313–348), Drobisch remarks: "He [Wundt] has preferred the freer form of lectures because of his conviction that textbooks and systems abound in a science in proportion to lack of knowledge, and that psychology

problems which have, till fairly recently, been prosecuted exclusively by psychologists; and it would borrow its equipment from both parent sciences, combining with psychological observation the methods of experimental physiology. It would single out actual instances of apprehension, feeling, and impulse for analysis, and it would analyze them, not directly, but through experimental variation of the relevant physiological factors. In time, it might provide the *Geisteswissenschaften*—history, law, politics, art, and religion—with a basis in natural science.

A suitable name for this novel enterprise would be *physiological psychology*,[6] or *experimental psychology*.[7] Either designation would announce the advent of a natural, explanatory science and would set it off from the current empirical psychology as well as from the newly launched *Völkerpsychologie*, both of which might well be termed descriptive sciences, or natural histories of mind.[8]

---

will never begin to progress unless an end is made to the writing of textbooks and systems. On this score we should like to ask Mr. Wundt. . . . Is not a systematic arrangement best designed for calling attention to gaps within a science?" In his autobiography (*Erlebtes und Erkanntes*, 1920, 206), Wundt recalls Drobisch's scathing criticisms ruefully. Cf. *Vorlesungen*, I, ix.

[6]The term *physiological psychology* occurs as a title in F. W. Hagen, *Studien im Gebiete der physiologischen Psychologie* (1847) and again in Leidesdorf and Meynert's *Vierteljahrsschrift für Psychiatrie in ihren Beziehungen zur Morphologie und Pathologie des Centralnervensystems, zur physiologischen Psychologie, Statistik, und gerichtlichen Medicin*, which began publication in 1867. Wundt himself employs the term in an article, *Neue Leistungen auf dem Gebiete der physiologischen Psychologie*, which he contributed to the first issue of the quarterly.

[7]Wundt seems to have coined the phrase *experimental psychology* in 1862 (Beiträge, vi). As we have not seen Bautain's *Psychologie expérimentale* (1839), we cannot tell whether *expérimentale* in that title means "experimental" or "empirical."

[8]We have not thought it worthwhile to analyze in detail the six chapters dealing with the "physiological properties of the nervous system," especially since a complete translation of the corresponding portion of the fifth edition is available.

The most important item in these chapters is the formulation of four "general laws of the central functions" (231): (1) the principle of connection of elementary parts: every nerve element is connected with other nerve elements, and only when so connected does it become capable of physiological function; (2) the principle of indifference of function: no element performs specific functions; the form of its function depends upon its connections and relations; (3) the principle of vicarious function: when the function of any element is inhibited or destroyed, it may be taken over by other elements, provided that they have the necessary connections; (4) the principle of localized function: every distinct function has a distinct place in the central organ from which it issues; i.e., a place in which the elements have the connections required for carrying out the function. The last three principles, we are told, are interrelated: vicarious function presupposes indifference, and qualifies localization. Wundt takes sharp issue, on the one hand, with Flourens's "principle of the indivisible function of the cerebral lobes" (226 and 234) and, on the other hand, with the "hypothesis of the specific function of the neural elementary parts" implied both by phrenology and by the Müllerian doctrine of the specific energy of nerves (226 and 232).

Sensation

Sensation is, unquestionably, the simplest psychological phenomenon; but it is never observed in isolation. To determine its underived properties, one must, in the manner of Condillac, first abstract from it all that it owes to its connections of the moment or to its history: relations in space and in time, feeling tone, attribution to specific source. The remainder will consist of intensity and quality.[9]

Sensory Intensity

Sensory intensity is commonly accepted as a simple indicator of external energies. To quote Herbart, two lights shine twice as brightly as one light, and three strings sound thrice as loud as one string. Yet it is quite obvious that such a relationship between sensory intensity and stimulus energy does not hold at the limits of sensitivity.

Only the lower limits have been investigated in detail, and even there only such approximate values as the following are available. In an illumination 1/300 as bright as moonlight, we can just see a white paper strip at a distance of 5.5 meters; if a cork weighing 1 mg drops 1 mm, we can hear it from a distance of 91 mm; we can feel a weight of 2 mg; we can sense a temperature 1/10°C. higher than that of the skin. The stimulus threshold varies, moreover, with quality, place, and extent of stimulation: it goes up to 50 mg on certain parts of the skin; and it goes down for light and for temperature as area of stimulation is increased.

Between the lower and the upper intensive limits,[10] discrimination is measured in terms of the differential threshold, which varies somewhat with method of experimentation (just noticeable differences, average errors, right and wrong cases). All these methods, however, have yielded, at the hands of Weber and Fechner, the same generalization: sensory intensity is proportional to the logarithm of the intensity of stimulus. Thus it is that a shadow cast by moonlight disappears in lamplight, while a shadow cast by lamplight disappears in sunlight; for

[9]Cf. H. Helmholtz, *Handbuch der physiologischen Optik* (1867, 438): "I conclude that, in perception, whatever can be eliminated or reversed by causes of demonstrably empirical origin is not properly sensation, but the product of experience and habituation. It will be shown that, if we follow this rule, we must refer to sensation nothing but quality, and to experience and habituation most of the spatial perceptions."

[10]Wundt invents the term *Reizhöhe* for the terminal limen.

the same reason, stars are invisible in the daytime. On the other hand, slight differences in brightness between two clouds may be seen by the naked eye and through dark glasses with equal distinctness. The logarithmic relationship is also exemplified in the case of apparent stellar magnitude; and it has been experimentally confirmed in vision and in hearing, for pressure and for warmth (but not for cold), and for lifted weights.

The generalization of the facts of intensive discrimination that bears Weber's name is thus sufficiently assured. Exceptions to it, where any have been demonstrated, rest upon specific physiological causes. For Weber's law itself, however, an immediate physiological ground is lacking. Observations made upon motor nerves, stimulated electrically at various stages of fatigue, suggest by inference that between stimulus intensity and intensity of process in sensory nerve a simple proportionality prevails. Weber's logarithmic law may, consequently, be regarded as a psychological law, expressing the relationship of sensation to neural process. It will be shown later that the relationship holds for quality as well as for intensity.

Sensory Quality

Each of the four special senses—hearing, sight, smell, and taste—provides a distinct continuum of highly differentiated qualities, although in taste and in smell the form of the continua is not apparent. The skin and all the remaining sensitive areas of the body may be regarded, with Johannes Müller, as one general sense organ, the organ of the less differentiated sense of feeling.

Intermodal differences are sufficiently accounted for by differences in the constitution of the sense organs. Thus, the more primitive sense of feeling functions through undifferentiated and directly stimulated nerve endings, some of which are rendered more sensitive by accessory bulbular (Krause) and corpuscular (Meissner, Pacini) structures. That temperature and touch rest upon different modes of stimulation of identical fibers is suggested by the confusion of the two at low intensities. The ear reacts first as a whole, but the cochlea with its basilar membrane superimposes an analytic mechanism. In the eye are the rods and the cones, every one of which is the seat of many complex chemical reactions. A lesser variety of chemical reaction-modes will allow for the discrimination—by way of smell and taste—of acids, bases, salts, ether oils, etc.

Such extraordinary functional specialization at the receptor removes any theoretic need for ascribing, with Müller and Helmholtz,[11] specific energies to peripheral or central nerves—an assumption that is, in any case, incompatible with evolutionary tenets, the principle of indifference of neural elements, and other established facts. Qualitative variety may, instead, be referred to heterogeneous molecular processes induced through receptor stimulation and transmitted in their specificity to the brain. Repeated stimulation of the same sort will naturally predispose the adaptable nerve substance to a set type of molecular movement. In hearing and in touch, the molecular processes repeat the periodicity of the stimulus; in the case of sight, smell, and taste, the relationship is not so simple. An account of auditory and visual quality will illustrate these two modes of receptor function.

In general, auditory quality gives a faithful rendering of stimulus form. The simple sine wave is heard as a pure tone; the complex wave yields an analyzable sound; irregularity of waveform is reflected in the noise. When one considers the continuity of tone and the unanalyzability of noise, the parallelism, it is true, seems to lose its precision; but these exceptions may be respectively attributed to the temporal limits of perception and to the "narrowness of consciousness." The parallel is further modified in the case of pitch discrimination, where a logarithmic relationship obtains between sensation and stimulus. Here, moreover, the logarithmic function is not extracted from liminal determinations but is plainly exhibited in the comparison of finite values.

The simple—or saturated—colors lie, like the simple tones, in a linear series. The color line, however, returns on itself and—with the purples— forms a closed figure, which becomes a triangle when degrees of color saturation are added. Since we regard color quality with its neural correlate as a continuous but complex function of stimulus, the color triangle may be taken as a graphic representation of that function. Color differences are measured in liminal terms, and the colors coinciding with maxima and minima of differential sensitivity—red, yellow, green, and blue—have a more pronounced quality than the other colors, which are sensed as transitions.

---

[11]Wundt had earlier followed Helmholtz's views concerning specific energy (cf. *Grundzüge*, 346 f. with *Vorlesungen*, I, 182), theory of vision (cf. *Grundzüge*, 332 with *Vorlesungen*, I, 158), and theory of hearing (cf. *Grundzüge*, 348 with *Vorlesungen*, I, 184).

Upon these issues, and others to be noted later, Wundt remained in agreement with Helmholtz down to the third edition of his *Lehrbuch der Physiologie*, which he published the same year (1873) in which he sent the *Grundzüge* to press. Cf. *Lehrbuch*, 494, 611, 671 f.

Tonal quality, being independent of intensity, is not influenced by fatigue; in the case of color, however, where quality changes with intensity, fatigue affects both. Color passes over into gray or black as the stimulus is continued; and unless contrast intervenes, the complementary afterimage—itself an indication of altered retinal sensitivity—is negative (less bright than the original impression). The same-colored afterimage is always positive (as bright as, or brighter than, the original impression) and implies lag of excitation, while the flight of colors may be explained by differences in the temporal course of retinal excitation.

The facts of color-blindness are compatible with the hypothesis that in vision, receptor activity is a continuous function of wavelength. Color-blindness means, as a rule, low sensitivity or total insensitivity for red, combined with low sensitivity for violet. Insensitivity for red occurs also in the normal retinal periphery, in the initial stage of atrophy of the optic nerve, and in many cases of simple amblyopia. The occurrence of green-blindness, blue-blindness, and achromatopsy lacks proof.

The most favorable conditions for contrast, as demonstrated in the Meyer and Ragoni–Scina experiments, are maximal difference of color tone; an optimal brightness difference (white on black is no brighter than light gray on the same black)[12]; an optimal saturation of inducing surface; zero saturation of induced surface; and absence of contours (in Fechner's experiment the contrast shadow persists when viewed through a tube). While, then, the last factor displays the influence of reproduction, favored by the perception of discrete objects, the others suggest that discrimination is relative in the case of visual quality, as it is in the case of intensity and auditory quality. Direct proof of this relativity may be found in the fact that brightness contrast remains undisturbed under wide changes of illumination, and no facts are contradicted by generalizing from this special case to the whole group of contrast phenomena. To dispose of the phenomena of contrast as illusions of judgment (Helmholtz)[13] is to ignore their palpable character and to exalt the secondary factor of reproduction, while to refer them to a supposititious interaction of retinal areas is to disregard the reproduction factor altogether. Rather

[12]Cf. 408.

[13]Wundt writes, "I then [*Vorlesungen*, I, 198; *Lehrbuch*, 626], adhered in detail to Helmholtz's theory of contrast; but the facts have convinced me of its untenability (*Grundzüge* 423)."

Wundt also recedes from his previous concurrence with Helmholtz in the explanation of color mixture (cf. *Grundzüge*, 387 with *Lehrbuch*, 609 f.), of afterimages (cf. *Grundzüge*, 398 f. with *Lehrbuch*, 620, 624) and of the flight of colors (cf. *Grundzüge*, 401 with *Lehrbuch*, 622 f.)

do the facts of sensation, taken together, require the positing of a general psychological law of relation, valid for quality as well as for intensity. Sensation, in both of its aspects, is a relative and not an absolute measure of neural process.

Sense Feelings

Sheer pleasantness and unpleasantness depend, in the first instance, upon degree of sensory intensity. Hence, these feeling tones are most noticeable in the lower senses, where qualitative distinctions are few, and there they contribute to the apprehension of self to mood and temperament. In the higher senses, qualitative variety is matched by a corresponding diversity of feelings, which enter into the aesthetic appreciation of external objects. High tones are gleeful, low tones have dignity; loud tones give the impression of power and exaltation, soft tones are low-spirited; there is rejoicing in a fast, moodiness in a slow tempo; and clashing, discordant feelings arise from the interplay of fundamental with overtones and the intrusion of beats. Similarly, cheer is found in white, gravity in black; excitement in yellow, depression in blue; and between these poles stand the neutral grays, the tranquil greens, and the instable reds. Affective analogies—such as obtain between deep tones and dark colors and are implied in terms like *color tone, tone color, cold and warm colors, sharp tones,* and *saturated colors*—contribute further to aesthetic appreciation.

While feeling is thus originally determined by intensity and quality, it may be modified through associations. The feeling tone of black, for example, is enhanced by its association with mourning, but the association, in turn, rests upon the original feeling tone of black. Other affective connections, such as between green and the peaceful meadow, or between yellow and the cheering sunlight—instances of a remarkable harmony between sensation and external nature—illustrate the principle of adaptation to environment which has governed the development of the human eye.

The inconstancy of feeling is explained, in part, by sensory adaptation and summation. Yet such instances as the euphoria of convalescence and the thrill found in games of chance, in dramatic performances, and in other forms of play suggest that it is of the nature of feeling to rebound from one of its poles to the opposite pole. As Kant said, pleasure must be preceded by pain. The basis for this affective movement, and in fact for feeling itself, is to be found in the relation of sensation to consciousness, which continually oscillates between the opposed states of inhibition and facilitation. Pleasantness goes with facilitation, unpleasantness with inhibition; witness the assertiveness of pain, the easy flow of ideas when one is pleased, the frustration of sight by black, the clash of sensation in beats.

The psychological status of feeling is now apparent. Every sensation has its feeling tone just as it has its quality and its degree of intensity. But the three sensory determinations do not stand on a level; feeling is dependent upon intensity and quality and represents a secondary modification imposed upon sensation by the general state of consciousness. [14]

Apprehension

In the apprehension of existing and nonexisting objects, of external objects and oneself, sensations—supplied by peripheral or central stimulation—are involved. But these sensations are now ordered both in space and in time. Apprehension, therefore, rests upon a new, integrative activity. The two modes of integration, temporal and spatial, are found together, and in their earliest form, in the tactual perception of bodily movement; they are independently and more highly developed in hearing and in vision.

Tactual Perceptions

Tactual localization without the aid of vision implies, in the first place, a local coloring of cutaneous sensations, or local signs, whereby parts of the body are discriminated. Such local differences would account for the limits of localization (expressed in terms of constant error or two-point limen and pictured by means of overlapping "sensory circles") as well as for the effects upon localization of practice, sensitivity, and intensity of stimulus. The correlation of size of sensory circle with nerve supply of the skin points to a structural basis for local signature.

---

[14]The theory of feeling is given a different turn later in the chapter on "Consciousness and Attention."

Before, however, the bidimensional system and qualitative local signs can be converted into a spatial continuum, some precise and dependable metric means is required, and only in the fine intensive grading of the sensations of motor innervation is a device of this sort discoverable. Localization may, then, be referred to a synthesis of motor and tactual sensations resting ultimately upon a coordination of tactual and motor impulses, which presumably takes place in the optic thalmus but is also specifically represented in the cortex. In this psychological synthesis,[15] as in a chemical synthesis, the constituents—motor sensations and local signs—lose their identity in the product, spatial order; they cannot, therefore, be observed for themselves but must be inferred from the conditions—motor and cutaneous—of localization.

The early development of the spatial discrimination of parts of the body must have been favored by the unambiguous relation between motor and tactual sensations in bodily movement. The tactual exploration of objects would then lead to the perception of surfaces of varying curvature, and because of the predominance of rectilinear movement, the object surfaces would be fitted into a tridimensional framework. At the same time, the possibility of reproduction would render unnecessary a constant reliance upon both local signs and movement. Since bodily movement, with its regularly recurring accents or emphases, also provides a basis for temporal apprehension, it would seem that the earliest perception of all was that of movement, a perception in which temporal and spatial order—later developing separately in hearing and in vision—are given together.

Auditory Perceptions

Sounds owe their localization altogether to vision and to touch; specific factors are to be looked for in tensor tympani, pinna, and throat movement. The variety of sounds, their analyzability, and their precise attunement to stimulus course come into account in other ways: in the apprehension of rhythm and time, of melody, and of tonal relationship.

Related sounds are those containing common or coincident partials.

---

[15]How Wundt came upon the notion of synthesis, and the changes which it went through between 1858 and 1874, are related by E. B. Titchener, "A note on Wundt's doctrine of creative synthesis," American Journal of Psychology, 33, 1922, 351 ff. Cf. also Lehrbuch, 554 f.

Where coincidence is independent of the fundamental, as in the vocal sound and in timbre, relationship is constant. In the musical interval, on the other hand, there is a variable—or harmonic[16]—relationship between the constituent notes, the degree of resemblance depending upon the relative number and intensity of the common partials. The octave, double octave, and twelfth represent imperfect unisons rather than related tones, for in each case the higher note merely repeats partials already present in the lower note. The closest degree of kinship, then, is to be found in the fifth, with its three audible common partials; next come the fourth, the major sixth, and the major third, with two such partials; and lastly the minor third and other intervals, with but one. In major chords, where the difference tone furnishes a common fundamental, relationship is indirect. To such an indirect relationship pure tone-intervals owe their harmonic character, although associations may be contributing factors.

Suitable conditions for temporal perception and the perception of rhythm are first found in connection with bodily movement and later in connection with the visual perception of movement.[17] Hearing, however, affords the most adequate basis for both perceptions. Temporal discrimination is present in the simplest rhythm; every intensive rise is apprehended as a repetition and with every rise or fall a recurrence is anticipated. Duration is estimated in terms of the rhythmic unit and is correctly estimated only within the limits of rhythmic organization.

In melodic apprehension, qualitative variation is added to the intensive variation upon which rhythm is conditioned; hence the significance of variable tonal relationship (melodic repetition and the law of the tonic) for melody and of constant tonal relationship (rhyme and assonance) for poetry.

Visual Perceptions

The retinal mosaic is fundamental to visual localization. It provides the sensory material for spatial arrangement, and it determines the limits of the total field of vision and of local discrimination, or visual acuity. Since the cones have more numerous fiber connections and are more

[16]Earlier Wundt followed Helmholtz's theory of harmony (cf. *Grundzüge*, 370 f. with *Vorlesungen*, II, 68).

[17]Wundt alters his account of the perception of time in a later chapter (cf. *Grundzüge*, 513 and 681 f.).

closely packed than the rods, acuity falls rapidly from fovea to periphery. Discrimination varies also with form and size of stimulus object, and peripheral acuity in particular improves with practice.

The determining factor in visual localization, however, is ocular movement. The orientation of the eye and the direction and magnitude of its excursions are apprehended by way of sensations of innervation and tactual local signs. That these motor and cutaneous sensations enter into fairly uniform connections with retinal local signs is guaranteed by the laws of Listing and Donders, and when the eye is stationary, the impulses of innervation reproduce the appropriate tactual local signs. From the synthesis of these elements, as from the similar synthesis in touch, spatial arrangement results in the form of a surface. The distance of this surface from the eye is defined ,rather poorly, by way of accommodation; more precisely, by way of convergence; and, at a later stage of development, by the reproductive effect of perspective. Specifically, the influence of eye movement evidences itself in the orientation, form, and continuity of the visual field; in the displacement of objects owing to paralysis of eye muscle; in the discrimination of extents; in the overestimation of vertical distances (except in the case of such familiar figures as the circle) and of distances in the upper and outer portions of the field of vision; in the apparent inclination of verticals; in the overestimation of filled extents; and in the various illusions of visual movement.

This genetic theory of visual perception presupposes sensory and motor mechanisms that are ready to function—for purposes of spatial apprehension—at birth (or in the case of congenital blindness, as soon as vision is rendered possible); it does not derive perception from empirical inferences or from associations. Perception, which is the basis of experience, cannot itself be the result of experience, and the concept of association is quite different from that of sensory synthesis, since an association does not yield a new product.

The singleness of binocular vision rests not upon stimulation of identical points but, in the first instance, upon a common localization made possible by the synergy of binocular movement. Through repeated movements of fixation, a paired correspondence of retinal points becomes established which favors, but does not compel, single vision. Common localization is facilitated also by eye movement, by the presence of fixation lines (if not too long) and of secondary cues to localization, by familiarity of object, and by similarity of the binocular impressions.

The visual field is properly a plane: one cannot see two objects in the

same visual direction, at least not with equal distinctness. Of two sufficiently different impressions, one impression prevails altogether (perfect
mirroring, retinal rivalry and suppression), or one is more distinctly
perceived than the other impression (transparency and mirroring); if the
factors favoring each impression balance, luster appears.

Imaginative Apprehension

The sensory materials involved in perception recur, in conformity
with the rules of association, either as direct supplements to perception or
as discrete formations. Thus arise various forms of apprehension: memory and imagination, hallucination, illusion, and dream—all implying a
spread of excitation in the sensory areas of the cortex. Normally this
secondary excitation is weak, and the reproduced elements are faint;
hence, for example, pleasant incidents lose less of their body in recall than
painful (and therefore more intensive) experiences do. Cortical excitation
may spread further to motor areas, and in the case of hallucinatory objects
that follow the movement of the eyes and leave negative afterimages, a
centrifugal course of excitation is indicated. In the hallucinatory types of
apprehension, moreover, cortical sensitivity is high, and for various
reasons: absence of stimulation (silence is conducive to auditory, dark-
ness to visual hallucinations); excessive stimulation (hence the frequency
of visual hallucinations); or nutritive disturbances leading to an accumulation of products of decomposition in the cortex. To this last condition, a
source of automatic central stimulation, dreams and pathological hallucinations owe their incongruency; yet they draw largely upon reproduc-
tions instigated by sensory stimulation and affective tone.

Complex Apprehension, Generalized Apprehension, and
Perceptive Forms

Apprehension is enriched through the concurrence and reproduction of impressions of disparate modalities. This is exemplified in perceiv-
ing a sharp point, a grating noise, a heavy weight, an impending blow.
Movement also contributes to such complex apprehensions by way of the
sensory materials involved in gesture, speech, and writing. Pantomime,
onomatopoiea, and pictography exemplify the complication or fusion of

similar elements, while the association of sounds with visual and other disparate impressions was originally guided by analogies of feeling. For the most part, however, it is sheer habituation that has produced the intimate connection of object, word, and sign.

The change from a specific to a generalized or schematic apprehension of objects requires not a distinct process of abstraction but the normal operation of the laws of association. Generalization begins in perception: the features that recur in objects of the same class tend to stand out, while the variable features are neglected. In this way a schematic mode of apprehension develops, which, however, is not stable but easily resolves itself into a serial apprehension of specific objects within a class. Even animals may attain to this level of generalization, and the child who identifies a circle first as a plate, then as a pond, and then again as the moon is carrying out the process of resolution and thereby beginning to comprehend a class of objects.

Schematization, however, is adequate only for certain classes of objects, such as "circle" or "green." For most object classes the schema becomes too vague and the process of resolution too cumbersome (e.g., "color"). The realization of this difficulty, at first felt but vaguely, finally leads to the postulation of a generalized object. Such a postulate, or concept, implies no new psychological mode other than schematic apprehension. With the advent of the concept the verbal element in apprehension becomes more prominent, and the verbal symbol is then also pressed into service for the comprehending of relations (such as means and end), to which schematic apprehension is altogether inadequate. The abstract concept—the theoretical as a postulate of thinking, the practical as a postulate of action—develops out of an earlier stage of exemplificatory apprehension (e.g., idol worship precedes the abstract conception of god). To this derivation abstract concepts still owe their feeling tone and their appearance in correlative pairs.

When thinking of space or time—the two forms of perception—we apprehend a specific stretch of space or of time and not a symbol, as with other concepts. Yet their mode of derivation is similar. The geometric representation of the systems of color and tone neatly illustrate the formation of the space concept; by bracketing together color tone, saturation, intensity, and duration, we may even understand a space of four dimensions. It is, nevertheless, inadmissible to suppose, as Zöllner does, that space is curved; for while physical theory may—as it has already done—advance far beyond the direct evidence of perception, it must conform to the general perceptive forms of space and time. On the other hand, psychology has nothing to say concerning the reality of space or of any other concept, or even of the objects of perception; it takes all these for granted and then seeks to determine the conditions of their apprehension.

Aesthetic Feelings

At a level between sense feelings and emotions, one may place the varied class of feelings that color all apprehension, and whose basal modes are liking and disliking. Often indistinct, these "aesthetic" feelings are most obvious in tonal harmony and rhythm and in the symmetry and proportion of spatial form. But they are also to be discerned in recall and in recognition, in the simple understanding of a sentence and in the solution of a problem, in the ideas of the beautiful and the ugly, the sublime, the ridiculous, and the comic. It is evident that these feelings imply evaluation. They may be said to reflect the degree to which the diversity given in apprehension is unified. They thus express the general conscious status of apprehension, just as the sensory feelings indicate the status of sensation.

Consciousness and Attention

Conscious life does not begin with sensation, nor does it involve from the outset of consciousness of self, nor, finally, can it spring from unconscious inferences.[18]

Self-awareness and inference, both, appear at a fairly late period of development; they imply the use of concepts. The explicit awareness of self, moreover, presupposes, first, the perceptive discrimination of external objects from one's own body and, secondly, the differentiation of memory and imagination from perception.

The single sensation, on the other hand, is an abstraction. The sound

---

[18]In the last two clauses, Wundt negatives the fundamental ideas of the *Beiträge* and the *Vorlesungen*. Even sensation had been made out to be an unconscious inference (*Beiträge*, 445 ff.; *Vorlesungen*, I, 52 ff., 57 ff., 305.).

we hear has a certain duration; the color we see is localized. Synthesis operates from the beginning, and wherever synthesis, even of the most rudimentary kind, is rendered possible by conditions of central organization, some level of consciousness must therefore be assumed to exist. In animals possessing various levels of neural integration, the unitariness of consciousness is nevertheless guaranteed by the close interrelation of the various neural mechanisms. Some animals, it is true, exhibit signs of consciousness after decerebration; such consciousness, however, is not residual, but a new development.

Alongside of sensory synthesis and of association, a third psychological activity must now be recognized: attention or apperception. All objects are not apphended on equal terms. Under instantaneous illumination, several words can be clearly read; if, however, one is intent upon the precise form of a single letter, all the other letters become less clear; while with repetition the range of the attentive "point of regard" may increase. The same phenomena can be demonstrated with a combination of tones. The wider range of the whole conscious field of regard may be inferred from the limits of rhythmic complexity and of consecutive thinking.

While attention is favored by reproduction (as the aforementioned effect of repetition indicates), and also by stimulus intensity and visual fixation and contours, various facts bespeak for it a single primary subjective condition. Under attention, apprehension of disparate objects (for example, the sound of the bell and the sight of the pointer in the complication experiment) is unitary. Then there is the peculiar feeling that may be observed during the accommodation of attention. It bears a personal reference; it becomes fairly tense in expectation and surprise and in effortful thought, imagination, and recollection; it may be accompanied by innervation of the muscles about the eyes, ears, and head; it suggests, finally, innervational functioning. One may, therefore, conceive of the cortical innervation-areas as operating in two ways: they shunt the course of excitation back to the sensory spheres, whose activity is thus reenforced, and they also innervate the bodily musculature. It follows that between attention and voluntary action there is simply a difference in the relative emphasis of these two innervational modes. The central determination of all feelings, which we have earlier derived from the total state of consciousness, may now, also, be more specifically referred to innervation.

The Course of Apprehension: Association

The course of apprehension is regulated by the accommodation of attention. The shortest "physiological time"[19] is obtained under conditions permitting adequate accommodation: foreknowledge of the object reacted to and of the time of its appearance, and absence of distraction. Accommodation also governs the time relations both of perceived objects (cf. the "personal equation")[20] and of memorial objects (cf. the experiments on the comparison of time intervals).

The possibility of reproduction rests upon a facilitating aftereffect of cortical excitation. The aftereffect is of a functional sort, analogous to the effect of practice upon muscular movement or upon visual acuity rather than to the aftereffect of visual sensation. Such a dispositional aftereffect underlies the laws of association by spatial and temporal contiguity. These two laws, both of which imply a tendency of excitation to recur in the manner to which it has been habituated, may be combined into a single law of associative habituation. The law of similarity presupposes, in addition, a transfer effect of associative practice. Since the sensory areas of the cortex are dominated by the frontal areas of innervation, the laws of association cannot operate automatically. They are always subject

[19]Wundt here (*Grundzüge*, 733) reports experiments performed by himself and his wife.
[20]Wundt brought the "personal equation" into the laboratory in 1860, when he devised the complication experiment. In 1862, in the course of a general attack on Herbartianism, he made the bold announcement that this experiment disproved the metaphysical axiom upon which the whole Herbartian psychology had been erected. Herbart, by the use of his mathematical method, had demonstrated that the sum of ideas held simultaneously in consciousness was never less than two, while the relative displacement of bell and pointer in the complication experiment—so ran Wundt's argument—meant that we can apprehend only one thing at a time (*die Einheit der Vorstellung*). Cf. *Beiträge*, xxi (footnote), xxvii f., 335, 382 f.; *Vorlesungen*, I, Lectures III and XXIII, and 469; *Grundzüge*, v, 757; J. F. Herbart, *Psychologie als Wissenschaft*, sec. 44; E. B. Titchener, Wundt's address at Speyer, 1861, *American Journal of Psychology*; 34, 1923, 311; E. G. Boring, *A History of Experimental Psychology*, 1929, 247 ff., 341. Drobisch replied vehemently for the Herbartians in the review mentioned above. In the *Grundzüge*, Wundt tacitly drops the argument.
   Boring writes (*op. cit.*, 144) that "Müller's belief in the instantaneousness of nerve action was overthrown by Helmholtz's measurement of the velocity of the nervous impulse, but his view nevertheless persisted as the basis of Wundt's psychology of the 'complication.' " Cf., however, *Vorlesungen*, I, Lecture III, where Wundt writes "Just a few years ago, a German physiologist, Helmholtz, determined with precision the true rate of conduction of sensory and motor process in nerves" (33), and then uses Helmholtz's determination to support his own explanation of the complication experiment.

to the accommodation of attention, although this may sometimes, as in dreams and in the pathological flight of ideas, be fairly slack, and the guiding influence of accommodation grows stronger with proper training. What appears to be association by contrast really points to a peculiarity of attention: when accommodation continues for a long time in the same direction, fatigue sets in, encouraging a maximally different direction of accommodation.

Emotion, Impulse, and Temperament

Emotion and impulse are both expressions of innervational activity. In emotion, attention is, as it were, taken by surprise; in impulse, it is in a state of expectation.

In all pronounced instances of emotion, the affective situation inhibits the flow of ideas; if the emotion is pleasant, a sudden release of inhibition may follow; all emotions gradually subside and are replaced by moods. At the same time, the changing state of innervation and of feeling is reflected in sthenic and asthenic tonicity and in alteration of visceral function; this bodily reverberation is the same in all emotions of sufficient intensity.

The impulse is characterized by a forward reference to an affective situation, with appropriate motor consequences. Its two opposed modes of desire and resistance meet in the neutral mode of expectation. The mere accommodation of attention may thus be regarded as an elementary impulse. The more primitive impulses, like the early perceptions, command ready-made sensory and motor mechanisms; yet they are not mere reflexes. Their direction, at first vague, is defined only as apprehension develops. Nor does psychological development consist in the elimination or repression of the primitive impulses, but in the appearance of new and more varied forms, which, of course, bring with them the possibility of conflict.

Emotional and impulsive dispositions, or temperaments, vary more or less with individual, nation, race, and species. One may discriminate, with Galen, four temperamental types. Intense emotion and dark mood distinguish the choleric and the melancholic from the phlegmatic and the sanguine. While the sanguine and the choleric change their mood with the occasion, the brooding and the conservative types are not so easily distracted. Lastly, one may set off the affectivity of the melancholic and the sanguine against the activity of the choleric and the phlegmatic. Each temperament has its good and its bad points; the wise man will, therefore, cultivate all of them.

Action

There is no sharp cleavage between voluntary action, or action initiated by impulse, and nonvoluntary action. The impulse usually indicates the general direction of the action, without prescribing its specific course. Under repetition, intention may lapse altogether or may show itself only in starting the actional sequence and in bringing it to a close. Such facts cannot be accounted for by invoking now the agency of the will and now unconscious and mechanical determination. All actions are sustained by the operation of organic devices. In voluntary action, essentially the same mechanisms are involved as in nonvoluntary action, but initiation is cortical, since the impulse implies innervational activity. The course of apprehension resembles that of action: once started by apperceptive activity, it may be carried on by way of associative linkage with only occasional interference on the part of apperception. The two modes of innervational function thus behave in a like manner.

Expressive Movements

Expressive movements have various origins. The tonic and visceral indices of emotion are, for the most part, direct consequences of innervation; expressions of the mouth and nose are specific sensory reactions that have become integrated with diverse situations by virtue of a common affective coloring; and gestures can be traced to early perceptive situations. Speech began as vocal gesture; as such it may still be observed in the deaf-mute. Both speech and gesture presuppose a discreteness of perceived objects that is lacking in animals and in human infants. The further development of speech was aided by onomatopoiea and affective analogy. The comprehension of speech was facilitated by gestural comment, just as facial expression contributed to the understanding of gesture.

Concluding Remarks

All psychological processes—sensation, synthesis, association, and apperception—are physiologically grounded, and just as the organism is a unity of many parts, so mind, its inner counterpart, is a unitary connection of multiple processes. These principles suggest the monistic conception that the world consists of simple beings variously integrated and undergoing parallel changes externally and internally. When integration becomes sufficiently persistent and coherent—a level attained in animal life—the internal processes take the form of sensation and apprehension. In this sense, mind may be regarded, with Leibniz, as a mirror of the world.

10

Herman K. Haeberlin

THE THEORETICAL FOUNDATIONS
OF WUNDT'S FOLK PSYCHOLOGY*

Wundt's folk psychology constitutes an integral part of his philosophical system. In some respects it must be regarded as the crowning achievement of his thought, inasmuch as its theoretical foundations presuppose all his former work. In order to gain a proper setting for our critical considerations, we must begin with a somewhat detailed discussion of certain general concepts employed in Wundt's philosophy. Without a clear comprehension of these a criticism of his folk psychology would not be feasible.

Wundt's Concept of Creative Synthesis

The term *voluntaristic* characterizes Wundt's psychology—in contradistinction to that of other schools, such as the associationist, Herbartian, and others—as viewing all psychic phenomena as the expressions of the will, but of the will in the broadest possible sense of the term. To Wundt the will is not a metaphysical concept, as it is to Schopenhauer. It is rather a principle that states the fundamental nature of all psychic life, from the simplest to the most complex processes. It gives expression, in the form of principle, to the empirical facts about the mind—the psychological facts as they are borne out by an analysis of psychic experience and by an interpretation of psychological experiments.

*Published originally in *Psychological Review*, 1916, 23, 279–302.

Wundt regards the sensations (*Empfindungen*) and the feelings (*Gefühle*) as the two ultimate and irreducible elements of psychic life. They do not occur as concrete realities, being the abstract products of logical analysis. In the world of reality we only experience complex psychic phenomena compounded of those elements. The psychic elements are only real in the sense that they are constant components of all psychic experience. But no psychic phenomenon is merely the sum of the component sensational and emotional elements. Invariably it is something new over and above the sum of the parts that enter into the compound. Thus, all temporal and spatial ideas, for instance, are not equal to the sums of the separate sensations and feelings that constitute their elements. A chord is not equal to the sum of all its component tones: it is rather, on its psychological side, a new and unique experience. All psychic phenomena are, therefore, creative products of synthesis: they are, when seen from this point of view, acts of *will*. This justifies the term *voluntaristic* as referring to that fundamental trait of the mind by which all psychic processes are creative. As we see, Wundt extends the concept of creative synthesis from the highest forms of apperceptive processes—which we witness in intellectual and artistic pursuits, where the creativeness is so obvious—to the entire realm of psychic life.

The principle of creative synthesis, as the one cardinal principle of psychic life, embraces the three principles of psychic causality which Wundt cites; namely, the principle of psychic "resultants," the principle of psychic relations, and the principle of psychical contrasts.[1] They pertain to the same content viewed from different angles.[2]

A word must here be said about the counterpart of the principle of creative synthesis, namely, that of the heterogeny of ends (*Heterogonie der Zwecke*). According to Wundt, every causal relation when reversed becomes a teleological one, inasmuch as the two principles of cognition, causality, and teleology, do not exclude each other but are complementary modes of bringing phenomena into logical relation. Thus, the principle of creative synthesis, as a causal principle, can be reversed into a teleological one, namely, that of the heterogeny of ends. It applies to the same facts of psychic life as the former, but from a different point of view. What is cause and effect in one case is means and end in the other:

---

[1] *Outlines of Psychology*, 2d Engl. ed., 364 et seq.; *Physiologische Psychologie* (5th ed.), 3, 778 et seq.
[2] *Physiol. Psychol.*, 3, 787.

Es [handelt] sich eben bei dem Prinzip der Heterogonie um kein neues Prinzip, sondern nur um eine durch die besonderen Bedingungen nahegelegte
teleologische Umformung der causalen Prinzipien des psychischen Gesche-
hens.[3]

It is important to emphasize this relation of the two principles in order to
understand the significance which Wundt attributes to the heterogeny of
ends in the psychic development of the individuals as well as of the
group. It must also be stated in this connection that as an interpretive
principle of cultural phenomena not the causal principle but rather the
teleological one (the heterogeny of ends) is of paramount importance.
This is the case because the psychic phenomena in cultural development,
on account of their complexity on the one hand and the discrepancy of
their causes and effects on the other, are not interpretable progressively
from the causes to the effects, but rather regressively from the given ends
backward to the motives. Theoretically, the heterogeny of ends is a
principle of universal validity. Wundt elaborates its application especially
in connection with the interpretation of the development of ethical ideas
out of nonethical or rather preethical ones.

In keeping with the nature of psychic causality, according to which
an effect is not equal to its cause, the heterogeny of ends implies that in
psychic development the ends attained are not equivalent to the purposes
embodied in the motives. Between the motives and their ends there arise
as unintended by-products secondary "resultants" not implied in the
motives, and thus is brought about a constant discrepancy of motives and
ends. In a chain of motives and ends these unintended resultants, as well
as the purposed end, take the form of new motives. Thus, a constant
shifting of the purposes takes place, which leads Wundt to speak of a
heterogeny of ends.

The Concept of Psychic Actuality

The concept of creative synthesis is supplemented by that of psychic
actuality. This concept expresses the fundamental characteristic of
Wundt's conception of psychic life and distinguishes his psychology from
those other forms that conceive the psyche as a substance analogous to
that of the physical world. According to Wundt the phenomena of psy-

---

[3]*Physiol. Psychol.*, (5th ed.), 3, 789–790.

chology are *toto coelo* different from those of the natural sciences in their relation to the investigating subject. It is of the very nature of the natural sciences that their objects be thought to exist in an objective world distinct from the subject. They exist as if there were no subject. This conception of the purely objective world of natural phenomena becomes possible through an abstraction from the observing and correlating subject. This abstraction involves the postulation of a physical substratum to which all natural phenomena must be referred as to the underlying principle. The hypothetical substratum thus postulated takes the form either of matter or of energy. In this way the natural sciences view their phenomena through the medium of an auxiliary concept, namely, that of the substantiality of their objects. Over and against this, psychology does not approach its objects by way of an abstraction from the subject. It views them "immediately" (*unmittelbar*), since they are given in the consciousness of the subject itself. Those psychologists who postulate a soul substance ignore the intrinsic nature of the objects of their investigation and have fallen into the pitfall of an untrue analogy of the psychical with the physical world. In contradistinction to physical substantiality, Wundt characterizes the subject matter of psychology as the actuality of psychic life. This actuality defines "the nature of mind as the immediate reality of the processes themselves."[4]

The distinction between physical substantiality and psychical actuality determines likewise that between physical and psychical causality. The terms of the one form of causality are quantitative, those of the other are qualitative.[5] Physical causality is characterized by the quantitative equivalence of cause and effect—a fact which finds its expression in the principle of the preservation of energy. Psychical causality, as implied in the concept of the creative synthesis, involves qualitative disparity of cause and effect:

> Es gibt absolut kein solches [i.e., psychologisches] Gebilde, das nicht nach der Bedeutung und dem Wert seines Inhaltes mehr wäre als die blosse Summe seiner Faktoren oder die blosse mechanische Resultante seiner Komponenten.[6]

By juxtaposing the constant values of physical energy to the creative synthesis of psychic energy, Wundt gains specific psychological connotations for his concept of evolution.

[4]*Outlines*, 357.
[5]Wundt, *Logik* (3d ed.), 3, 276.
[6]*Logik*, 3, 274.

The Bearing of Creative Synthesis on the Concept of Folk Soul

Wundt identifies the growth of psychic life with the increase of qualitative *"Wertgrössen,"* which concept he contrasts with that of the quantitative, "Grössenwerte" of the physical world.[7] This clever play of words contains *in nuce* the essence of Wundt's philosophy. The concept *Wertgrössen* implies the teleological factor which Wundt introduces into his conception of psychic evolution. The idea of purpose (*Zweck*) is an integral part of Wundt's concept of voluntaristic psychology. The intrinsic nature of man in his psychic life. But, as we have seen, all psychic processes are voluntaristic, are products of a creative synthesis—are acts of will, if you like. These processes are therefore, by their very definition, purposive. Thus, the consistent conclusion is that the existence of man finds its purpose in the creation of psychic life;[8] but this purpose of existence is not limited to the life of man. The individual human being is but a link in the chain of psychic evolution. Life in the entirety of its expressions is the self-manifestation and self-evolution of the psychic. Nature as the physical prerequisite of the psychic is the "Vorstufe des Geistes"; and, inversely, the psychic is the "vorauszusetzender Zweck des organischen Lebens."[9]

The principle of creative synthesis defines the nature of this psychogenesis in terms of psychic causality. This principle, which, as we have seen, characterizes all our psychic processes as creative productions over and above their constituent parts, characterizes them, in short, as "voluntaristic," applies to all psychic life in general, from its lowest to its highest forms. From this point of view Wundt's position in the discussion of the relation of reflexes to volitions obtains its deeper significance. Volitions are not differentiated mechanical reflexes, but rather reflexes are mechanized volitions. Thus, in the successive stages of evolution the volitions lay claim to priority. Wundt demonstrates this by the fact that, even in the very lowest forms of life, reactions are not mechanical but purposive, and thus characterized in the same way as our own psyche.

Wundt's theory of psychogenesis gains its immediate significance for the concept of folk psychology through the fact that the universality of creative synthesis obtains not only for the continuous succession of steps

[7]Ibid., 276.
[8]Wundt, *System der Philosophie* (3d ed.), 2, 238–239.
[9]Ibid., 147.

which lead from our psyche down to inorganic nature, but also for that whole sphere of psychic life which, as Wundt assumes, leads beyond the individual psyche into the realm of the overindividual life of the community (*der Gemeinschaft*). The creative synthesis which characterizes the intrinsic nature of all psychic compounds, and of all interconnections of these compounds in the psyche of the individual, is found repeated, according to Wundt, in a strictly analogous way, but on a higher level of evolution in the psychic life of the community or the folk. The reality of the folk soul is involved in the extension of this principle beyond the individual psyche. As the psyche of the individual is built up in the form of a progression of superimposed syntheses, so the folk soul is a synthesis of syntheses: it is something creatively new, not equal to the sum of its elements, that is to say, of the individuals of which it is composed.[10] Wundt expresses this idea clearly in the following sentence:

> Aber wie nicht psychische Elemente in isoliertem Zustande, sondern ihre Verbindungen und die aus diesen entspringenden Produkte das bilden, was wir eine Einzelseele nennen, so besteht die Volksseele im empirischen Sinne nicht aus einer blossen Summe individueller Bewusstseinseinheiten, deren Kreise sich mit einem Teil ihres Umfangs decken; sondern auch bei ihr resultieren aus dieser Verbindung eigentümliche psychische und psychophysische Vorgänge, die in dem Einzelbewusstsein allein entweder gar nicht oder mindestens nicht in der Ausbildung entstehen könnten, in der sie sich in Folge der Wechselwirkung der Einzelnen entwickeln.[11]

The Folk Soul

Wundt maintains that the folk soul is no less real than the soul of the individual. In order to understand the line of thought that leads up to this assertion, it is necessary to recall what has been said about his conception of psychic actuality. The concept *soul*, as used by Wundt, does not refer to a substance, be it materialistic or spiritualistic, but rather to the immediateness, the actuality, of psychic experience. Thus, the soul of the individual, being deprived of the connotation of a substantialistic substratum, is an abstract term for an entity of concrete psychic experiences: "Unter der individuellen Seele verstehen wir die unmittelbare Einheit der Zustände eines Einzelbewusstseins."[12] This same conception of *soul* as

---

[10]"Darum ist das gemeinsame Leben niemals eine blosse Addition individueller Wirkungen," *Deutsche Rundschau*, 1891, 200.
[11]*Völkerpsychologie* (1st ed.), I, 1, 9–10; see also *Probleme der Völkerpsychologie*, 1911, p. 13.
[12]*System d. Phil.*, 2, 148.

psychic actuality leads Wundt to postulate the reality of the folk soul. As we have seen, he defines the folk-psychological phenomena as a sphere of psychical facts, which, while claiming the individual souls as their constituent elements, represent a new and peculiar creative synthesis distinct from the component parts. The concept *folk soul* refers in exactly the same way to the entity of these overindividual psychic facts as the individual soul refers to that of the psychic experiences of the individual. The essential connotation of the folk soul, like that of the individual soul, is that it is an actuality, not a substance. Now the psychic facts of the overindividual group, as empirical facts, are according to Wundt as real as the psychic life of the individual. Therefore, so argues Wundt, the term *soul* is equally justifiable and equally applicable in the case of folk-psychological phenomena as it is in that of individual psychology.[13] The axiom of voluntaristic psychology is "So viel Aktualität so viel Realität."[14] Therefore, the folk soul as an actuality is a reality.

A psychology, says Wundt, that abides by the conception of a soul substance can never comprehend the reality of the folk soul, because a soul substance is necessarily bound to the physical entity of the individual. "Ist die Seele ein beharrendes Wesen, wie die Substanzhypothese annimmt, ein geistiges Atom . . . , so hat selbstverständlich nur das Individuum wahre Realität."[15] To those who state that the folk soul is a fiction and a production of the mythological imagination, Wundt replies that the conception of the soul as a substance is mythological rather than that of the actuality of the folk soul, and hence of its reality.[16] The idea of a soul substance, says Wundt, is a survival of mythical animism.

This is the line of thought that induces Wundt to postulate folk psychology as an independent science, with its own particular realm of problems. Its existence is as justified as that of individual psychology. Wundt defines it as the study of the folk soul ("die Lehre von der Volksseele").

Wundt's plea for folk psychology is apparently founded on a rigid construction of logical thought. The well-balanced succession of premises and conclusions offers a good example of Wundt's argumentative brilliancy. The line of thought is enticing, and still the one decisive point in his argument for the reality of the folk soul is gained by a subtle *coup d'etat*.

[13]*Probl. d. Völkerpsychol.*, 1911, 13, 20.
[14]*Logik*, 3, 293–294.
[15]*Logik*, 3, 293; *Syst. d. Phil.*, 2, 188.
[16]*Völkerpsychol.*, I, 1, 8–9.

The *raison d'être* of folk psychology is at the mercy of the thesis of the reality of the folk soul. This reality, as we have seen, is based on the idea of psychical actuality—a concept taken from the psychology of the individual. In individual psychology the concept *actuality* acquires its meaning through the fact that the phenomena at hand are *immediately*[17] perceived in contradistinction to the mediate cognition of the natural sciences, which must postulate a substance as the extrasubjective substratum of their phenomena. The immediateness of experience is the fundamental connotation of psychic actuality. The condition in question is fulfilled in the case of individual psychology by the intrinsic and irreducible nature of consciousness. But what about the folk soul? The folk soul is by definition an overindividual synthesis. The psychic phenomena of the folk soul are by definition not contained in the psyche of the individuals as such, but immediate psychic experience is—again by definition—confined to the consciousness of the individual. How then can there be an *immediate* experience of an overindividual synthesis? And what sort of a meaningless thing is an overindividual actuality of psychic life? But if there is no overindividual actuality, then there can be no folk soul. The one falls with the other. The *contradictio in adjecto* which we here encounter in Wundt's argument lies in the following premises: psychic actuality is the immediateness of experience; the folk soul is an overindividual synthesis. Wundt bridges the gap by ignoring at the decisive point in his argument the "immediateness" of psychical actuality.

The Relation of the Individual to the Group

Having discussed in abstract terms the flaw in Wundt's plea for folk psychology by pointing out his self-contradictory usage of concepts, let us investigate for a moment somewhat more concretely the same break in argumentation from another point of view, namely, from that of the relation of the individual to the group.

Wundt states categorically that folk psychology deals with the psychology of language, religion (*Mythus und Religion*), and custom. These three types of cultural phenomena are the achievements *par excellence* of the folk mind (*Volksgeist*). Not the individuals, but the group (*die*

---

[17]I use the terms *mediate* and *immediate* for Wundt's terms *mittelbar* and *unmittelbar*. *Indirect* and *direct* would only convey the meaning approximately.

Gemeinschaft), is the creator of language, religion, custom. Of course, the group consists physically of a number of individuals, but those folk-psychological phenomena, so argues Wundt, represents a higher synthesis that transcends the scope of individual consciousness.[18] He says:

> Sie [i.e., die Erlebnisse und Erzeugnisse geistiger Gemeinschaften] unterscheiden sich dadurch von den Synthesen des individuellen Bewusstseins, dass sie sich aus Bestandteilen *eines* Bewusstseins niemals erklären lassen, sondern auf einer geistigen Wechselwirkung vieler beruhen, die sich zu den genannten Vorgängen ähnlich verhalten, wie die Vorstellungsund Willenselemente des Einzelbewusstseins zu den zusammengesetzten Vorstellungen und Willenshandlungen des einzelnen.[19]

Misled by the analogy between the synthesis of psychical elements in the individual and the synthesis of the individuals in the group, Wundt becomes entangled in the illusory problem of the relation of the individual to the group.

This problem is no less an illusion than the old one of the relation of the particular to the universal, of which indeed it is but a specific application. The illusory nature lies in the fact that when speaking of the particular and the universal, we are not operating with concepts of different objects but rather with different conceptual abstractions of the same object. The individuals are the group, and the group is the individuals. The two terms represent different modes of conceptualizing the same thing. Wundt puts the problem thus: Is the individual as such, or is the group as such, the creator of language, religion, and custom? He states correctly, in opposition to the intellectualistic school of psychology, that it is not the individual as such, but at once he falls into the opposite error, and asserts that the group as such, the overindividual synthesis, is the creator of cultural phenomena. Wundt's position is no more consistent than is that of his adversaries. Logically, a collective term is an abstraction from its analytic components, and the latter again are an abstraction from the former. Correspondingly, in our case the group is an abstraction from the individuals, and the individuals are an abstraction from the group. Thus, Wundt's juxtaposition of the individuals as such, and the group as the overindividual synthesis, is an absurdity. A result of the contradictions in which Wundt becomes entangled is the vagueness with which he continually treats the relation of the individual to the group as soon as he attempts to demonstrate this relation concretely.[20]

[18]*Probl. d. Völkerpsychol.*, 24.
[19]*Logik*, 3, 295.
[20]See, for instance, Wundt, *Menschen- und Tierseele* (4th ed.), 509.

The error in Wundt's position is determined from the outset by the way in which he formulates his problem: Is the individual as such, or is the group as such, the creator of language, religion, and custom? The difficulty thus involved arises from a confusion of the two distinct points of view from which the individual can be conceived. From the one point of view the individual is the subjective entity as experienced "immediately" (*unmittelbar*) in consciousness. This subjective individual experiences himself as autonomous. It is the individual of psychical actuality and of indeterminism. From the other point of view the individual is society and he is history. He is determined psychically by his cultural milieu. He is the individual of determinism and the object of culture history. We avoid the problem of determinism versus indeterminism, and we do not, as Wundt does, entangle ourselves in its meshes, if we distinguish clearly between these two points of view. Wundt gains the concept of the group as an overindividual synthesis by viewing the individual only from the first point of view, namely, as an autonomous nomad.[21] Of course, the individual as such cannot be brought into *rapport* with culture-historical problems when approached from this standpoint. Since language, religion, and custom are by definition psychical and historical phenomena—in short, cultural phenomena—the only point of view from which their study is conceivable is that of culture history. But from this point of view, the individual, as we have seen, is history, he is society; he is, in brief, the ζωὸν πολιτικὸν.

To conceive the individual historically—and by this I mean at the same time socially and culturally—as an autonomous entity is as meaningless as to study the course of a river independent of the geology of its bed. The ζωὸν πολιτικὸν has *sui generis* a psychohistorical setting, it has a culture. And this culture is nothing accessory, it is not cast in the mold of an autonomous individual, but language, religion, custom *are* from the historical point of view the individual, they *are* the group, they *are the* ζωὸν πολιτικὸν.

The result of which Wundt's distinction between the individual soul and the folk soul leads is nicely borne out by the following analogy, to which he repeatedly calls attention in his different works. In his individual psychology, Wundt designates the ideas and the emotions as the analytic components of the psyche and defines the third class of psychic phenomena, the volitions, as a synthesis of the former two. Since ideas,

[21]*Syst. d. Phil.*, 2, p. 204.

emotions, and volitions thus make up the individual soul, Wundt, consistent with his idea of higher syntheses, is induced to find the corresponding division in the folk soul. He actually goes so far as to correlate language, religion (*Mythus und Religion*), and custom—the elements of the folk soul—with the ideas, emotions, and volitions, respectively, of the individual soul:

> Die Sprache enthält die allgemeine Form der in dem Volksgeiste lebenden Vorstellungen und die Gesetze ihrer Verknüpfung. Der Mythus birgt den ursprünglichen Inhalt dieser Vorstellungen in seiner Bedingtheit durch Gefühle und Triebe. Die Sitte endlich schliesst die aus diesen Vorstellungen und Trieben entsprungenen allgemeinen Willensrichtungen in sich. . . . So wiederholen sich in Sprache, Mythus und Sitte gleichsam auf einer höheren Stufe die Elemente, aus denen sich der Tatbestand des individuellen Bewusstseins zusammensetzt.[22]

The superficiality of this analogy is manifested by the altogether arbitrary selection of the attributes of language, religion, and custom. I can conceive of no reason why mythology and religion, for instance, should not be correlated just as well with the ideas or the volitions as with the emotions. Furthermore, it must be borne in mind that Wundt's tripartite division of culture into language, religion, and custom—a division which is of course convenient for the above analogy—is in itself altogether arbitrary. Why social organization and technology, for example, should not find coordinated divisions is incomprehensible. The correctness of this statement is, indeed, demonstrated by the fact that in his latest work on folk psychology, in his *Elemente*, Wundt himself ignores the tripartite division in favor of a consideration of all categories of cultural phenomena. The above analogy between the elements of the individual soul and those of the so-called folk soul is no less crude than the analogy sometimes drawn between the state and a physiological organism on the basis of certain superficial similarities.

The Psychogenesis of the Folk Soul

In his folk-psychological terminology, Wundt introduces the concept *social will* (*Gesamtwille*), which, analogous to the concepts *folk soul* and *social mind* (*Gesamtgeist*), corresponds on the social side to the will of the individual. To be sure, the distinction which Wundt makes between the

[22]*Probl. d. Völkerpsychol.*, 29–30; see also *Logik*, 3, 232; *Völkerpsychol.*, I, 1, 26, 27.

concepts *folk soul, social mind,* and *social will* is frequently far from being clear. He is inclined to use especially the term *Gesamtwille* in a way that demonstrates clearly to my mind the line of thought that leads him to the idea of social life as an overindividual synthesis. My point is—and it is probably profitable to state it at this point—that Wundt derives the idea of the folk soul from the collective actions of the group as an *organized* social entity. At times one even gets the impression that it may be derived in a superficial way from the legally organized state of the present day. For instance, while trying to demonstrate that the reality of the group is of a higher order than that of the individual, Wundt states:

> Der praktisch bedeutsamste Beweis scheint mir freilich darin zu liegen, dass die Normen des Rechts nur aus einem realen Gesamtwillen jene ver- pflichtende Kraft schöpfen können, vermöge deren sie ihre unbedingte Herrschaft über den Einzelwillen behaupten.[23]

It is significant that Wundt cites criminal law as a specific example. A similar specification of the social will in terms of organized society is expressed in the following passage:

> Nun findet sich der Wille des Einzelnen eingeschlossen in einer Wil- lensgemeinschaft, die mit ihm in fortwährender Wechselwirkung steht, so dass er, vom Gesamtwillen beeinflusst, selber wieder nach Massgabe der erreichten individuellen Entwicklung diesen bestimmt. So ist der Einzelne zunächst Mitglied eines Stammes, einer Familie, einer Berufsgenossenschaft, dann bei sich erweiternder Willensentfaltung Glied einer Nation, eines Staates, um schliesslich mit diesen höheren Willenseinheiten teilzunehmen an einer . . . Willensgemeinschaft der Kulturvölker.[24]

Bearing this rendering of the social will in mind, and recalling that language, religion, and custom are, according to Wundt, the creations *par excellence* of the folk soul, it is fair to infer that these cultural achievements are conceived by Wundt as created by the group as an *organized* social unit. That this is his meaning is implied in the following statement:

> In der Tat bilden ja Rechtsordnung und Staat nur hoch entwickelte Formen eines gemeinsamen Lebens, das von frühe an in der eine Volks- oder Stam- mesgemeinschaft verbindenden Sprache, in den ihr eigentümlichen re-

[23]Wundt, "Ueber das Verhältnis des Einselnen zur Gemeinschaft," *Deutsche Rundschau,* 1891, 203.

[24]*Syst. d. Phil.*, 1, 389. It is interesting to note that in a chapter of his *System der Philosophie* (2, 188–211) devoted to the evolution of the social mind ("Entwicklungsformen des Gesamtgeistes") Wundt treats exclusively of the forms of social organization beginning with the tribe and leading up to the modern state. Here he ignores all other possibilities of a broader aspect of cultural development, in spite of the fact that the *Gesamtgeist,* by way of definition, pertains to the psychogenesis of culture at large.

ligiösen und mythologischen Anschauungen, endlich in den für alle ver-
bindlichen Normen der Sitte sich äussert.[25]

While from an *a priori* point of view it may seem plausible enough
that language, religion, and custom are the evolutionary products of the
social group as such, it is easy for modern anthropology to point out that
the homogeneity and continuity of development as implied in the
psychogenesis of the organized group are not borne out by empirical
data. We do not find types of language, of religion, of mythology, of
custom grouped in such a way as to justify us in viewing cultural evolution as a single line of development. For instance, we find the
Athapascan-speaking Navaho in absolute social isolation from the remote northern Athapascans, and with a culture characteristic of the
southwestern area. Again, we find the Tewa-speaking inhabitants of
Hano living in the closest social and cultural relations with the Hopi, in
spite of the difference of tongue. The Plains area shows a great diversity of
speech associated with a great similarity of other cultural factors, especially of material culture. Anthropology furnishes numerous instances of
the constant dissociation in the distribution of cultural elements.

Wundt's folk psychology pretends to be based on empirical facts, but
is it not rather an unhistorical construction, inspired by the *a priori* idea of
the manifestation of the folk soul in the organized social group? When I
protest against the identification of the folk soul with the organized
group, I do not mean to question, of course, the social factor in cultural
development. That would be an absurdity. The point lies in another
direction. The question is whether we can conceive the development of
culture, language, religion, and custom in the form of a single line of
psychogenesis, as implied in Wundt's idea of the *Gesamtwille* and the
constructive development of the social group.

I emphasize the "single line" of development, because Wundt's
psychogenesis[26] represents psychic evolution as a *typical* and universally
valid succession of developmental stages. He thus intentionally abstracts
from the heterogeneity and multiplicity of the lines of development as
they are presented to us empirically in the history of culture. Wundt's
idea of psychogenesis is determined by his postulate of the purely psychological, nonhistorical nature of all folk-psychological problems. The
fundamental question is whether such an abstraction from all concrete

---

[25]Wundt, in *Deutsche Rundschau*, 1891, 198.
[26]*Elem. d. Völkerpsychol.*, 4.

historical data is methodologically permissible. Quite apart from other theoretical considerations Wundt's method is condemned, in the eyes of the anthropologist, by the fact that while positing the psychology of cultural development as the particular object of folk psychology, it ignores completely an account of the inherent schematism of its unilinear construction, the two fundamental psychological problems of cultural development, namely, that of culture areas and that of cultural diffusion. These two complementary psychological problems transcend the realm of the unilinear psychogenesis of the organized group as such and thus find no place within the dogmatically limited sphere of Wundt's would-be social will (*Gesamtwille*). What is the psychological significance of cultural specialization within certain geographical areas—a specialization quite distinct from the distribution of language, and in no way limited to social units? What is the psychological interpretation of the relation of cultural centers—those focal points that appear like the crests of waves—to the outlying fringes of the areas? What are the psychological situations that quicken the diffusion of borrowed cultural elements? What are those that retard or exclude the diffusion? What are the factors that determine on the one hand the passive absorption, on the other the active assimilation of borrowed traits? These are all real psychological problems. They apply specifically to those cultural phenomena which Wundt's folk psychology seeks to comprehend—to such phenomena, for instance, as sound shifts, the psychical transformation of religious ideas, and the heterogeny of custom. But Wundt's folk psychology ignores such problems in favor of a construction which, while ingenious, blinds us by its very nature to the real psychological problems as presented by the empirical facts.

I have tried to demonstrate that Wundt derives his concept of the social will from the group as an organized social entity with collective modes of action. This derivation is characteristic of Wundt's attempt to arrive, through a process of conceptualization, at a purely psychological construct, to be operated with in a would-be science of overindividual syntheses. This construct is the folk soul. Inasmuch as the problems of folk psychology are to be purely psychological, the folk soul must be conceived as a psychological actuality *abstracted* from the concrete historical phenomena. But where is this purely psychological something demonstrable, since all cultural developments are given as concrete historical phenomena? It is not difficult to understand why Wundt, in this dilemma, seizes upon the collective actions of the organized group as a tangible realization of the social will, and thus, in his terminology, of the folk soul. But one dilemma is not annulled by the addition of a new one. The construction of a typical and unilinear psychogenesis of language, religion, and custom is contradicted, as we have seen, by the culture-historical phenomena themselves, from which the folk-psychological construction is supposed to abstract. The net of contradictions in which Wundt thus becomes involved is caused, as will be shown, by his *a priori* assumption that in the study of cultural phenomena a separation of the psychological from the historical point of view is methodologically feasible.

The "Typical" Nature of Folk-Psychological Inductions

Before entering on the discussion of this final point of our criticism, it is necessary to dwell for a moment on Wundt's proposition that the inductions of folk psychology are of "typical"[27] significance. This is a fundamental point for Wundt, inasmuch as it is a direct expression of the "purely psychological" bearing of folk psychology and thus implies his idea of the absolute distinction between psychology on the one hand and history on the other. According to Wundt, the phenomena of psychology are "typical"; those of history, "singular" (*singulär*).[28] Individual psychology deals with the psychical processes of individual consciousness, insofar as they are "typical."[29] The processes of folk psychology as an essential branch of general psychology are characterized in the same way: "Gegenstand einer psychologischen Disziplin kann . . . überall nur das Allgemeingültige, Typische sein."[30] The concept of the *typical* in folk psychology is derived from the corresponding concept in individual psychology by means of Wundt's general analogy of the individual soul as the microcosmos and of the folk soul as the macrocosmos. This analogy, with its derivative concepts, appears plausible enough as long as it remains in an ethereal sphere of abstractness. As soon as such ideas are elaborated for specific application, they become self-contradictory. That this is precisely what happens to the concept *typical* I shall attempt to

[27]I use the term *typical* to convey the meaning of Wundt's terms "*typisch*" and "*allgemeingültig*."

[28]I would call attention to the specific sense in which I use the term *singular* in order to make it correspond to Wundt's "*singulär*." It is the contrasting term of *typical*.

[29]*Logik*, 3, 162.

[30]*Logik*, 3, 230.

demonstrate presently by means of certain inconsistencies in Wundt's considerations.

The subject matter of folk psychology—language, religion, and custom—is originally given in the form of "singular" phenomena and is thus subject priorily to a purely historical consideration. From these "singular" data of history, however, the "typical" material of folk psychology is gained by means of analysis and comparison. The "typical" something that is thus supposedly found is referred to by Wundt as the "common attributes of the folk mind" (*allgemeine Eigenschaften des Volksgeistes*).[31] Then, again, he speaks of the products of the refining process as the "universal laws of psychical evolution" (*universelle geistige Entwicklungsgesetze*).[32] In another connection, however, Wundt explicitly states that the general psychical laws that are borne out by folk psychology are necessarily already completely contained in individual psychology. He says:

> Darum ist es von vornherein ausgeschlossen, dass in der Völkerpsychologie irgendwelche allgemeine Gesetze des geistigen Geschehens zum Vorschein kommen, die nicht in den Gesetzen des individuellen Bewusstseins bereits vollständig erhalten sind.[33]

By combining these two propositions of Wundt we arrive at the conclusion that the laws of folk psychology, which are supposed to characterize the attributes of the folk soul, are not at all characteristic of the folk soul, inasmuch as they are but applications of individual psychology. The contradiction thus incurred demonstrates the meaninglessness, on the one hand, of the term *typical* in folk psychology and, on the other, of the juxtaposition of the individual soul and the folk soul.

There is another point of view from which the "typical" nature of Wundt's folk psychology can be criticised. As we have seen, its "typical" significance implies theoretically that the subject matter of folk psychology is "purely psychological"; that is to say, nonhistorical. In order to ascertain what this "typical," nonhistorical something is, we naturally turn to Wundt's work on folk psychology itself. What we find here differs strikingly from what the theoretical foundations have led us to anticipate. The three spheres of folk-psychological investigation are, according to Wundt, the purely psychological problems of language, religion, and

---

[31]*Probl. d. Völkerpsychol.*, 28.
[32]*Probl. d. Völkerpsychol.*, 24; see also *Logik*, 3, 240.
[33]*Logik*, 3, 227.

custom. [34] Those of language and religion are dealt with in his large work on the subject; those of custom, in a part of his *Ethik*. A glance at the contents suffices to show that in reality Wundt's folk psychology, far from dealing with "purely psychological" problems, consists of psychological interpretations of a hypothetical *historical* construction. The content is certainly not nonhistorical: it differs only from the usual conception of history in that Wundt has replaced the empirical account of historical developments by a historical construction which he regards hypothetically as the general course of the development of all language, religion, and custom. The "purely psychological" of Wundt's theoretical postulates reduces and transforms itself in the actualized product into a "generalized historical." Thus, the unscientific character of the "typical" attributes of the folk soul is proved by the very process of their elaboration.

The point just made is borne out still more clearly in the case of Wundt's latest work on folk psychology, his *Elemente der Völkerpsychologie*. Here we have before us a constructive history of human culture embracing the past, present, and the future—a brilliantly worked out scheme of the development of mankind through a number of successive cultural stages. This historical framework is constructed mosaic-fashion by fitting the traits of different cultures together and by letting the presumably higher forms succeed the presumably lower ones. The selection of traits necessary for building up in this way a ladder of evolutionary stages characterizes the ensuing edifice as purely hypothetical. What objective criteria, indeed, have we for determining one culture as "higher" than another—for placing the Australian totemism, for instance, on a higher level than the types of "primitive man" which Wundt adduces? From the empirical point of view, cultures are not differentiated quantitatively by varying degrees of development, but rather by the qualitative heterogeneity of their psychic specialization. The idea of *degrees* of evolution can only be determined by an extraneous code of evaluation. In Wundt's case this code is clearly supplied by his purely ethical norm of the development toward a humanitarian ideal *("Entwicklung zur Humanität")*, as elaborated in his *Ethik*. In his *Elemente*, this normative conception is, as already discernible from the table of contents, responsible for the arrangement of the empirical data of culture history in a preconceived order of hypothetical stages.

[34]*Völkerpsychol.* (1st ed.), 1, 1, 24.

Wundt's *Elemente der Völkerpsychologie,* we repeat, is a historical construction. That Wundt himself conceives this work as historical is demonstrated by its subtitle, *Grundlinien einer psychologischen Entwicklungsgeschichte der Menschheit.* But, according to the explicit theoretical foundations, the *raison d'être* of folk psychology rests on the purely psychological, nonhistorical nature of its problems. Now a historical subject matter evidently does not become purely psychological and nonhistorical, nor does it become typical in Wundt's sense by forcing it into the mold of a hypothetical construction. It is generalized history, and Wundt has in the subtitle named the child by its right name, but by doing that his theoretical foundations of folk psychology negate themselves. The *Elemente* prove to be the *reductio ad absurdum* of the science of the folk soul.

Psychology and History

The incompatibility of the theoretical foundations of folk psychology and their actualization—the gap, in short, between the word and the deed—centers about Wundt's failure to apperceive clearly one fundamental problem. This problem, as I conceive it, is that of the relation of history to psychology. We have already discussed his notion of the "singular"-historical and the "typical"-folkpsychological. Wundt does not always give the same connotations to these concepts. One mode of using them has been discussed above. Let us for a moment dwell on a variant form.

Wundt's large work on folk psychology deals exclusively with what is commonly known as primitive culture, in contradistinction to the culture of documentary history. Wundt motivates the limitation of the scope of his investigations by stating that the early development alone of language, religion, and custom exhibit a *typical* psychogenesis, not yet vitiated by the conscious actions of individuals. These early stages of development are, according to Wundt, common to all peoples, because they are determined by universal psychological motives.[35] In the later stages single individuals become in an increasing degree the determining factors[36]; then the phenomena are no longer "typical," they are "singu-

[35]*Probl. d. Völkerpsychol.,* 22.
[36]*Ethik,* 3d ed., 2, 364.

lar." The typical phenomena of the early stages present psychological problems and are therefore the domain of folk psychology. The phenomena of the later stages, due to their "singularity," are nonpsychological and thus pertain to history. Wundt expresses this idea by saying that the field of history begins where that of folk psychology ends[37]; but in his later work, the *Elemente,* Wundt tacitly ignores altogether this distinction between the earlier and later stages of culture. In his *Elemente,* as we have seen, he presents a construction of the whole cultural development of mankind, barring the above-said limitation. In fact, the fourth and last stage in this book, called "die Entwicklung zur Humanität," is conceived by Wundt as a period which we have by no means completed at the present day.

The distinction Wundt makes in his large work between psychology and history is of dubious scientific value and is refuted by the contents of his later work. The notion that history applies to phenomena of individual making, in contradistinction to the psychological creations of the folk soul, is arbitrary and implies a superficial conceptualization of history. The historical phenomena of conscious individual origin are in no way *essentially* distinct from the development of language, religion, and custom. Both groups of phenomena are historical, and both presuppose the psychological setting of culture. This bears directly on the criticism I made on a previous page of Wundt's theory on the relation of the individual to the group. The difference between the individual creations and the phenomena of language, religion, custom is not given objectively in the objects themselves, as would have to be the case if "history began where folk-psychology ended"; but the difference is rather determined by the angle from which we ourselves view the objects. Let us take an example. Wundt states that the history of literature is the successor of the psychology of language. [38] The former deals with the historical creations of individuals; the latter, with the psychological genesis of the folk soul. This distinction is plainly unmethodological, because Wundt contrasts and brings into an identical line of development two fields of research that are not comparable on account of the different subjective points of view adopted by the scholar, in spite of the common historical nature of the empirical objects. The psychology of language does not *develop into* the history of literature, as Wundt would have it. It is rather the focus of our interests that shifts.

[37]*Völkerpsychol.* (1st ed.), 1, I, 25.
[38]*Völkerpsychol.* (1st ed.), 1, I, 25.

A similar confusion of the relation of psychology to history is demonstrated by the way in which Wundt delineates the difference between ethnology and folk psychology. In the relation of these two sciences Wundt rescues the "purely psychological" (!) nature of folk psychology by defining ethnology as a genealogy of peoples. Its problems are not psychological. Wundt says:

> Die Ethnologie ist eine Wissenschaft von der Entstehung der Völker, ihren Eigenschaften und ihrer Verbreitung über die Erde. . . . Hier können scheinbar kleine Kunsterzeugnisse und ihre Abänderungen in hohem Grade bedeutsam sein für die Feststellung einstiger Wanderungen, Mischungen oder Uebertragungen.[39]

These migrations, mixtures, and borrowings associated with the repression of psychology savor suspiciously of Graebnerian diffusionism, which this ethnologist has thought well to formulate as "the method of ethnology." It seems probable that this "Kulturkreislehre" has been fatal to Wundt's conception of ethnology.

Enough has been said, I think, to show that Wundt has failed to bring psychology and history into a harmonious relation with each other. This is proved by the mutual contradictions of the theoretical foundations of folk psychology, as well as by the gap between these foundations and their actualization. Graebner pretends to solve the problem of the relation of psychology to history by ignoring it. For him psychology does not exist, and history is something that serves as a bait for his "Kulturkreislehre." Wundt sees the reality of the problem and answers it by drawing a sharp line between history and psychology. With this distinction the raison d'être of folk psychology stands and falls. The impossibility of this distinction leads to the self-negation of folk psychology in Wundt's Elemente.

A criticism of Wundt's folk psychology and of its theoretical foundations has a deeper bearing than the mere fact of pointing out logical discrepancies. The significant fact is that in the case of Wundt's folk psychology a most ingenious attempt to mark out clearly a distinction between psychology and history has failed. Wundt has devised a remarkable foundation of concepts upon which to build up a new science of the folk soul. His concepts of the higher synthesis, the social mind, the reality of folk-psychological actuality, etc., are all seemingly firmly anchored in a monumental philosophical system, but Wundt's conceptual scheme

[39]Elem. d. Völkerpsychol., 5.

breaks down when applied. His failure is significant, since it proves the inconsistency of drawing a line between history and psychology. That history without psychology is an impossibility is proved by Graebner; that a nonhistorical psychology of culture, a folk psychology, is likewise a misconception is proved by Wundt. It would seem to me that history, when taken in its broad sense as the history of culture, is intrinsically associated with a psychological point of view. The relation of psychology to history is much the same as that of physics to physiology. Historical phenomena are interpreted psychologically as physiological processes are interpreted in terms of physics. The general skepticism that this form of the relation of psychology to history encounters is due, I believe, to two causes; first, to the disreputable role that popular psychology has played; and, second, to the unaccustomed novelty of thinking of history in its broadest possible sense as the history of culture (*Kulturgeschichte*).

What an intrinsic association of psychology and history can attain is well exemplified by numerous individual passages in Wundt's works on folk psychology, when we abstract from all his theoretical foundations. There we find psychological interpretations of historical phenomena executed with a brilliancy characteristic of Wundt's genius. Such interpretations of Wundt will mark the monumental significance of his work long after folk psychology as such will have been recognized as an *"Unding."*

INDEX

DATE DUE

DATE DUE			
FEB 2 3 '82			
FEB 27 '82			
GAYLORD			PRINTED IN U.S.A.